Corporate Truth
The Limits to Transparency

Adrian Henriques

London • Sterling, VA

First published by Earthscan in the UK and USA in 2007

ISBN: 978-1-84407-390-0

Typeset by MapSet Ltd, Gateshead, UK
Printed and bound in the UK by Bath Press
Cover design by Nick Shah

For a full list of publications please contact:

Earthscan
8–12 Camden High Street
London, NW1 0JH, UK
Tel: +44 (0)20 7387 8558
Fax: +44 (0)20 7387 8998
Email: earthinfo@earthscan.co.uk
Web: **www.earthscan.co.uk**

22883 Quicksilver Drive, Sterling, VA 20166-2012, USA

Earthscan is an imprint of James and James (Science Publishers) Ltd and publishes in
association with the International Institute for Environment and Development

A catalogue record for this book is available from the British Library

Library of Congress Cataloging-in-Publication Data

Corporate truth : the limits to transparency / Adrian Henriques.
    p. cm.
  ISBN-13: 978-1-84407-390-0 (hardback)
  ISBN-10: 1-84407-390-4 (hardback)
   1. Business ethics. 2. Social responsibility of business 3. Industries—Social
aspects. I. Title.
  HF5387.H465 2007
  658.4'08—dc22

                                                              2006101422

The paper used for this book is FSC-certified and
totally chlorine-free. FSC (the Forest Stewardship
Council) is an international network to promote
responsible management of the world's forests.

Contents

Boxes, Figures and Tables

BOXES

FIGURES

TABLES

Acknowledgements

The chapter on corruption was based on research originally commissioned by the DfID.

I should like to thank the following for their support, comments and suggestions in the course of preparing the book: Brendan O'Dwyer, Stephen Walker, John Christensen, Chris Marsden, Helena Paul, Rob West, Rob Gray, My-Linh Ngo, Jorgen Randers, Richard Murphy, Geoffrey Chandler, Jonathon Porritt, Oliver James, David Nussbaum, Paul Scott, Roger Adams and Mary-Jane Rust.

Acronyms and Abbreviations

3G	third generation mobile phone technology
ASB	Accounting Standards Board
CEP	Council for Economic Priorities
CFS	Co-operative Financial Services
CSO	civil society organization
ECPHR	European Convention for the Protection of Human Rights
EITI	Extractive Industries Transparency Initiative
EMAS	Eco-Management and Audit Scheme
FDA	Food and Drug Administration (US)
FDI	foreign direct investment
FRC	Financial Reporting Council
FSC	Forest Stewardship Council
GAAP	generally accepted accounting principles
GRI	Global Reporting Initiative
ICAEW	Institute for Chartered Accountants in England and Wales
ICCPR	International Covenant on Civil and Political Rights
ICESCR	International Covenant on Economic, Social and Cultural Rights
ICSTIS	Independent Committee for the Supervision of Standards of the Telephone Information Services
ICT	information and communications technology
IGF-1	Insulin-like Growth Factor 1
ILO	International Labour Organization
IMCB	Independent Mobile Classification Body
IMF	International Monetary Fund
ISO	International Organization for Standardization
NDA	Nuclear Decommissioning Authority
NGO	non-governmental organization
OECD	Organisation for Economic Co-operation and Development
PCC	Press Complaints Commission
POS	point of sale
PR	public relations
rBGH	recombinant bovine growth hormone
RFID	radio frequency identification
SRI	socially responsible investment
UDHR	Universal Declaration of Human Rights
UNEP	United Nations Environment Programme
WTO	World Trade Organization

'I am convinced not only that what I say is wrong,
but that what will be said against it will be wrong as well.
Nonetheless, a beginning must be made …'
ROBERT MUSIL (1880–1942), TR. BURTON PIKE AND DAVID S. LUFT

'The truth is rarely pure, and never simple.'
OSCAR WILDE (1854–1900)

1

Approaching Transparency

Companies and the potential of transparency

Today's world is characterized by increasing concentrations of power through economic growth and globalization. We have larger and more dominant companies affecting a greater and greater part of our lives, in both the developed and developing worlds. We also have political processes which, while technically democratic, seem at times to operate in dealings with companies well beyond the margins of propriety.

Over 70 years ago, Berle and Means wrote that:

> Corporations have ceased to be merely legal devices through which the private business transactions of individuals may be carried on. Though still much used for this purpose, the corporate form has acquired a much larger significance. The corporation has, in fact, become both a method of property tenure and a means of organizing economic life. Grown to tremendous proportions, there may be said to have evolved a 'corporate system' – as there once was a feudal system, – which has attracted to itself a combination of attributes and powers, and has attained a degree of prominence entitling it to be dealt with as a major social institution. [...] We are examining this institution probably before it has attained its zenith. Spectacular as its rise has been, every indication seems to be that the system will move forward to proportions which stagger imagination today [...] they [management] have placed the community in a position to demand that the modern corporation serve not only the owners [...] but all society. (Berle and Means, 1933, p1)

Corporations clearly now have a huge impact on our lives – who does not work for one or buy their products or negotiate their way around their lorries in the street or see their factories or offices? Many of us will also 'own them' through pension plans. Yet how many of us feel it possible to control them? Or even perhaps, more modestly, that they are under someone's control? So they appear to suffer from a democratic deficit. Whether their impact is good or bad, we have little control over them. In remedying that deficit, the first need is for knowledge – for companies to be transparent about what they do and what effect they have on us and the world.

In more recent years we have seen corporations challenging our assumptions and values in many ways: from the placement of soft drinks in schools to the implications of cabinet ministers and political parties receiving funds from companies; from corporate scandals involving the collapse of huge multinationals to the European Commission sponsoring the idea of 'corporate social responsibility'; from the cautious support of some non-governmental organizations (NGOs) for corporate self-regulation to vigorous attacks on it from other NGOs; from the development of courses on corporate responsibility in universities to the enactment of new legislation.

It may not be a surprise that we hear about most of these issues, which affect almost all of us, from newspapers rather than from companies. And some may feel that there is enough information available already. We have the media: we have newspapers; we have the internet; we have television; we have radio. If we have information coming at us from all sides, is there really a need for more transparency?

The problem with the media is twofold: first, the media for the most part are themselves large companies with powerful interests which can preclude an unvarnished access to truth. And second, the media have to sell their information. Routine misery does not usually constitute a story, so the truth has to be 'sexed up'. If today, as the sayings go, the media are treacherous friends and reporters the whores of truth, how do we move beyond what stands in for truth? What is to be done and what kind of transparency or truth should we legitimately expect from companies themselves?

To move beyond the media story we need to recognise that transparency cannot be purchased wholesale. One thing it requires is painstaking attention to detail. Yet transparency is not just a technical issue of communication, but a moral issue for us all. The fundamental argument of this book is that transparency is required wherever power is exercised. And where power is abused, transparency is doubly necessary. In the world of public life, a misdeed hidden is twice the crime. To wrongly accept money or gifts for yourself or your family may be bad; but to lie about it subsequently will be far worse. Lack of transparency seriously compounds moral failure.

So transparency should be a central element of any real accountability in corporate life. Yet currently both accountability and transparency fall far short of what most of us might like to see. In the last decade, there has been a big rise in the number of corporate reports produced which describe how companies are tackling social and environmental issues. While this counts towards an increase in transparency, the quality of many of these reports is not encouraging. As a result there is a continuing decline in confidence and trust in the corporate sector from an already low level. In any case, transparency alone is not enough. For full accountability, action to improve corporate impacts is also necessary, as well as transparency about them.

Corporations do have positive and beneficial effects. But they also have negative and detrimental effects. Transparency is required for them all. It is not

2

helpful to attempt to set off one against the other. Consider the building of a beautiful and functional building, with negligible environmental impacts: this is positive. But if the building process led directly to the loss of a life, how can this be taken into account? Does it diminish the positive effects in some way? Should transparency require that all effects are laid out for inspection?

Companies themselves are much more enthusiastic about being transparent about their positive impacts, but rather more reluctant when it comes to the negative ones – particularly when the bad effects are intimately connected with the good ones. As a result, much of this book has to focus on negative impacts and the reasons why it is difficult to be transparent about the negative.

Even if it is accepted that full transparency is central to ethical behaviour, there is still much confusion over how far to go. There is uncertainty about the significance of current reporting practices and doubt about what transparency should actually mean in practical situations. In the end, what is it really possible for companies to say about themselves? Is the demand for full transparency simply unrealistic, or is transparency a necessary part of what companies will have to do?

Perhaps there is too much at stake for companies to be truthful and transparent. For some, the term 'corporate truth' will be an oxymoron. Companies are not to be believed as they are immensely powerful. Such sceptics may agree with the approach attributed to Michael Moore that 'you should just start from the position that anyone important is lying. Force them to tell the truth. Trust, but verify.'

Today, in the face of unjust wars, ethnic cleansing, communities forced off their land and environmental degradation, transparency seems almost too modest a demand. Clearly transparency is not remotely the final remedy for the ills of the world – but it is a first step. Transparency is necessary for those wronged so that they may claim some redress, or at least an acknowledgement of their pain. Without transparency, the task of those wronged becomes far harder. And if it is too hard, such injustices are far more likely to have a violent resolution.

For the powerful, transparency is necessary so that they can release their grip on themselves and allow themselves to change, which is otherwise psychologically hard to do. But transparency is difficult to deliver for governments, companies and other powerful groups, as it seems to require moral perfection in advance. Revealing poor performance feels humiliating. What politician can admit an error without already having solved the problem?

The message of this book is that it does not have to be like this. Transparency does indeed lead to a moral obligation to improve performance. Yet the courage to reveal faults should be received with a period of grace in which they may be addressed.

Transparency for shareholders

It is true that from the shareholder point of view transparency may affect reputation and profits positively or negatively in the short term. In the longer term it is much more likely to put their true prospects on a firmer footing, yet this does not mean that it is possible to develop a general business case for transparency. If it were possible to set out a general business case for transparency (or good social performance in general), someone would have done it by now and companies would just be getting on with delivering it. So the fact that it has not happened is significant and suggests that there is no general business case for transparency.

However, there is no business case for transparency in the same way that there is no business case for proper financial accounting or for honest advertising – or even for mining diamonds. Even to ask the question in this way shows a poor understanding of how business cases work, as I have argued elsewhere (Henriques, 2005b). Business cases are normally constructed at a much more precise and detailed level than this. It is doubtful if there is a 'business case' for anything in such general terms, except making money!

There is, of course, a general theoretical argument that greater transparency must lead to more efficient markets. This follows on from basic economic theory that markets perform better when information about products is available and there is also symmetry in the information available to producers and consumers. However, it is not possible to discover from this general theory what the particular costs and benefits of practising transparency for a given company are likely to be. It must also be acknowledged that some instances of transparency will have adverse effects on particular companies. This is consistent with the general argument about economic efficiency, which does not imply the preservation of specific companies but is a claim about the workings of a market as a whole.

There are some business arguments for good social performance in general. Over the past 30 years some 127 studies have been undertaken on the value of social performance to business, involving companies from South Africa to the US. The main finding has been that:

> *a clear signal emerges from these 127 studies. A simple compilation of the findings suggests there is a positive association, and certainly very little evidence of a negative association, between a company's social performance and its financial performance.* (Margolis and Walsh, 2003)

While it is possible to make some serious methodological criticisms of some of the underlying studies, their consistency is impressive. For a given business, however, they do not guarantee success. After all, quite consistently with all these studies, some businesses will have attempted to be responsible and enjoyed no financial benefit at all. And, of course, transparency is not the same thing as 'good social performance in general'.

More fundamentally, the argument for transparency is a moral one, not a financial one. The less transparent business as a whole is, the less anyone might want to live in the world which resulted. This book argues that transparency is part of the moral baseline for business conduct, rather than an optional extra to be adopted when it doesn't adversely affect the bottom line. To ask whether there is a 'business case for transparency' suggests that it might be legitimate to place shareholder interests above a moral imperative – which is ethically absurd. After all, if there were a business case for deception and fraud, would that make it a good idea? Down that road Enron lies.

Having said that, there are different ways of being transparent, some more expensive than others. And there may also be specific business advantages for being transparent, say, about the impact a company's new construction site may have on the local community, so that there is less opposition, or even support, for the project over its lifetime. It is clearly a good idea to make the best of transparency.

One area in which there actually is a business case for transparency is where 'transparency' means the absence of corruption, which is discussed in Chapter 12. Since corruption is an economic phenomenon – clearly with attendant social and environmental consequences – it is not surprising that it has fairly direct adverse economic consequences. Some of these are spelt out in Chapter 12.

It is also possible to suggest that there are, in general, business advantages for transparency over secrecy and deception. These would include greater trust, greater stakeholder understanding and lower transaction costs such as legal fees. What is not possible is to quantify such advantages for the general case – or to take proper account of the attendant costs. Yet often the greatest obstacle to transparency is not really financial, but a matter of personal pride and embarrassment. While this can be made to appear like a matter of corporate reputation, it is more usually a matter of the personal survival of a number of individuals.

About this book

Transparency is 'a good thing' – that is the basic premise of this book. But how far can you or should you go in being transparent? And in particular, what transparency should we expect of companies? What transparency do we actually get from companies? And what are the limits of transparency?

The aim of this book is therefore to describe the nature and limits of corporate transparency, how far it is possible for companies to tell the truth, how far they should be required to tell the truth and when they might have a right to keep information secret. Its purpose is not to pass some kind of overall moral judgement on companies in relation to their stakeholders, which would be futile. There are three main themes:

1   A description and assessment of the current transparency practices of companies. This includes their reporting, both financial and non-financial, and the numerous other ways in which companies reveal themselves. It also describes the practical challenges and issues which drive companies to behave as they do.

2   An exploration of the nature of transparency itself and particularly its moral character. The basic claim is that wherever power is exercised, there should be transparency.

3   An unravelling of the complex nature of companies and their relationships to their stakeholders. Companies can be seen both as actors in their own right and also as mechanisms for reconciling the often conflicting demands of stakeholders. This reconciliation reflects the balance of power between stakeholders and so is important to an understanding both of the moral nature of transparency and also of some of the mechanisms which companies use to avoid transparency.

The first part of this book assesses the current practice of transparency by companies, particularly in the West. Chapter 2 presents two case studies of the practical difficulties facing companies trying to be transparent. The issues raised include the personal investment of company staff in addressing corporate transparency. These include dealing with personal shame, corporate pride and the desire to be perfect in the face of relentless commercial pressures, all of which compromise the ability to be transparent. They also make clear that simply saying the word 'transparency' is not enough.

Chapter 3 attempts to clarify the multitude of concepts and buzzwords, such as corporate social responsibility (CSR) and ethics, which sometimes confuse this whole field. It argues that the impacts of power relationships provide the foundation for the moral case for transparency. The chapter also sets out some practical ways to assess the truth of companies and their behaviour.

In an attempt to reveal 'the truth' of companies, Chapter 4 examines what companies really are and how they are structured. The chapter discusses the idea of companies as a legal fiction and the analogy of companies as 'persons', showing how that peculiar analogy informs their functioning in many different ways. It argues that we may even have to accord companies some degree of 'personality' if we are to expect them to behave ethically.

Chapter 5 examines the field of human rights and the competing rights brought into play to demand, and to refuse, transparency. The language of human rights provides an authoritative framework to set out the moral basis of transparency in some detail. The chapter explores the relationship between formal human rights and the shifting legal basis for transparency. It also reveals the surprising extent to which companies themselves claim 'human' rights to justify their activities.

Chapter 6 turns to the role of the individual within a company and its relationship to transparency. If there is some moral obligation on companies to be transparent, how does that affect those who work within them? This chapter describes the way employee ethical codes function and how that relates to personal transparency, from personal disclosure to whistleblowing. It is argued that since power abhors the light of transparency, if any real degree of transparency is to be achieved, we must have the maturity to tolerate imbalances of power and imperfection – both in ourselves and in those of whom we demand transparency.

In Chapters 7 and 8, the principal official means of transparency by companies – reporting – is examined. This takes us through the territory of voluntary as well as involuntary or mandatory reporting. The chapter approaches reporting historically, starting with financial reporting. It demonstrates that such transparency that has been achieved has been hard won. It has only resulted from a struggle between those who wanted it (the majority of stakeholders, from shareholders to local communities) and company management, which, on the whole, whatever its theoretical remit, did not. In other words, today's transparency has resulted from the power struggles between companies' different stakeholder groups, not as a result of a rational business case produced by company management. It also shows that the struggle for transparency is a continuing process.

Chapters 9 to 13 in the second part of this book mainly concern a number of specific, 'difficult' subjects about which it is hard to be transparent. What makes an issue difficult for some is that it results from the close connection of the issue to the core business: for example, how do you make a media company transparent? How can you be open about intellectual property or trade secrets? Where transparency appears to involve giving away the essence of the business, it will seem like a bad idea. So what can be said of these things? And what should be said?

Chapter 9 examines the media, rather than a particular issue. Transparency – about others – is of course the core business of the sector. It is not surprising that the media, and particularly the news function within it, raises a number of particularly difficult and important issues concerning transparency. The chapter analyses issues such as editorial independence and the idea of a 'brainprint', and suggests how the sector can practically be transparent about itself.

Chapters 10 to 13 cover tax, commercial confidentiality, corruption and lobbying. These are all areas about which companies do not like to talk. They are also issues which have large impacts on corporate stakeholders and for which a reasonable degree of transparency is possible. Tax is an issue because, especially for globalized companies, there is a mismatch between what countries, being geographically bound, can control and what companies, having international power, can do. This makes transparency over tax both important and hard to achieve. In its structure and as a transparency challenge, tax is a paradigm for a number of other issues including arms control, gambling and personal data protection. For all of these activities international companies can take advantage of the limited power of countries.

Commercial confidentiality is the ultimate catch all argument against transparency. While the competitive nature of capitalism does demand some protection for commercial ideas, commercial confidentiality is greatly overused as a defence against transparency. Given the changing balance between the public and private sectors, it is also beginning to threaten basic democratic processes.

Corruption has a corrosive effect on the functioning of business worldwide and damages all who come into contact with it. It is also illegal. This combination means that it is very difficult to acknowledge and eradicate. There are nevertheless useful transparency strategies and ones which can have very beneficial economic consequences.

Lobbying challenges us to consider the proper role of companies in a democratic society. Lobbying by companies to affect legislation and other decisions is widespread and presents many ethical issues. Lobbying is also closely associated with complicity. Both issues require the greatest integrity and far greater openness, from government as well as from companies.

In conclusion, Chapter 14 provides a summary of the main findings on the limits of transparency. It articulates the basic rules for the limits of transparency and explores how far the same rules may be expected to apply to public and voluntary sector organizations. Finally, some hopes – or perhaps dreams – are offered as to the potential of a world of transparency.

2

Case Studies

LICENTIOUS TO OPERATE

Telecommunications – A growing industry

The telecommunications industry – from phone providers, internet service providers and mobile phone companies to communications hardware manufacturers and many others – is experiencing rapid growth and huge change. This is raising large commercial issues, but also moral ones. In particular, third generation mobile technology (3G) makes pornography more accessible than ever. How far should we expect telecommunications companies to be open and transparent about this? How far can they be?

> Public carriers in North America, Europe and Asia Pacific have increased their capital expenditures two years in a row now and are expected to increase them again for a third consecutive year in 2005. [...] Carriers in the three regions are expected to increase their capital spending by 6 per cent to just under $190 billion in 2005 after nine per cent annual growth in 2004. Many of the increases reflect investments in next generation technologies. (Mitchell, 2005)

Much of this growth involves new technology, such as a shift from fixed line to wireless or mobile phones. The convergence of computing and data communications technologies takes it a step further, with more traditional telecommunications technology used for the internet and the use of the internet to carry voice calls. According to Infonetics, '[each of the 18 North American, European, and Asia Pacific carriers interviewed] spent an average of $2.9 billion in 2005 on next [generation] mobile and wireless broadband equipment and will spend $4.1 billion in 2007, a 41 per cent increase.' (Webb, 2006)

Growth and change on this scale poses a commercial challenge, as well as questions of propriety over the way in which such change affects the workforce and consumers. As one of the drivers of this convergence trend is 3G, these moral issues concern 3G also. Commercially, 3G was very expensive (McIntosh,

9

2000; Milmo, 2001). In the spring of 2000, five companies paid between them nearly £22.5 billion for the UK licences for the use of this technology, representing about £3000 per customer. The next task was to invest in the infrastructure and technology at a cost of between £1000 and £3000 per customer. The initial reaction of stock market investors was to sell telecommunications shares, which slumped. A year later around of a third of those in the industry thought it would take at least ten years to recoup the investment.

So the pressure is on to recoup the investment. Of course there are big opportunities presented by the many consumer benefits of 3G. The technology will allow a global unification of mobile phone technologies, allowing phones to be used seamlessly from Japan to Europe and the US. It will make wireless access to the internet practicable for the first time. It will also enable the downloading of music and even TV and film routine. In addition to, or rather because of, all these technical innovations, it will also make pornography much more easily accessible.

The presence of pornography within Western societies is perhaps at its highest level ever. Will 3G be responsible for pushing this even higher? Has it created this demand or is it just servicing it? One view is that the history of new visual technology is also the history of the rise of pornography – consider projection cinema, video tape, DVDs and the internet. Pornography may also be said to have generated the cash to permit the development and wide deployment of these technologies (Gibson, 2003). Whatever the cause, it is now possible to access pornography from all the major telecommunications operators, cable and satellite TV companies, internet service providers and hotel chains – all of them household brands.

How much will the 3G licences be dependent on such material? Estimates vary from 5 per cent to 20 per cent of the total market for mobile phone content:

> The market for erotic content for mobile devices will be worth $2.3bn by 2010 compared with just under $1bn this year [...] the entire mobile phone content market, including music and gaming, is $43bn by 2010. Adult services will account for just five per cent of the market. (Wray, 2005)

Mobiles and sex

It may be true that the sexual mores of Western society are becoming more relaxed towards sex and pornography and that it is unclear whether increased demand has led to increased supply or vice versa, but what should the companies involved do and say about these issues?

To answer that at all systematically, it is necessary to ask who the stakeholders involved are. Some of the main stakeholders in a mobile phone company involved in pornography include:

- adult consumers;

- children;
- the people depicted in pornography;
- those who manufacture the content;
- the service providers who deliver it; and
- the staff of service providers.

Adult consumers may in turn be divided into those who do not mind it or care about it either way, those who like it, and those who dislike it. The industry's fundamental strategy has been that pornography is acceptable, if as an adult consumer you wish to have it. Consequently, service providers have sought to provide pornography only to that group which wishes to have it available. However, this stakeholder analysis masks the complex reality of sex addiction, which comprises people who both like and dislike it and are consequently bound up with compulsive behaviour. This is important because this actually vulnerable group is not well served by strategies which seek to divide consumers such that to each is given only what they desire.

Children are not involved in legal pornography and child pornography is not supported by the industry, although it is often admitted that it is very difficult to prevent telecommunications infrastructure from being used to deliver it, especially without breaching the right of the general public to privacy. Beyond this, the industry's strategy has been that children should not be allowed to access pornography of any kind. However, this approach has not been wholly successful. According to the UK Office for National Statistics, '[among] 9 to 15 year olds in the UK who went online at least once a week, 72 per cent had visited a chat room and 47 per cent had seen pornography online' (ONS, 2005, p178).

In relation to children, the mobile phone companies have adopted clear policies for their protection. In 2004, the mobile phone operators established a code of practice (IMCB, 2004) to regulate content on mobile phones. They then also established the Independent Mobile Classification Body (IMCB) to agree a classification framework, essentially to determine what content it is acceptable to provide to those less than 18 years of age. Content deemed unsuitable for children includes certain images or games relating to horror, drugs and violence as well as sex.

Those depicted in pornography, men as well as women, are one of the most vulnerable groups of all. However, consultations with this group are most unusual. Nobody asks them what they want. Nevertheless it may be expected that at least some of those involved may feel neither ashamed nor abused. It is difficult to reconcile this perspective with any kind of across the board restrictions.

Those who manufacture the pornographic content are looking forward to good business from the advent of 3G. The major brands are unlikely to risk contaminating their reputation by manufacturing it directly, but they have been reported as signing contracts under which others would provide it to them (Nicholson, 2002).

There is a complex value chain of different companies with different roles, all involved in delivering material over mobile phones. This may include those

11

who interface with the customer, those who provide handsets, those who operate the network of masts or the communications networks linking them, those who provide the customer billing services, and so on. If pornography is delivered, all of these are involved in delivering it. The list of stakeholders above is therefore relevant to all these different types of company. Somehow the responsibility must be shared, and the role of each acknowledged. A mobile phone company, for example, cannot simply argue that because other parties have some responsibility, they can be absolved of any.

The mobile phone operators do not give very much attention to the issue of pornography as a whole (other than that of illegal material). It is in fact very hard to find out what their position is in relation to the issues raised by the various stakeholders, other than children, discussed in this section. It seems to be an issue which is hard to talk about. This is particularly true for staff in these companies.

Talking about 'adult content'

While all mobile phone company staff are involved, at some remove, in the provision of pornography, they do not like to talk about it. As a result of talking at a meeting of a number of parties involved in the telecommunications industry, I have come to appreciate just how difficult it is to talk about.

When first raised, the issue of pornography is greeted with avoidance or silence, especially from women. This may be followed by nervous laughter or ribald suggestions from the men. Another strategy is to use euphemisms in order to talk about it without mentioning it. The most prevalent of these is 'adult content', which sounds much less troublesome, if not positively responsible. But this does not really help communication or resolve the issues.

Why is it so hard? One obvious reason is that pornography and sex are very personal issues which few people talk about much in any context. To talk about sex in a professional context is even harder. I suspect that most of the women in this position find it too distasteful to easily consider it dispassionately. It may be that the men have been tempted by pornography in their personal lives. So the stakes are high at a personal level.

At a corporate level, the stakes may also be high. We have seen how the commercial potential for pornography is significant, but pornography is defined and regarded very differently across different cultures. Even attitudes within Europe vary quite markedly. Yet each of the operators has some kind of presence right across the world, including in Islamic countries, where any such material is completely unacceptable.

Part of the difficulty seems to be technical. There is no widely accepted language or framework with which to talk about different levels or grades of pornography in order to work out how far a given image may be acceptable to a given audience. While it is true that the issue is not yet mature, in the sense of being widely acknowledged with workable and accepted strategies readily available (AccountAbility, 2005a, p55), it is also relevant that it touches on issues about which staff themselves may not have reached a level of personal maturity which will allow them to acknowledge the issues to themselves. Beyond that comes the further maturity required to be able to talk about these issues to the other stakeholders affected.

Meanwhile, each of the mobile operators carefully maintains a brand image which gives no hint of any problems or issues. Of course they are not alone in this fantasy; somewhat remarkably all brands project an image of perfection. As Naomi Klein (Klein, 2000) has pointed out, this is a risky strategy.

The problem is not likely to go away. O2 sees the issues in this way:

> *Consumer demand, as mobile telecommunications become more sophisticated, could mean that mobile devices increasingly become a channel for adult content such as pornography, gambling, financial services and other intensive push-marketing. Internet operators, broadcasters, regulators and governments have already wrestled with this issue with varying degrees of success. To date, this type of content has not been a significant issue in mobile communications, not least because voice and simple messaging services are poor channels for the delivery of adult content. The emergence of data-rich services could change this situation. As the new 2.5G and 3G services, offering internet access and the transmission of sophisticated video and audio content, come to market, this issue will become ever more important. (O2, 2005)*

Pornography brings together the challenges of both personal and corporate transparency. It is unlikely to be resolved in a socially acceptable way unless the problems are openly acknowledged, stakeholders are actually consulted and individuals in these companies are able to talk openly about the issues.

TRANSPARENCY UPON TRANSPARENCY

The following interview has been transcribed from a report and interview broadcast at 7pm on Monday 22 May 2006 by the UK's Channel 4 News. Victoria McDonald (VM), from Channel 4 News, asked whether McDonald's were worried about a potential PR disaster as a result of Eric Schlosser's new book, *Chew on This* (Schlosser, 2006), being released at the same time as a new 'Bigger Big Mac'. Steve Easterbrook (SM), UK Chief Executive of McDonald's, responded:

> *Well, at McDonald's we're really acting as a progressive company and we're very proud of our 31 years here in the UK. But I think we've made more changes in the last 3 or 4 years than we have in the previous 27. And we will continue to change. And we'll continue to run the business in an increasingly transparent way and allow people to find out the real truths about McDonald's themselves.*

VM asked where all the recent books and films about McDonald's have got it wrong.

SM: *There's a lot of curiosity around our brands and sometimes that curiosity can lead to myths, and I believe that the way I want to run the business is with increasing transparency. Transparency. And just allow people to separate the facts from the fiction a little. Because we have a good story to tell. And I'm keen to make sure that I can communicate that to people.*

VM: *Well what are the fictions in this?*

SE: *Well there's always myths about McDonald's and my job is to run the business in an increasingly transparent way, so that we can separate the facts from the fiction and communicate the good story that McDonald's has to tell.*

VM: *But give me one example of where there's been a myth that you've had to rebut.*

SE: *Well there's always a lot of curiosity around the brand. And that can sometimes lead to myths. And what I plan to do is to run the business with increasing transparency and allow people to separate the facts from the fiction themselves. And allow them to understand McDonald's themselves and come and see about the real McDonald's.*

VM: *But you've just answered the question in the same way three times, but you haven't given me an example.*

SE: *That's right, but I'll allow people to read the book for themselves. But from my perspective what I'm concentrating on is running the business and I plan to run the business in an increasingly transparent way.*

[...]

VM: *Why can't you give me any figures for how the salad sales are going?*

SE: *Well we look to grow all aspects of our business, so we concentrate on our traditional menu, on our breakfast menu, on our drinks and our desserts and on our toasted deli sandwiches. And my focus is on growing all aspects of our business going forward.*

VM: *I still remain unconvinced by your salads because of your inability to tell me exactly what portion of your sales they consist of.*

SE: *Yeah, I'm not going to go into specifics over how our sales break down by different areas of the business. But what I am committed to doing is growing all areas of our business.*

Background

Facts supplied by McDonald's:

- 67,000 UK employees.
- 1200 restaurants in the UK.
- 17,000 UK and Irish farmers are suppliers.
- On average customers visit 3 times a month.

Facts quoted by Channel 4 News from Eric Schlosser's book:

- 2.5 million UK customers visit McDonald's everyday.
- £300 million a year spent on advertising food to children.
- 1 million children (1 in 6) are obese.

From Channel 4 News:

- In America it has been estimated that 98 per cent of customers never order a salad at McDonald's.

3

Coming to Terms with Transparency

TRUTH

A book on transparency with the word 'truth' in its title needs to say something about what truth means. While this is definitely not a technical philosophical treatise, it is still important to capture our intuitions about truth in a workable way. So what do we mean when we say something is true?

At one level, the truth is what ought to be known, or what should be told. It is related to ethics. The truth about a company is what we should all be told about it. The immediate assumption is that truth involves 'skeletons in the closet', scandal and hidden machinations. And, of course, sometimes it does. But it also involves a full and systematic picture of the company. The reason that 'the truth' about a company appears to imply something negative probably results from the fact that a very large majority of corporate communications are wholly positive in character. When problems are acknowledged the solution is always already at hand, if not completely implemented. Such magical corporate spin makes for scepticism and suspicion.

But if we are looking for a fuller, more systematic truth about a company, what will it look like? I think it is possible to set out some heuristics, or rules of thumb, for what the truth about a company should look like. The literature of philosophy abounds with theories about truth and, for our purposes, they all have something useful about them. They each capture one kind of intuition about what the truth looks like. The result here, then, will not be a surprising new theory of truth, but a set of practical tools. Together these represent a pragmatic approach to judging corporate reports and statements. And in practice they should underlie the formal auditing of such reports.

Some of the main philosophical theories of truth, each of which can be said to underlie or inspire an important perspective on what should be told about companies, are:

- correspondence theory;
- coherence theory;

17

- consensus theory;
- constructivist theory; and
- pragmatism.

Correspondence theory suggests that statements are true because they correspond to an underlying reality. This is perhaps the most basic intuition about truth, suggesting that truth can be verified with evidence. If you read that a company has poisoned a river killing all the fish in it, but you live on that river and it seems much the same as it always has, then the statement that the company has poisoned the river will not seem to be true. Companies also make statements for which it may be inherently hard to find evidence, since they are primarily designed to be expressive rather than containing any fact. Examples of statements of this kind are lists of corporate values or logos such as 'every little helps'. If we are to judge such statements as 'true', we need to know *what* it is that helps, *how* little it may be and still help, *when* (and maybe *where*) the help will arrive, and above all *who* it is that is helped.

Unfortunately, even for more straightforwardly declarative statements, it is not always easy to verify what a company has said. In many instances a powerful aid is the coherence of what is said. The coherence theory of truth suggests that truth resides in the consistency of a statement with other statements; it can be regarded as the 'internal' verification of a statement. In relation to corporate truth, it is of great significance to discover that contradictory statements are being made. When there is inconsistency between two statements, it casts doubt on both.

The consensus theory of truth suggests that truth is what people agree it to be. While this is in a sense a much more modest idea, it can upset those who believe that the truth is objective and in some sense 'out there'. In a court of law, for example, the truth is what the court decides is true; for scientists it is what scientists have generally agreed upon (although the reasons scientists give themselves will doubtless be of a different nature). At any rate, in practice it is hard to argue with the idea that what we usually take as the truth in most cases is simply what we have heard others say. What proportion of what we believe does anyone actually verify by considering the evidence? In practice, consensus is a useful starting point for further investigation, and it will usually define the terrain which has not yet been explicitly verified, but may need to be in the future.

However, in the context of companies and their pronouncements, it is critical to ask who has agreed upon the truth. More sharply, which stakeholders belong to the consensus in question? The management may believe, say, that the staff in general are paid pretty well. However, the opinion of the staff may be quite different. There are two different truths here, and each needs to be acknowledged. The constructivist theory of truth suggests that truth is developed through social processes; the development of stakeholder groups is an example of this. The most important implication for corporate truth is that the views and opinions of each stakeholder must be respected. Their expression of their experience is their truth. In contrast, it is interesting to note the very prevalent presentation of 'stakeholder dialogue' in terms of surveys of *percep-*

18

Figure 3.1 *The ring of truth*

tion. The assumption behind this formulation is that it is *only perception* and the truth may be otherwise. This does not respect the stakeholder's truth. It appears to allow a stakeholder opinion to be expressed, while managing at the same time to discount it.

Finally, pragmatism, which has a bad name. Although pragmatism was originally an attempt to operationalize the concept of truth, it has been associated with the idea that truth is simply what is convenient and that what is held to be true is something that can be cynically manipulated. However, the idea of pragmatic truth raises the important question of which version of events is actually used, in other words of what the truth is in practice. If different stakeholders have different versions of events, which version prevails? The significance of this question is that it reveals the balance of power. And the revelation of power, and where it lies, is perhaps the most fundamental corporate truth of all.

ETHICS

Good business is all about honesty and fair dealing; if you can fake that you've got it made! (attributed to Groucho Marx)

Groucho Marx's insight is that ethics is a practical affair. It is the practice of aligning actions with words, or action with transparency. And to the extent that

19

our identity is determined by our behaviour it is also the practice of defining who we are. One thing is particularly important about this view. Moral behaviour does not happen instantaneously: people need time to work things out. If we are to expect progress, impatience will work against us.

Business ethics today has come to be identified with the topic of the ethical behaviour of individuals within organizations, particularly in the discharge of their ordinary commercial activities. The focus is usually on challenges such as conflicts of interest or the temptation to bribery or other corruption. In this context, the existence, appropriateness and use of a corporate code of conduct are important and central issues. This topic will be addressed further in Chapter 6.

However, ethics has a much greater role than this in relation to business. In many ways, ethics can be said to define the scope of what it is important to be transparent about. In the end the most interesting question and the greatest driver of demands for transparency is how far the company itself does 'good things' and 'bad things'. This must certainly include what happens to an investor's money, but also whether or not the company is producing products which are damaging in some way, or whether staff are subjected to abuse or, more hopefully, whether their activities are of net benefit to society and the environment. In this wider sense, business ethics has to refer to a company as an ethical actor in its own right, over and above the ethics of its employees. Chapter 4 will make a more detailed case for treating companies as 'people', and, if we do that, the need for them to be moral ones.

The varieties of ethical experience

The terms 'moral' and 'ethics' do not enjoy a single, consistent usage. They are derived from the Latin and Greek words, respectively, for customs – in other words what people do. And they are each still used in this sense (mores or ethic). However, they are also each used to mean several other things: first, as adjectives (moral or ethical) to describe what is good; second, as abstract nouns (morality or ethics) to mean a set of judgements about the goodness or badness of actions (for example 'his morality was poor'); and third, mostly by philosophers (moral philosophy or ethics), to mean a theory which explains why some things are good and others bad. Finally, for completeness, the theory of what 'good' is in itself is sometimes called 'meta-ethics'.

Ethics is also a name for various theories which have been developed over thousands of years. Three principle intuitions have been consistently identified by many writers, and much ethical argument has been generated by attempts either to prove one intuition superior to the others, or to combine elements of two or more. These three principle intuitions have been articulated in the philosophies of virtue ethics, duty ethics and utilitarianism.

Virtue ethics is founded on the primacy of virtue or character as the basis of morality. This approach has perhaps not been as richly articulated as the other approaches to ethics, but its origin has been attributed to Aristotle and it has been set out by Lawrence Blum (Blum, 1980) among others. For virtue ethics, moral worth resides above all in the *values* and *characteristics* of moral agents and their intrinsic disposition. Courage, honesty and kindness are the sorts of qualities which should be admired and may be called good.

Duty ethics is founded on the importance of conforming to *principles* in moral behaviour. In this view, a person motivated other than by duty is not behaving morally. It is a very common view, for example, that if a company gives money to a worthy cause only to look good, then that action is not particularly meritorious. It may even be held to be wrong, since the motivation may be entirely selfish.

Utilitarianism, of which John Stuart Mill and Jeremy Bentham were perhaps the most famous exponents, holds that the moral worth of an action should be judged from its consequences. A moral judgement of a person or company will therefore require an assessment of their performance; what matters is *results*. This perspective is integral to modern economic theory, which links consumer choice closely with satisfaction.

Each of these intuitions matter, and little is to be gained by claiming that only intentions, only results or only duty matters in judging the actions of a company. It is possible for someone to have the best of intentions, but not to know how to put their intentions into practice and to fail miserably; yet their intentions remain good. On the other hand a person may have selfish intentions, ingeniously carry them out and yet produce something of value to others. This belief is behind the invisible hand view of the free market, as described by Adam Smith:

> It is not from the benevolence of the butcher, the brewer or the baker that we expect our dinner, but from their regard to their own interest. (Smith, [1776] 1999, p119)

Finally, it is possible for a company to have good intentions and clear principles and yet to do things which seem inevitably likely to produce bad results. Google's decision to comply with the request from the Chinese government for censorship could be regarded as consistent with their motto 'do no harm', since the company itself is not directly harming anyone. However, it is also very likely to lead to further repression.

In fact, a moral judgement about a company cannot be complete unless all three intuitions have been brought to bear. In advance of a proposed action, an appeal to character and principle may be all there is to go on. However, the judgement about performance has perhaps a privileged status in regard to *repeated* action, or deciding whether to do something again. It would be astonishing if consideration of what happened last time did not play a major role in deciding whether or not to do that same thing again. So much so that to knowingly repeat an action which caused harm must lead one to question the intention and principle behind it.

Applied ethics – Shell

The practical application of these ethical frameworks can be illustrated by a very brief review of some of the statements about its governance in relation to employees made by the Shell oil company. For Shell, as for many companies, 'ethics' means the extent to which a company lives up to the values which the company or their stakeholders hold. 'Values' are those behaviours and intentions which the company or its stakeholders consider to be important.

One way in which companies like to establish their moral credentials is to publish their values. Shell's declared values are 'honesty, integrity and respect for people' (Shell, 2006a). A virtue-based critique of Shell might capture our intuition as to its character; it might ask questions such as whether more should be expected of Shell, whether these values are consistent and whether they had been realized in practice. It might also go further and ask whether there are other values, such as the pursuit of profit, which are of considerable significance to Shell, while for some reason not being listed as core values.

Duty-based analysis is concerned with the policy implementation of such values – it answers our question as to whether the company really means to deliver on its values. Shell makes a number of statements about the responsibilities of its five main operating companies. These have included the following statement about the instructions given to these companies in respect of employees:

> To respect the human rights of our employees and to provide them with good and safe working conditions and competitive terms and conditions of employment. To promote the development and best use of the talents of our employees; to create an inclusive work environment where every employee has an equal opportunity to develop his or her skills and talents. To encourage the involvement of employees in the planning and direction of their work; to provide them with channels to report concerns. We recognize that commercial success depends on the full commitment of all employees. (Shell, 2005)

Beyond this, a deontological critique of Shell's position might further enquire whether there were detailed policies and procedures on pay and conditions relating to its staff. A utilitarian analysis would go even further in this direction, asking what happened after all the good intentions and the effort to implement them. Such an analysis would seek detailed data on, for example, what employees were actually paid and how this compares to the local context. This is one example of the kind of information requested from companies in their public reporting using the Global Reporting Initiative (GRI) guidelines.

Morality and the law

The relationship between morality and the law matters to transparency. It is commonly held that CSR, for example, does not include behaviour mandated by law. From this it would follow that there is no particular need for trans-

22

parency over the legal activities of a company. If CSR is only about going beyond the law (in a positive sense), then CSR reports need concentrate only on voluntary behaviour.

This perspective relies on a rather over-simplified view of the law and of its relationship to morality. The relationship of companies to the law is not simply one of compliance. Companies help shape the law, through lobbying and consultation. Their role in that respect, and the consequent needs for transparency, are discussed in Chapter 13.

In addition, what is legal is not simply the same as what is moral. There are clearly laws which need to be changed. The very existence of the political system shows that views of what is right are constantly changing. It is also the case, as the proponents of CSR might argue, that there are many more good things than are prescribed by law.

Yet what also matters from an ethical perspective, and therefore in relation to transparency, is why a company is complying with the law. Is it because they want to do the right thing? Or because they could not get away with anything else? What would happen if it turned out to be cheaper to disobey the law than to abide by it? The lack of a 'business case' is a common occurrence, especially in relation to regulated aspects of business.

So, to be fully transparent, a company cannot be silent on its relationship to the law. Quite apart from motive and any influence on the laws themselves, what also matters is the extent of compliance actually demonstrated. It is naïve to assume that if there is a law, a company will always obey it. There is, in fact, already a history of companies disclosing their breeches of the law in some areas, the most notable being in the area of environmental regulation. However, whatever the actual practice, and whether it is called 'CSR reporting' or not, there is a need for transparency to extend over legally regulated activities.

SUSTAINABILITY

'Sustainability' has enjoyed a greater variety of definitions than most words. I will not attempt to produce a final definition, but given that sustainability is often used to define the boundaries of what companies ought to be transparent about, it is important to understand some of the main ways in which the word is used.

The original definition of sustainability carries the sense of 'capable of being sustained'. As applied to companies, this suggests that they would be able to carry on their operations indefinitely. Most of the argument has been around the conditions under which that might be possible. The most fundamental point is that, the boundaries of a company being quite arbitrary, it is not very meaningful to describe a company, in isolation from the whole ecosystem in which it exists, as sustainable. Sustainability is a property of the global system, not of any one of the entities within it in isolation. Of course, the contribution of all the entities within it matter, but it is not always possible to be sure how much they matter without some kind of global accounting. Only in a very few areas (such as the Montreal Protocol) is there any kind of global accounting for the effects of companies on the global ecosystem.

The way in which sustainability is defined varies with the stakeholder group to which the person doing the defining belongs. For example, to define sustainability as the ability of an organization to make reasonable profits in the long term suggests that sustainability is being defined in terms which benefit shareholders. That is clearly part of the picture, but so are the views of other stakeholder groups. From the point of view of a local community concerned about noise and disruption, for example, sustainability includes the absence of such unacceptable impacts. Similar arguments will apply to all other stakeholder groups.

What is useful about the concept of sustainability is that it defines a set of issues for which a minimum degree of performance is demanded. As applied to companies it is taken to set out the environmental, social and economic issues for which the performance of companies matter. It therefore also maps out the scope of issues for which transparency matters.

Just as the definition of sustainability can be problematic, so it is far from straightforward to define precise meanings for the terms 'environmental', 'social' or 'economic', which are commonly taken to combine to determine the overall sustainability impact of an organization. Fortunately, it is not necessary to do so definitively here, although it is important to say something about how they relate to each other and about the nature of the social dimension of sustainability. The division into environmental, social and economic aspects is not well-formed in that while individually any given impact can be allocated to one or another aspect, it can often be allocated to more than one. In other words, the categories overlap. This is particularly true of the social and economic categories, although it is also true of environmental impacts, as will be argued below.

The nature of social impacts causes a lot of difficulty for companies that are interested in trying to understand them. This appears to be because the science of the social is somehow less quantitative, technical and defined than the science of climate change, for example. However, this is a somewhat illusory view, both because the practical (in other words social) implementation of the protocols for greenhouse gas emissions require continuing maintenance of the interpretation of protocols, but also because, for a company, the domain of the social can be fully described as the set of stakeholder relationships into which it enters.

Of course, this does not remove the work necessary fully to define and understand what those relationships may be, but it does mean that the concept of sustainability can coherently be defined to include 'the social'. What the concept of sustainability alone does not do is indicate those to whom these issues matter. As I have argued elsewhere (Henriques, 2004), for every issue there is a stakeholder and for every stakeholder there is an issue. Transparency over sustainability for an organization, therefore, should include disclosure of those to whom the relevant sustainability issues of an organization matter.

Environmental issues may appear to be somehow different, as they are issues for which the stakeholder may not be obvious. For this reason many organizations find it convenient to treat the environment as another stakeholder, which can appear odd. One of the main reasons environmental issues appear not to have a corresponding stakeholder is that they often affect a very wide range of people (as do CO_2 emissions), or the people who will be affected may not yet even exist (such as those who may be affected by radioactive waste). However, the stakeholders for other environmental impacts, such as noise pollution, will be clearly identifiable. In the final analysis, someone must care about any given environmental issue, as otherwise it could not have been identified.

ACCOUNTABILITY AND RESPONSIBILITY

'Accountability' and 'responsibility' are names for ways to manage power relationships. In the running of an organization, if someone has power over a budget, for example, then they will (usually) be asked what they have done with it and how the money is being spent. They will be held accountable as they have power over company money. They will be asked to account for their activities.

Between an organization and all its stakeholders, the situation is – or should be – the same. When an organization affects its stakeholders, it is likely to be asked to account for its activities. Currently, the main area in which companies are legally required to account for their normal, lawful activities is in relation to shareholders for financial performance. This is examined in more detail in Chapter 7, which deals with reporting.

Transparency is therefore necessary not only over what impacts an organization has had, but also over how an organization has managed those impacts and the associated stakeholder relationships. Transparency is required, then, over organizational responsibility and accountability. Stakeholders have a (moral) right to know what is going on when it affects them.

What is the difference between accountability and responsibility? They are apparently closely related, but are they the same? The dictionary is not helpful in distinguishing between the two. The Oxford English Dictionary, for example, defines 'accountable' as 'bound to give an account, responsible, explicable'; it defines 'responsible' as 'liable to be called to account, answerable, morally accountable, capable of rational conduct, apparently trustworthy'.

'Responsibility' has more of a moral overtone and appears to be a softer requirement. In relation to corporations it is used in three main ways:

1   the acknowledgement of power and impact;
2   taking action or refraining from action appropriately; and
3   responding to its stakeholders – either with words or with deeds.

In 2006, the ISO Working Group on Social Responsibility (where the label 'social' is largely redundant) produced a working definition of organizational responsibility, which defined it as:

The actions of an organization to take responsibility for the impacts of its activities on society and the environment, where these actions:
- *are consistent with the interests of society and sustainable development;*
- *are based on ethical behaviour, compliance with applicable law and intergovernmental instruments; and*
- *are integrated into the ongoing activities of the organization.*

(ISO, 2006b)

Although this appears to use the term to be defined within the definition, its main function is to define organizational responsibility as a subset of moral behaviour. From the corporate perspective this is a comfortable position to take, as it suggests the organization is in control. Accountability, by contrast, because of the association with legally prescribed activities, is less comfortable to live with and may even be thought very threatening.

In practice, the 'accountability' of corporations is also used in a number of ways. The first is a legal sense, as we have seen. In this sense, the accountability of a corporation implies being able to hold it to account through submission to the legal system. This also entails that the courts may impose sanctions on a corporation.

Another meaning of accountability derives from its use within organizations in relation to the role of individuals in management positions. In this sense, accountability refers to the obligation to explain actions and their outcomes – the overspend of a budget, for example.

Accountability has also been used by civil society organizations to extend the parallel between stakeholder accountability and shareholder accountability to formalize responsibility in three ways:

1 taking responsibility for actions and their consequences;
2 giving an account, or explaining what has happened; and
3 responding systematically to stakeholder concerns.

This has been elaborated most by the AA1000 Standard. The original AA1000 Standard (ISEA, 1999), produced by the organization AccountAbility, then called the Institute of Social and Ethical Accountability, included a number of principles setting out what accountability for organizations might mean in practice; these are:

- inclusivity (of stakeholders in organization management);
- completeness (of management processes and communications);
- materiality (of management processes and communications);
- regularity and timeliness (of management processes and communications);
- quality assurance (of accountability processes);
- accessibility (of communications);
- information quality (of communications);
- embeddedness (of accountability processes); and
- continuous improvement (of performance).

CORPORATE SOCIAL RESPONSIBILITY

What is 'Corporate Social Responsibility (CSR)'? Although the concept of CSR has a considerable academic history, as Archie Carroll has documented (Carroll, 1999), I will suggest here that CSR is today more a social phenomenon than a coherent concept. To do so will involve looking at the variety of ways in which the term is used and some of the reasons behind this variety.

> *CSR, sometimes called responsible business practice or corporate responsibility, has no single definition but essentially covers how your business can make a positive contribution to your local area.* (CoC, 2006)

> *We know that CSR cannot be imposed, or directed from above. It is voluntary.* (Quintin, 2004)

> *The Government sees CSR as the business contribution to our sustainable development goals. Essentially it is about how business takes account of its economic, social and environmental impacts in the way it operates – maximising the benefits and minimising the downsides.* (CSR, 2006)

So, while everybody knows that CSR stands for corporate social responsibility, I am not convinced that anyone knows what it means. It has come to be identified with the range of ideas and initiatives concerned with what companies should do, and how they should do it, that has grown up since the closing years of the last century. So one interpretation of CSR is simply 'companies being ethical'.

There are those who will immediately suggest that companies in general are very rarely ethical, being overwhelmingly driven by the pursuit of profit, and that therefore the very nature of CSR must be empty. For those who believe that companies can, despite this, be ethical, there is unfortunately a great diversity in the nature, quality and quantity of ethical behaviour which companies display and label CSR. For example, environmental reporting, philanthropic donation, negotiating with unions and many other activities have all been called CSR. This might be acceptable, but very few have attempted to define what it is in all these diverse activities which makes them all part of CSR – other than their being ethical, of course.

As a result, the term has been embraced by many, hotly contested by some, but carefully defined by no-one – and so is also being abandoned by others who have lost any confidence in CSR being more than three letters in search of PR.

Some of this can be seen from the way alternative terms to CSR have been suggested. Some people have challenged what the 'C' in CSR stands for, or whether it should be there at all. Is CSR only about corporate behaviour? Or should it also embrace NGOs and government? Those in companies, when they are feeling overwhelmed by the demands for responsibility, ask why the NGOs which call for corporate responsibility should not also demonstrate their own. So might corporate social responsibility not be renamed 'organizational social responsibility'? This is the position from which the International Organization for Standardization (ISO) is trying to work, as we have seen. Their solution is to drop the 'C' altogether:

> *SR applies to more than just private companies. Corporate social responsibility, CSR, has been broadened to include governmental agencies and other organizations that have a clear interest in showing how they work.* (ISO, 2006a)

The reaction of NGOs, at least, has been to acknowledge that there is a need to demonstrate an efficient use of their resources for the purposes of their mission. However, NGOs also question the motives of those who insist that NGO organizational aims, which are explicitly designed to improve social, economic or environmental outcomes, should be challenged in the same way as those of organizations designed for another purpose entirely.

One of the main tasks of government is to formulate policies which improve the social, economic and environmental outcomes for their country. However, to deliver and enforce those policies, governments need to operate a large organizational machinery, which has impacts of its own. While the effectiveness of government policies is the mainstay of traditional politics, the impacts of public sector organizations themselves is largely unknown. Both are legitimate aspects of organizational responsibility.

Others have challenged what the 'S' stands for – or at least whether it should be confined to the sphere of the social alone. After all, the environmental performance of companies is also a matter of great social concern. Given the dominating concern with carbon emissions, it could be argued that the greatest 'social' issue facing companies is in fact an environmental one. There have been calls for the 'S' to be dropped in consequence; this would leave the term as 'corporate responsibility' – or perhaps, following the suggestion above, just 'responsibility'.

The difficulty of pinning down the social is illustrated by the treatment of health and safety issues. Somewhat surprisingly, health and safety has been treated as an environmental issue for some time and often falls within the managerial responsibility of the environmental manager. The UK Health and Safety Executive defines CSR in this way:

> *Corporate responsibility covers a wide range of issues, including the effects that an organization's business has on the environment, human rights and third world poverty. Health and safety in the workplace is an important corporate responsibility issue.* (HSE, 2006)

Few have challenged the 'R' for responsibility, but then even fewer have defined it, although this is hard to do, as we have seen. But, as we have also seen, it has been positioned in contrast to accountability as in some way less onerous. In

1999, admittedly the pioneering Wild West of CSR, a very senior manager in a mining company declared that he was entirely happy to be responsible, but that when he heard the word 'accountability', he 'reached for his gun'.

CSR is therefore commonly presented by companies as the voluntary expression of their desire to undertake voluntary activities for a wider social benefit. This has particularly included reporting. However, for NGOs, what matters is a systematic attempt to take responsibility for all company impacts, including those prescribed by law, and to be transparent about them. If that does not happen voluntarily, then legislation is necessary:

> We believe the voluntary approach to corporate accountability has failed; we are calling on the UK Government to enact laws that will ensure making profits is done within the context of businesses' responsibilities to their stakeholders and their obligation to ensure their businesses are sustainable long term [...] companies should [...] report against a comprehensive set of key social, environmental and economic indicators. With a standardized approach comes the ability to measure companies' operations and performance – here in the UK and abroad – and compare them with other businesses. (CORE, 2006)

A common view on CSR from the NGO community is that it is simply about PR:

> Since CSR will not bring an end to destructive activities for as long as they are profitable, can it really be described as 'responsibility'? (Fauset, 2006, p9)

CORPORATE CITIZENSHIP

Some have opted for the term 'corporate citizenship' instead of CSR. However, what is meant in practice by corporate citizenship turns out to be hard to distinguish from most of the definitions of CSR:

> Topics related to corporate citizenship can include (but are not limited to): corporate responsibility, stakeholder relationships, public policy, sustainability and environment, human and labour rights/issues, governance, accountability and transparency, globalization, small and medium-sized enterprises (SMEs), as well as multinational firms, ethics, measurement, and specific issues related to corporate citizenship such as diversity, poverty, education, information, trust, supply chain management, and problematic or constructive corporate/human behaviours and practices. (JCC, 2006)

Taken as defining something different from CSR, corporate citizenship has three important implications. First, that companies are people and second, that they are in some sense 'members' of society, in the same way that human citizens are. This suggests that they would naturally work in harmony with their society; in other words that 'corporate citizens' are also 'good citizens'. Yet for multinational companies, with operations across the world and wholly-owned subsidiaries in many different countries, it is not obvious what 'their society' might mean in practice – particularly when there are significant differences in the values people hold in the countries in question. And third, the concept of corporate citizenship also raises the crucial question as to what place companies have in running society. Corporate citizenship suggests that companies, as well as human citizens, have formally defined rights and responsibilities. However, beyond obeying the law, to which all companies pay lip service, very few would suggest that they should have additional rights in running society. Yet in the UK, until 1969, businesses did have a vote. This right is retained to this day within the City of London. In the City almost all businesses have the right to nominate a number of voters based on the number of their employees. Whatever the formal justification of this, it remains anomalous and is widely regarded as undemocratic, particularly since the business vote considerably outweighs the local residential vote.

THE POWER OF TRANSPARENCY

Transparency means conveying the truth. The origin of the word is to carry something across. What should be carried across is the truth. So transparency means seeing clearly.

It is ironic that the word 'transparency' seems itself to be both rather hard to define and to have two apparently different meanings. On hearing the word, usually the first thing we think of is glass; glass is transparent because light passes through it and so you can see what is behind. But there is also another meaning, such as when we say that someone behaved transparently – in other words you can see what they were up to. In this case the light is *reflected* by the behaviour, making it visible. As a result, there is no agenda, nothing hidden.

So transparency can be a property of glass, or of the things you can see through the glass. Both of these senses are important. Very often, campaigns for transparency (for example, against corruption) focus on honesty about what has happened. What is requested, in order to change behaviour, is that actions normally hidden are revealed. Yet what they must in practice often focus on is that the procedures for conducting such transactions are declared so that they allow light to be shed on the underlying behaviour.

David Heald (Heald, 2006b) has developed a theoretical schema for analysing transparency which distinguishes between:

- 'transparency upwards', in which the superior/principal can observe the behaviour of the subordinate/agent;
- 'transparency downwards', in which the ruled can observe the conduct of the rulers;

30

- 'transparency outwards', in which those subordinates inside an organization can observe the behaviour of those outside it; and
- 'transparency inwards', in which those outside an organization can observe what is happening inside it.

This framework is useful as it illustrates some of the ways in which power may be operating around an organization. The upwards–downwards dimension is explicitly described in terms of hierarchy and upwards transparency is also characterized as surveillance. Conversely, downwards transparency, particularly in a public governance context, is fundamental to accountability. Outwards transparency is also an important tool for organizational control. Finally, inwards transparency is the basis for inclusion and its lack is broadly equivalent to exclusion. In one way this book is about showing in some detail how all transparency can be reduced to 'transparency inwards' as all the parties interested in transparency will be stakeholders of a company and so, on a rigorous analysis, 'outside' it.

As applied to companies, there is a moral case, and therefore a need, for transparency when there is a significant power relationship between a company and one of its stakeholders. 'Power relationship' here means that one party is able to dictate to the other at least some of the terms of their relationship. The following chapter will further argue that a power relationship between a company and one of its stakeholders is actually equivalent to a power relationship between (at least) two of its stakeholders. Usually the power relationship exists between shareholders or management on the one hand and other stakeholders on the other.

Yet the issues about which stakeholders care are the same ones with which sustainability is concerned. Since sustainability issues are those which result from a particular company's social, environmental and economic impacts, the power to produce these impacts is at the same time a power to impose them on others, in other words on stakeholders. It follows that requiring transparency over power relations entails transparency over sustainability impacts. At times one formulation or the other will seem more natural. However it is formulated, though, the struggle over transparency in relation to a particular impact is how the power relationship between two stakeholders will often express itself.

4

What is a Company, Exactly?

Part of corporate truth is being clear as to the actual nature of companies. It may seem unusual to devote time to the issue of what a company really is, but it is important for at least two reasons. First, companies are not what we usually think they are. And second, if we are asking companies to be transparent, what kind of response should we expect? What should we expect them to be transparent about?

Most of us imagine that we know a lot about companies – we shop in them, we get annoyed with our bank, we enjoy TV shows, and so on. As a result, our common sense view is often that a company *is*:

- its buildings;
- the people who work in them; and
- the brands or other intellectual property that we see or use.

Yet actually a company is none of these things. Companies may make use of all of them, and more, but a company is not the same as any of them. So if we are asking companies to be transparent, what are we expecting to see?

This question will be approached through examining what a company is at several different levels, starting with the most fundamental, its legal basis, moving through successively less tangible layers and finishing with a review of brands, which will consider the 'psychology' of a company. The most striking thing about the various layers of what a company is is that many are remarkably similar to perfectly ordinary people. The sections below will therefore review the arguments and surprising ramifications of companies as persons, which lays the foundation for how the corporate world can borrow from personal morality to legitimize any lack of transparency.

REAL COMPANIES, LEGAL ENTITIES

Why do people form companies? Probably the most important advantage of companies today is 'limited liability'. Sole traders and partnerships are liable for all their debts in full. However, the shareholders in 'companies limited by shares' (which is the most usual form of company) enjoy a limit to their exposure. In practice, the maximum financial risk which the shareholders in a company must bear is determined not by the impact their company may have had, but by the amount its shareholders have invested in it. For some of the early companies of previous centuries, the rationale for this was that the share-holders were banding together and undertaking significant risks (such as discovering new lands or building railways) *for the public good*. Despite the change in motivation among shareholders today, the form of limited liability and its attendant advantages for shareholders remains.

If you ask a lawyer what a company or corporation is, the immediate response is likely to be 'something which can be sued'. This eminently practical reply also serves as a preliminary operational definition of a company, but we would still need to distinguish companies from ordinary people, who can also be sued. Further thought from our imaginary lawyer will elicit that companies are legal entities which can be the subject of rights and can take action.

In legal terms, a company is a 'person'. The concept of person dates back to that of the mask of an actor on a stage (*dramatis personae*), someone who was known through the sound which they made. For the millennia of Roman law, a person has been someone who could initiate, or respond to, an action at law. This is also the position in all modern legal systems today.

The law does not recognize intrinsically different kinds of person. Before the law, corporate persons are just the same as individual, flesh and blood persons (what we might call people). Yet there clearly are vast differences between Microsoft Inc. and you and me. To account for this, those who have to make sense of it typically take one of three positions.

The first is the fiction theory, which holds that the idea of a legal person is simply a 'legal fiction'. Although corporations can take real action, and can improve or ruin people's lives, they do not really exist. The second is the aggre-gate theory, which suggests that you can simply reduce companies to the actions of ordinary people, particularly company directors. And the third is the reality theory, which claims that companies do have an underlying reality, but one which is *created* not by the law but by society. The role of the law is simply to recognize and make use of such pre-existing persons.

If a company really exists, where does it live? This is not a silly question and had to be settled in law. In the case of the Egyptian Delta Land and Investment Company Ltd *v.* Todd (1928) it was argued that despite being regis-tered in the UK, the Egyptian Delta Land Company conducted virtually all of its business in Egypt and should therefore not be required to pay income tax on its earnings in the UK. One of the Law Lords, Lord Buckmaster, included in his reasoning the following from an earlier case:

> *Registration, like the birth of an individual, is a fact which must be taken into consideration in determining the question of residence. It may be a strong circumstance, but it is only a circumstance. It would be idle to say that in the case of an individual the birth was conclusive of the residence. So drawing an analogy between a*

*natural and an artificial person, you may say that in the case of a
corporation the place of its registration is the place of its birth, and
is a fact to be considered with all the others.* (Egyptian Delta *v.*
Todd, 1928)

The outcome of the case was that the Egyptian Delta Company was considered
resident in Egypt, not the place of its incorporation – and did not have to pay
UK income tax as a result.

In practice, most large companies actually themselves comprise other
companies or subsidiaries. One reason for this is that most countries require
commercial activities to be carried out by organizations registered within their
jurisdiction. So a large multinational will have at least one company for each
country in which they operate.

CORPORATE ANATOMY AND PHYSIOLOGY

How do such complex entities actually work? The organized behaviour of large
companies is a considerable achievement requiring much attention and effort –
usually called management. The overall purpose of a company, however, is
achieved through 'corporate governance'.

Sir Adrian Cadbury (Cadbury, 1992) defined corporate governance as 'the
system by which companies are directed and controlled'. This has led to an
extensive literature on the composition of formal committees and their relationship to shareholders. Attention has focused particularly on the board and its
directors, how directors are selected, the roles they have, and the background
and training necessary.

Although Cadbury was writing about the financial governance of companies in relation to shareholders' interests, it is also possible to consider
governance in the context of stakeholder interests more generally (see, for
example, Henriques and Richardson, 2004). From this broader perspective,
the governance of a company extends into general management and includes a
wide range of values, principles, mission statements, procedures, policies and
indicators.

There have been a number of attempts to introduce structure into this
apparently amorphous set of management practices with a view to understanding CSR. Significant examples are the 'pyramid' of Archie Carroll (Carroll,
1991) and its development by Donna Wood (Wood, 1994). As elaborated by
Wood, there are three significant levels – principles, processes and products
(or outcomes) – to take into account. Her approach, which she called 'corporate social performance', was designed to include a range of stakeholders.
However, it needs to be emphasized that it should be applied to shareholders
(and other investors), as much as to other stakeholders, in order to be generally applicable.

This structure or schema is based on what is increasingly common business
practice, which includes:

- a set of articulated values or aspirational material which purports to set out what the organization is aiming at for a variety of stakeholders; targets are a quantified expression of what the organization is aiming at;
- a set of policies and guides to decision making which indicates how the organization is seeking to realize its values through the actions of its employees and as an organization; and
- a set of indicators which are designed to capture how it has actually performed in relation to its aspirations.

Such a schema is inevitably simplified, but it can be applied to every stakeholder. Another formulation of a similar, systematic approach to stakeholder interaction is provided in Wheeler and Sillanpää's book *The Stakeholder Corporation* (Wheeler and Sillanpää, 1997).

The Global Reporting Initiative (GRI) calls for disclosure of the same range of elements, with the requirement that reports should include material about strategy, targets and policies, and also detailed indicators of performance. In practice, it is certainly rarely true that an organization clearly and systematically sets out these three levels in relation to its performance for any one stakeholder. It is also true that the articulation of these three levels is very rarely evenhanded across the various stakeholder groups of the organization.

As we have seen, there is a correspondence of this three-part schema with the three kinds of ethical theory outlined in Chapter 3. Thus virtue ethics is most relevant to company aims, duty ethics to policies and utilitarianism to actual performance. This is important, since if the scope of what companies should be transparent about is defined by the field of their moral responsibility, it will be helpful to be clear about what the most suitable approach to ethics at each of these levels may be.

COMPANIES AND STAKEHOLDERS

Companies are to stakeholders as bodies are to cells. It is possible to think of our bodies as 'nothing but' the collection of cells which compose them. Yet it is also possible to describe our bodies as coherent entities with purposes and actions of their own. In the language of complexity theory, our bodies can be said to be emergent entities that cannot be completely described in terms of their cells. Both views are valid.

A similar divergence of perspective applies to companies. It is possible to describe them entirely in terms of their stakeholders. In this respect, companies are 'empty' and their activity is simply the coordination of stakeholders' activities. In this view, it is important to remember that both shareholders and company management are stakeholders, rather than being somehow the same as the company. Yet it is also possible to describe companies as moral agents, with coherent purposes other than that of any particular individual or stakeholder.

The consequences of this for transparency are that it is legitimate to ask a *company* for transparency, rather than simply an individual within it. In this perspective, transparency results when an organization talks about itself to a stakeholder.

On the other hand, the stakeholder perspective also helps to clarify that, in practice, we, that is one stakeholder, will be asking for transparency about the activities of another stakeholder. Given the prevailing power relationships, this will typically be a request for transparency about the activities of management or of shareholders. In this perspective, transparency is a relationship of openness between stakeholders.

It will be clear by now that stakeholders are critical to a company and also to assessing its performance. But what are stakeholders? The traditional definition, which derives from Edward Freeman's work (Freeman, 1984), defines a stakeholder as 'any person or organization which affects, or is affected by, an organization'. It is very important to point out that whether or not a person or organization is a stakeholder is a matter of fact, not of judgement by the organization (or by the person) concerned. Of course an organization may decide to ignore or pay little attention to stakeholders, but that does not somehow make them cease to be a stakeholder, it just means they are being ignored. Indeed, which stakeholders an organization acknowledges is perhaps the single most critical piece of information in assessing an organization's ethical performance.

The nature of the relationship between a stakeholder and a company will be different for different kinds of stakeholders and will change over time. A variety of different ways are used by companies to analyse their stakeholders. Typical examples are:

- the relative power of the stakeholder and the company: can the stakeholder, perhaps a regulator, affect or influence the company?;
- whether the stakeholder has a legal or commercial relationship with the company of some sort – in this respect, for example, customers and suppliers are different from local communities or NGOs; and
- how often the company interacts with the stakeholder: there may be daily or much less frequent interactions.

These sorts of analysis are typically used to plan the company's relationship to a stakeholder. In general, stakeholders which have little power (or greater vulnerability) and no commercial relationship with the company and which interact infrequently with the company will tend to be ignored and the corresponding social or environmental performance will suffer accordingly. The converse is also true: powerful, commercial stakeholders with which the company interacts often will be privileged. And clearly these three dimensions are often independent, potentially giving rise to a complex ranking of stakeholders.

In terms of transparency, those stakeholders that are highly ranked using the above analysis are treated to additional transparency. Those with little influence are ignored. When impacts on vulnerable stakeholders are considered, the communication is typically addressed to NGOs, which may be promoting the vulnerable group's interests and which may be capable of influencing public opinion, rather than to the stakeholder themselves. This perspective is behind the production of social or sustainability reports addressed to 'opinion formers'.

This corporate behaviour pattern is based on perceived corporate interest, not stakeholder interest. The debate during the UK review of company law about the 'materiality' of issues as a determinant of what should be reported was based very largely on what is material to a company, rather than what is material to a given stakeholder. This gives rise to the absurd and immoral position that, for a large company, the loss of a single life at work may be regarded as non-material and therefore not necessary to report.

One way to understand what is happening in terms of stakeholder relations is to consider each company–stakeholder relationship as a principal–agent relationship. This has often been used to examine the relationship between shareholders and a company or its managers. The classic problem is how far the principal (the shareholder) can trust, control and incentivize the agent (company management). Economic theory suggests that where the agent's behaviour is known to the principal, transparency improves the outcomes for that principal (Holmstrom, 1979; Holmstrom, 1999; Prat, 2006). It is also interesting here to note that this problem is stated in terms of how two different stakeholder groups can or should relate to each other.

However, it is also possible to generalize this kind of analysis in two ways. First, *each* stakeholder can relate to company management in this way, and indeed to the other stakeholders. And second, each such relationship can be considered as a 'principal–agent' relationship as well as an 'agent–principal' relationship. So, for example, the company management to shareholder relationship is often (and perhaps more usually) considered from a day-to-day management perspective as one in which the shareholder is a provider of capital to be managed, rather than one in which the management is performing a job for the shareholder.

Similar shifts in perspective can be applied to different sets of stakeholder relationships. A consumer, for example, can be considered as the principal in relation to the shareholder: if they don't buy, the shareholder loses money. But, from the perspective of the marketing department, the consumer may be considered as an agent to be directed and controlled into a more profitable relationship with the company. Similar kinds of remarks could be made about other stakeholder relationships of the consumer, to suppliers, for example.

The implications of all this for transparency are considerable. First, from a formal economic perspective, the relationship cannot work well when the various stakeholders have different interests (which will often be the case) *and* there is an information asymmetry between them concerning the agent's performance (see, for example, Sappington, 1991). It follows that company performance is optimized when there is maximum transparency. This is far from the situation today.

Second, considering company management as the agent for the spectrum of company stakeholders opens the door to the idea of 'stakeholder governance'. This would generalize the considerations which apply to the traditional idea of corporate governance to include the interests that the variety of stakeholders have in a company, many of which are not primarily economic. Closely associated with the idea of governance are the information needs on which it rests. This is another way of saying that stakeholders need to have information in order to control or influence how a company impacts on them.

Finally, as we have seen, from the stakeholder perspective all transparency is cross-stakeholder transparency. Consequently, any power relationship between a company and a stakeholder can always be re-described as a power relationship between two stakeholders. Furthermore, because very often each individual occupies a number of different stakeholder roles in relation to the same company (as customer, employee and shareholder, for example) it follows that transparency can typically be thought of as required in the public interest.

WHO COUNTS AS A STAKEHOLDER?

So who counts as a stakeholder? The traditional list for a company includes:

- shareholders;
- suppliers;
- customers;
- the community; and
- staff.

It must be said straightaway that this list will need to be extensively tailored for every company – and also modified for non-corporate organizations such as voluntary or public sector organizations. Yet even for a private company, the list needs careful interpretation. For example, the investors in a company include not only shareholders but probably also bondholders and lending institutions such as banks.

Suppliers are often a very diverse group of stakeholders. One way of thinking about them is to consider general suppliers, product suppliers and the suppliers to suppliers, or the supply chain. The majority of active companies will have general suppliers; they may deliver stationery, cleaning services, power or transport. Unless the company manufactures stationery or one of the products or services which are considered general supplies, these suppliers will not be core suppliers, in other words those who deliver the raw material for the main products which the company sells. Beyond both general and core suppliers are the suppliers' suppliers. While companies may have no direct commercial relationship with these, they are, in practice, powerfully affected by the purchasing decisions of large companies.

If you ask a company how it treats its suppliers, it may respond in a variety of ways, by giving a heart-warming example of a time when it went beyond the call of duty in supporting a supplier, perhaps when the supplier was in difficulty; detailing the average price paid for its supplies, compared to the market average; or providing an analysis of the time it spends with its suppliers giving its purchasing policy.

Customers are important to all companies. Indeed, companies often say that they are customer-driven and will do whatever their customers require. It should also be pointed out that companies are also keen on influencing their customers in a variety of ways. For example, a bank may persuade a customer who can barely afford it to take out a loan. There is therefore a responsibility which extends from the company to their customers.

Another stakeholder which needs particular attention is 'the community'. For some companies, the identity of the community may be fairly clear. An example might be the fenceline communities of people who live or work in close proximity to company facilities. So companies which have significant operational sites near residential areas, for example, can clearly identify the community in question. However, for many, if not most companies, the identity of the community is far from clear. It turns out that 'the community' is often shorthand for 'society in general'. In practice, it is often used to refer to the recipients of company philanthropy. ING (UK), for example, is based in Reading; they say on their website that:

> We are committed to helping our local community and continue to support Turners Court Youth Trust (www.turnerscourt.org.uk), a local charity that strives to help vulnerable children and families in the Reading area. As well as creating and delivering fundraising activities, our staff show their commitment by running after-school clubs at local schools and can donate money via our payroll giving scheme. They have even put on a production of Cinderella for the local community to enjoy, with money raised through ticket sales going straight to the charity. (ING, 2006a)

Whereas in the US, ING say the following:

> ING DIRECT is the exclusive sponsor of the 'Degas, Sickert and Toulouse-Lautrec: London and Paris, 1870–1910', a special exhibition [which] focuses on the impact of Edgar Degas on Walter Sickert and his contemporaries in Britain, and features many works by Henri de Toulouse-Lautrec, as well as paintings by Pierre Bonnard, James Tissot, and much more. (ING, 2006b)

Coming to staff, we need to remember that stakeholders are 'other' than the company – in other words they are not the same thing. This may seem an obvious thing to say, but the lines can get blurred, particularly when considering staff as a stakeholder. For this reason, stakeholders are often divided into 'internal' and 'external' stakeholders. What this usually means is that staff are considered internal and all other stakeholders are external (occasionally shareholders are also considered internal stakeholders).

This perspective seems very clear in a report from the Swiss technical communications company Swisscom:

> Put simply, Swisscom consists of infrastructure and employees. Our networks form the backbone of our operations, enabling us to offer a full range of products and services. Our employees ensure that these offerings are of the highest quality and reliability, so that they

deliver maximum added value for our customers. Infrastructure and employees are the foundation of our company's success. They are the alpha and omega of Swisscom. (Swisscom, 2006)

However, this way of speaking is actually very unclear, because nowhere is it said what staff are internal to – except maybe its buildings from time to time. They are no more the property of the company than are its customers. There is nothing they are 'inside'. What this usage reflects is that staff are encouraged to consider themselves as part of the company and to *identify* with it as far as possible. The company's values are important elements of this strategy. Yet the company's values are usually really staff values. These values are usually chosen to reflect the values which senior management would like staff to hold, so that their work is more helpful to the company's goals. Even if staff were entirely compliant and adopted such values wholeheartedly, this approach does not make staff any more 'inside' the company, however.

Similar arguments apply to shareholders. They might form a company specifically in order to separate themselves from the possibility of loss, from which the legal form of the company insulates them to some extent. So it is hard to argue that shareholders are internal to the company. It may be suggested that shareholders will inevitably be identified with the financial goals set out by senior management, and while that may often be true, it is hard to see what it is that they may be considered 'inside'. It follows that senior management themselves should usually be considered as an additional, separate stakeholder group. Yet it is a group about which often little is known. As Anthony Sampson has written:

much less is known about [...] directors and their boards than about politicians and their cabinets, and their chief executives are much less exposed to public criticism, and less accountable to voters, even after they have been the subject of fierce controversy. (Sampson, 2004)

So, using the stakeholder view, when the stakeholders of a company are stripped away, what is left? One answer is simply the legal form and the various assets which the company owns – although these belong in turn to the owners of the company, the shareholders. If the company is, in effect, reduced to its legal rights and some borrowed assets, what does it actually do? The answer is that a company is a way of organizing stakeholder relationships. That is all a company does. All the efforts of management are concerned with relating one set of stakeholders to another: buying things from suppliers, altering them with staff and selling them to customers. In the end the idea that companies, as persons, are a legal fiction implies that they are empty. There are no truly 'internal' stakeholders, except by a somewhat shaky psychological process of identification. There is nothing inside, nobody at home!

AGENTS OF MORALITY

The ghost in the corporate machine

It was suggested earlier that the scope of the things about which a company ought to be transparent is defined by the boundary of their moral reach. What does that say about the nature of companies? If companies are no more than (legal) fictions, then, as fictions, perhaps they are not really morally responsible for anything. This might seem to give them complete freedom of activity. However, as Donaldson points out (Donaldson, 1982) the consequence is more likely to be to remove the justification for a limit on regulation, on the grounds that if they cannot be regarded as moral and able to control themselves accordingly, then they had better be very tightly controlled by laws.

What those, like Ladd and Velasquez (Ladd, 1970; Velasquez, 1983), who argue that 'corporations are not morally responsible for anything they do' mean is that corporations are entirely conceived, built and operated by human beings and there just isn't anything left when you have removed humans from the picture – that companies can be reduced to individual humans. This is an instance of the aggregate theory described above; it takes the stakeholder perspective one stage further. In this view, to hold companies to account it is necessary to hold one or more individual humans to account; to talk in any other way is just shorthand:

> *Saying that a corporation is morally responsible for some wrongful act is acceptable only if it is an elliptical way of claiming that there are some people in the corporation who are morally responsible for that act and who should therefore be blamed or punished.* (Velasquez, 1983, p13)

One problem with this perspective is that, like many reductionist theories, it fails to appreciate that complex systems sometimes cannot be reduced to their parts. This view was not shared by Margaret Thatcher, who famously denied the existence of society (Thatcher, 1987), although she did venture so far as to suggest that the family existed as well as individuals. But just as individuals are not only the collection of their individual cells, and we can't escape our moral responsibility by asking the cells responsible to step forward, so companies must also be more than the collection of humans who operate within them.

While a common sense view of companies might be that they can't really do things 'under their own power', in practice most people treat companies as moral persons. We are all quite ready to blame companies for their acts, even to prosecute them for manslaughter, for example, or sometimes to praise them. Yet one issue with this perspective is that a common sense view of a company, whether admired or resented, is also that it is not a person in the sense in which individual humans are. Perhaps in consequence there has been philosophical debate as to whether it is proper to confer 'personhood' on companies, and therefore whether they can be said to be moral agents and so responsible in a moral sense for their actions and omissions.

42

There are still some companies which claim that they are just economic agents with no responsibility beyond economic efficiency. On that score, when these same companies also make substantial, purely voluntary charitable donations, they are performing an immoral act. This appears to be the position of Helmut Maucher, who declared that 'ethical' decisions, for philanthropy, for example, can be immoral because they cost a company money, which is against its moral obligation (Maucher, 1994).

Other companies realize that they are powerful actors in today's global society and as such they are indeed moral agents. Some of the latter embrace CSR. The CSR perspective, as we have seen, appears to take for granted that companies are persons, and indeed goes further, considering them, as 'corporate citizens', to also enjoy rights and duties and certainly to be capable of moral standing. Behind the challenge and counter-challenge of NGO campaigns against companies lies the assumption that both parties are moral agents, whatever the apparent size of their respective moral surpluses or deficits.

When we think of a moral relationship, we usually mean a relationship between two ordinary people. But some ordinary people are considered too young or too ill to be capable of moral action. So when can an ordinary person be said to be capable of moral acts? Peter French and Kevin Gibson (French, 1979; Gibson, 1995) have defined some conditions which appear to work for ordinary people and, they are keen to show, also work for companies. The conditions are first, that the person is liable to be held to account for their acts, and second, that they actively intended to do them, or that they passively (negligently) failed to do something. The active form of the second condition (in which there is an intention) is based on the structure of criminal law, while the passive form (implying negligence) is based on that of civil law.

Ordinary people, naturally enough, fulfil these conditions quite readily – as the workload of the court system attests. The task is to show that companies also do, and in particular that they have intentions of their own. French's main argument to this effect hinges on his rather technical claim that descriptions of the acts of a corporation are not in general reducible to descriptions of the acts of its members or employees. He claims that corporations typically have an internal decision structure ('CID') which 'licences the predication of corporate intentionality' and so enables moral agency.

At this point, some may feel some sympathy with the reductionists and want to deny that corporations exist. It may feel as though we have proved the existence of a 'ghost in the machine', some kind of independently existing mind that 'does the intending' for the company, which is otherwise just the sum of its actions accomplished by individuals in the ordinary way. But there is no escape from the dilemma, as it would after all be just as possible to apply the same arguments to ordinary people, denying that there was any conscious intention which couldn't be accounted for by the activity of their cells.

Making companies moral

Fortunately there is a very different way of looking at the nature of moral personality which allows corporations to be considered moral agents and which accounts for our natural intuitions about morality. As I have proposed elsewhere (Henriques, 2005a), from a common sense point of view, people and companies do moral (or immoral) things, because that is how we see them – and because of how they think about themselves.

In the experience of most parents, children definitely don't start out capable of moral behaviour. But they mostly end up that way. How do children become 'moral agents'? What happens is that in the midst of everyday activities, parents project a moral capability onto their children and eventually children project it onto themselves. Probably from the moment that process starts, they are, quite validly, treated as moral agents.

Companies are also thought of as moral agents, as John Browne of BP puts it:

> *The fundamental definition of ethics is about the conduct of the relationship between one person to another. The issue of ethics and business is about the relationship of one entity to everyone with whom we come into contact.* (Browne, 2004)

It is also useful to imagine an experiment designed to see if it were possible to tell the difference between identical behaviour with moral implications carried out by a company and by an ordinary person. Would it be possible to tell the difference? Consider the actions of an individual sole trader against those of a limited company of similar turnover engaged in the same activities. It is easy to imagine a situation – perhaps that of a refusal to pay compensation or acknowledge obvious fault – in which, without knowing which was which, it would not be possible for anyone to be sure.

The antipathy towards the idea of corporations as moral persons is probably more about the idea of corporations judging others than as organizations able to take praise or blame. Yet there are several good reasons to think of corporations in this way. The first is that they often set out statements of their values, by which they propose to judge their own actions or invite others to judge them. The second is that they readily make judgements about the apportioning of blame or praise to other organizations and individuals. Of course the values and behaviour which corporations display may not be the same as those they profess and the judgements they make may be ill-founded. But corporations obviously share these deficiencies with people, and so this cannot count against them. What does count is that they engage in behaviour which is functionally identical with that of individuals in considering others as moral agents.

TOWARDS A CORPORATE PSYCHOLOGY

If the idea of companies being capable of moral agency seems odd, the idea that they have a mind or personality as well will seem even more so. Yet to try a company for a criminal offence, it is important to establish the state of mind of the company, just as it would be for an individual. In order to try a company for a crime, it is necessary to establish not only that the act in question has been committed (*actus reus*) but also that there was an intention to do so (*mens rea*). Under the 'identification doctrine' which is most usually applied in such cases, the conduct and state of mind of the company's senior management is regarded as the conduct and state of mind of the company. It appears that the aggregate theory is what is applied by the courts in practice.

This approach seems more plausible for smaller companies. It may seem possible, for example with small companies, that the mind of the founder becomes so linked to the company that it is difficult to tell the two apart. Manfred Kets de Vries (Kets de Vries and Cooper, 1996; Kets de Vries and Miller, 1984) has shown convincingly how this can happen and the pathologies which can result. Joel Bakan in *The Corporation* (Bakan, 2004) has suggested that the legally mandated fixation on the pursuit of profit results in pathological behaviour – that is in behaviour which would be judged psychopathic if it were exhibited by an individual.

Yet companies spend great sums of money to convince people that they are more than just their employees: they develop brands.

But are brands really minds? And are they the minds of companies? The prime reason brands are developed is to control the perceptions which others, particularly a company's customers, have of a company or its products. The Brand Company puts it this way:

> *What is a brand? Brand is the proprietary visual, emotional, rational and cultural image that you associate with a company or a product. When you think Volvo, you might think safety. When you think Nike, you might think of Michael Jordan or 'Just Do It'. When you think IBM, you might think 'Big Blue'. The fact that you remember the brand name and have positive associations with that brand makes your product selection easier and enhances the value and satisfaction you get from the product. [...] While Brand X cola or even Pepsi-Cola may win blind taste tests over Coca-Cola, the fact is that more people buy Coke than any other cola and, most importantly, they enjoy the experience of buying and drinking Coca-Cola. The fond memories of childhood and refreshment that people have when they drink Coke is often more important than a little bit better cola taste. It is this emotional relationship with brands that make them so powerful. (Brand, 2006)*

Whether or not brands are actually the same thing as the mind of a company, they clearly have a powerful effect on both the company and (at least some of) its stakeholders:

When you walk into Wal-Mart you are usually greeted by a
precious, mother-like lady who hands you a cart and says, 'Welcome
to Wal-Mart'. You buy, not because the cart is large, but because
the lady who greeted you established a relationship. When Sam
Walton began Wal-Mart years ago in Arkansas, he went to his
suppliers and said, 'I want to develop a partnership with you'. That
same philosophy has been transferred to how Wal-Mart treats its
customers and may explain why Wal-Mart is so successful. (Wong
and Wong, 2002)

The idea is that the homely, helpful, non-threatening image is strongly linked to
the company and its products. Wal-Mart goes to considerable lengths to ensure
its staff identify with the company, including morning group inspiration sessions.
Brands are perhaps the conscious parts of the corporate 'mind', carefully
maintained and presented. But companies have an unconscious too, and the
more the unconscious is ignored the more it fights for attention. In *No Logo*
(Klein, 2000), Naomi Klein carefully linked the bright, appealing image which
brands convey with the darker, damaging activities that they may also undertake. These may include poor labour conditions in the supply chain, exploitative
staff conditions or adverse environmental and health impacts. For example,
Nike has been strongly criticized for labour conditions in its supply chain, Coca-
Cola for its impact on water availability and Wal-Mart for its hostility to union
representation. Yet all these companies have strong and carefully maintained
brands. Maybe that is not so surprising: the defining characteristic of the unconscious, of course, is the difficulty of admitting to its very existence.

This difficulty with self-examination is a very psychological trait. Is it
psychologically feasible that companies have minds? According to analytical
psychologist Andrew Samuels, 'it is not absolutely necessary to have a patient
in human form in order to do psychotherapy or analysis' (Samuels, 1993, p30).
From a psychological perspective, however, companies, along with the rest of
the world, do not make very satisfactory patients, Samuels continues:

[depth psychologists] having issued them with a request for therapy,
the world has not shown up for its first session. The world is
ambivalent about its therapy [...] reluctant to be a patient.

This reaction, at least as far as companies go, is not that surprising, given that
the perfection of the brand is front of mind. With the kind of narcissistic disposition which a good brand instils, how *could* any fault be admitted?

It may not be worth pushing the idea that companies have minds to the
limit. The whole concept of 'mind' is so hard to define, in any case, that it is
difficult to see how the question could be fully resolved. But it is, as we have
seen, illuminating to consider the parallels between individual minds and corporate ones. This has two consequences. The first is that, for those who wish to
change companies' behaviour, it is important to bear in mind that any successful approach is invariably psychological on several levels.

The second is that, to the extent to which the parallel holds, the brands which companies maintain are very clearly psychologically immature. Characteristic psychological reactions to threats are to tolerate no imperfection, to be highly manipulative in getting their way and to be highly defensive when challenged. Just as with children, it does little good just to scold and punish. Tantrums will result. What process might help them to grow and develop into more mature, open and wise ways of functioning? There is no doubt that any work to increase transparency must acknowledge these issues, as I have argued elsewhere (Henriques, 2001a), and at least bring the same maturity to the matter which one would like to see from companies.

5

The Right Perspective

To talk of 'human rights' is to talk about the most widely accepted, non-religious articulation of morality to date. The spectrum of human rights includes rights in relation to information and to privacy. If transparency has the moral dimension suggested above, then how transparency fits with the language of human rights is very important. Two key issues are discussed in this chapter:

1   While the legal support for human rights underpins their moral authority, it also has the bizarre consequence of companies being able to claim 'human' rights.
2   The right to privacy provides a moral basis for a limit to the demand for transparency.

Most discussion of business and human rights treats human rights as defining a responsibility for a baseline or minimum level of performance which should not be breached. It is acknowledged that practical challenges in areas such as conflict zones can make such standards difficult to meet. It is also acknowledged that:

> *companies will have no defence if they are not transparent. Mistakes will be made, but if they are openly acknowledged, if they are made in the context of policies and practices that reflect the breadth of a company's responsibilities, they will be accepted as mistakes, not condemned as crimes.* (Chandler, 2003)

WHAT ARE HUMAN RIGHTS?

Rights are claims to entitlements. Human rights are usually taken to be those embodied in international law. Yet human rights have a moral as well as a legal expression. While the legal aspect of rights is important, it is also vital to ground the discussion with an exploration of their moral character. This matters, I believe, because the moral nature of rights is more fundamental than any particular legal expression, however powerful in practice that legal expression may be.

From a moral perspective, a human right is something which all humans possess by virtue of being human. Nothing more is necessary. (There may be controversy about the boundaries of the human, however, especially in relation to conception and the morality of abortion.) Collectively, human rights are a demand for respect and an acknowledgement of the essential dignity of individuals. Specific human rights refer to particular aspects through which such essential dignity should be realized.

It is usually asserted that to have a right, someone or something else must have a duty or be obliged to satisfy it. This arises from the legal expression of rights based on a corresponding entitlement, but it is not an essential component of their moral expression. The moral character of all rights lies in the inherent goodness or desirability of the object of the right, such as free speech. It remains a good thing even in the absence of any immediate prospect of realization. Such an 'abstract right' may be asserted to attach blame to those who would prevent others enjoying it.

In everyday use, the word 'right' is used very broadly in this way, to imply or underline the moral outrage which people feel if they are denied what they regard as their right. Whatever the merits or otherwise of such abstract rights, they do underline the fact that rights appear to be of most relevance and significance when they are breached; their peaceful enjoyment generally goes unremarked.

Human rights in the stricter definition are of course a subset of the many rights which may legally be claimed by humans; they are those of the most fundamental importance and the highest moral stature. They are *constitutive* of being human, as Donelly puts it: 'human rights are a sort of self-fulfilling moral prophecy: "Treat people like human beings and you will get truly *human* beings"' (Donnelly, 1989).

SETTING THE LAW TO RIGHTS

Before the modern state, the concept of rights was ill-defined. The English Magna Carta of 1215 set out the rights of (some) subjects against their monarch, provided for due legal process and protected against arbitrary demands by the King. It is credited with being the first legal charter of rights. In the late eighteenth century, the US and France enshrined rights in their constitutions. These were initially limited in their application, in particular applying to men rather than women, but were eventually extended to be of quite general application.

The United Nations developed the concept of rights in a number of ways with the adoption of the Universal Declaration of Human Rights (UN, 1948). This declared human rights to be inalienable – in other words all people have a right to rights. There is no status which a person might have (such as being convicted of a crime) which would mean that they have forfeited their rights. It also articulated the rights to which all people could lay claim and extended the domain of rights to social, economic and cultural areas. The Universal Declaration of Human Rights (UDHR) was not, however, designed to be a legally binding document.

Some 20 years later a number of key international instruments which did have the potential to be legally binding began to be signed. Of these, perhaps the two most significant were the International Covenant on Civil and Political Rights (ICCPR) (UN, 1966a) and the International Covenant on Economic, Social and Cultural Rights (ICESCR) (UN, 1966b). A large majority of countries in the world have bound themselves to implementing all the rights in both these agreements through their national legal systems. There are some very significant exceptions, however. To date, the US has not ratified the ICESCR and China has not ratified the ICCPR.

The particular area of human rights concerned with the workplace, or labour rights, has a parallel recent history. The International Labour Organization, which pre-dates the rest of the UN system, having been formed in 1919, has developed numerous conventions. In 1998 it adopted the Declaration on Fundamental Principles and Rights at Work (ILO, 1998), which promotes freedom of association and the right to collective bargaining, the elimination of forced and compulsory labour, the abolition of child labour, and the elimination of discrimination in the workplace. Of the many instruments adopted by the ILO, two of the most significant are the Convention concerning Forced or Compulsory Labour (ILO, 1930) and the Freedom of Association and Protection of the Right to Organize Convention (ILO, 1948). While a large majority of the countries in the world have bound themselves through their legal systems to implementing these conventions, to date, neither the US nor China has ratified either of them.

Human rights, as a legal concept today, in states which have implemented them in their law, concern the claims of a person in relation to the obligations of the state. In other words, human rights may be claimed by a person against a state, which has the corresponding obligation.

WHO HAS THE RIGHT?

In all the major legal systems of the world, there are only two sorts of entities that have legal status: 'persons' and the state. Organizations such as the civil service, hospitals and local councils are considered part of the state. As you may expect, individual people are considered persons. The concept of persons, however, extends also to groups, such as partnerships. And crucially it also extends to companies.

This means that corporations have human rights. While it may seem absurd to imagine that companies should have the right not to be tortured or to take part in cultural life, a court will have to allow a corporation to claim human rights against the state. This has indeed been done successfully. In practice, it has been used mainly to defend the right to the 'peaceful enjoyment of posses-sions'. It is possible to imagine it also being used to defend against 'unlawful interference with [...] privacy, family, home or correspondence'.

As the state alone (including the government and institutions established by the government) has responsibility for implementing human rights, it follows that that corporations do not have obligations for their implementation under human rights law. For the same reason, people, particularly human individuals, do not have human rights defined in relation to corporations. Of course corporations may have obligations under other, national, laws but that is entirely a matter for national legislation.

A natural response to this, given the growing power of companies, is to define at least some obligation for large companies to support the application of the human rights of individuals. A working group of the United Nations Sub-Commission on the Promotion and Protection of Human Rights (the main subsidiary body of the Commission on Human Rights) examined the impact of multinationals on human rights. This resulted in the Draft Norms on Human Rights (UN, 2003b) which set out how corporations can help to implement human rights in line with the general obligation on 'every individual and every organ of society' to promote human rights set out in the UDHR. Corporations, however, having sought legal advice, have insisted that they have no legal obligations under human rights laws and so have comprehensively rejected the Draft Norms.

Andrew Clapham (Clapham, 2006) has argued that since the power of companies has increased through globalization and the retreat and disintegration of states, then states have an obligation to monitor the activities of companies which might breach human rights. This has not happened systematically. Clapham also suggests that the idea of *complicity* with human rights violations, which is built into the UN Global Compact, points quite directly towards holding corporations accountable for human rights violations in a more formal sense. Such a line of thought would ultimately suggest that companies would gain a much more direct connection with the state, if not formally gaining the status of 'entities of the state' that would make them directly accountable under existing human rights legislation.

RIGHTS AND TRANSPARENCY

The relationship between rights and transparency is complex. First, rights can rarely all be satisfied simultaneously, so in order to determine which rights (particularly the rights to information and privacy) should prevail, it is necessary to consider how the interests of other stakeholders would be affected. This potentially involves the right to know, the right to free speech, the right to remain silent and the right to privacy. Second, of these various 'rights', only the right to free speech and to privacy are defined as human rights under the main UN covenants, although Article 19 of the Universal Declaration does say that people should have the 'freedom to hold opinions without interference and to seek, receive and impart information and ideas through any media and regardless of frontiers'. And third, the right to privacy is not very well defined in conventions or in practice.

Does all this amount to a right to know with an attendant duty of transparency? Except under carefully defined circumstances there are few *duties* on anyone's part to 'speak' or disclose information. The exceptions, as far as companies are concerned, have primarily to do with financial matters: companies have to disclose their financial performance to shareholders and individuals have to disclose their financial performance to the state in order to be taxed.

One way to argue for an apparently 'new' human right, such as transparency, is to show that other human rights cannot be realized unless the new right is also realized. In this case, transparency could be shown to be necessary for the achievement of other rights. Patrick Birkinshaw has argued just this (Birkinshaw, 2006), at least in relation to achieving the objectives of freedom of information legislation. He concludes that:

> *When power is exercised on our behalf, or our sufferance, we are not treated as full members of that community if power wielders deny us information about why they are using their powers the way they did or are doing.* (Birkinshaw, 2006, p55)

An exactly similar argument could be made in relation to the power of corporations.

Is it possible to define a set of 'communication rights', or at least a set of moral expectations, under which a right to transparency over power relationships, particularly between companies and their stakeholders, can find a natural place? To answer this there are three critical questions that are addressed in the following sections:

1   How far does a corporate right to privacy justify its silence?
2   Do we have a right to know?
3   Do companies have to tell the truth?

PRIVACY, DECENCY AND PROPERTY

Does the right to privacy mean that corporations can remain silent? Companies are very interested in the personal information of individuals at a number of levels, despite resistance from many. They are, on the other hand, most reluctant to provide information about themselves. This reluctance reduces any moral right or justification for their own privacy.

One area in which the right to privacy has been extensively tested is that of the battlefield between famous individuals and the demands of the press. (The implications of this for the media companies involved is discussed in Chapter 9.) The way we think about personal morality and obligation is often transferred and shapes what is considered appropriate for corporate morality. It is instructive, therefore, that while celebrities may be only too happy to give interviews in order to further their careers, when it is a matter of something embarrassing, or where publicity would damage their financial interests, they will usually try to prevent it. Thomas Nagel has argued that privacy is an essential component of a civilized society (Nagel, 1998) and that people should not be expected to reveal details of their private life and that to do so will often simply aggravate otherwise calm social relationships.

One of the main purposes of data protection legislation in many jurisdictions is to prevent the disclosure of personal information held on a computer by anyone, including private companies. The UK Data Protection Act (UK Legislature, 1998) was designed with information such as age, sex and addresses particularly in mind. Unusually for a piece of legislation, it specifically defines 'personal data' as that relating to 'living individuals', so excluding companies from its protection.

Should we therefore avoid transparency in order to have a quiet life? The answer depends on what our interest is. For those newspapers 'interested' in the sex life of a film star, the interest is simply prurience; no-one significantly benefits from disclosure. It might also be argued that disclosure is 'in the national interest', particularly when the sex life of a politician is at issue. However, the concept of 'national interest' is very poorly defined. Scott Burchill has argued (Burchill, 2005) that although the phrase 'national interest' is commonly used in diplomacy, it is a highly problematic concept and a poor guide to understanding the motivations of foreign policy – a concept more of convenience than clarity. The reason for this is that 'the national interest' combines two separate ideas: something supporting an emotional feeling of belonging and something supporting the policy goals of the state, considered as an organization. So if it is questionable whether 'the national interest' should be used to persuade people to make a sacrifice, it is scarcely more legitimate to suggest that the national interest justifies discovering details of someone's sex life.

On the other hand, the politician (and to an extent the film star) have a degree of power over the lives of others. This can justify a degree of disclosure. Yet the power of a politician, whatever they may think, does not consist of their sex life, but in the decisions they may make in the course of their political life. Disclosure of the details of decisions which affect the life of others is therefore justified. However, the disclosure of such political decisions is resisted on the basis of arguments which are fairly close to invoking the idea of the national interest.

What of corporations? The same arguments apply – in other words wherever their decisions exert power over and affect the lives of others, it is reasonable to expect those decisions to be transparent. Yet corporations do not often approach disclosure in this spirit, but are often determined to protect their own privacy.

In practice, two of the areas in which individual privacy rights have been especially contested and elaborated are perhaps the profiling of genetic material and radio frequency identification (RFID). Genetic information, held in DNA molecules within each of our cells (and those of all other living things), can both identify an individual uniquely with a high degree of accuracy and also reveal likely characteristics of that person. This can include traits such as predisposition to disease. RFID tags are a radio-based technology which can be embedded in clothing or other personal items and could be used to track the movements of individuals. In both cases, companies can discover more about an individual than the individual concerned may reasonably wish them to know (see, for example, Peslak, 2005).

Those seeking to defend privacy in these areas have in the main argued that the information in question is private and therefore privately owned, so that, as Everett suggests (Everett, 2003), other parties do not have an automatic right to its use. While this may work as a short-term tactic, it is in fact reducing the right to privacy to an entirely different kind of right, the right to property. There is, of course, a defined human right to be able to possess property (in Article 17 of the UDHR), but this is not the sort of thing which may be sold, rights being inalienable. Indeed, the idea of owning the right to information of this sort gives rise to absurdities, as Lori Andrews of the Institute for Science, Law and Technology at the Illinois Institute of Technology put it when talking about patenting human genes: 'It's like patenting the alphabet and charging people every time they speak.' (Neus, 2005)

TRANSPARENCY: A RIGHT TO KNOW?

Do we have any right to know?

Article 19 of the UDHR grants everyone the right to freedom of opinion and expression, including 'to seek, receive and impart information and ideas through any media and regardless of frontiers' (UN, 1948). This right is further elaborated in Article 19 of the Civil and Political Covenant to include any media. However, it also says that the exercise of such a right carries 'special duties and responsibilities' which are permissible provided they are explicitly included in legislation, in order to 'respect the rights and reputations of others' or for the 'protection of national security or of public order [...] public health or morals' (UN, 1966a).

The Aarhus Convention (Aarhus, 1998) covers participation in decision making and access to justice in relation to environmental matters. It was formulated by the EU states, but has also been signed by some non-EU countries, such as Tajikistan and the Ukraine. As Kofi Annan has said:

> although regional in scope, the significance of the Aarhus Convention is global. It is by far the most impressive elaboration of principle 10 of the Rio Declaration, which stresses the need for citizen's participation in environmental issues and for access to information on the environment held by public authorities. As such it is the most ambitious venture in the area of environmental democracy so far undertaken under the auspices of the United Nations. (Annan, 1998)

However, access to information under the Aarhus Convention contains a number of exceptions to be 'interpreted in a restrictive way' in order to protect confidentiality, including that of commercial parties. And of course it only applies to public bodies, including local government, but not to private companies directly. However, if a private company works for a public body, then it may be possible to request information under the convention from the public body for which they worked – unless, of course, the company or the public body object on grounds of confidentiality.

The US, the UK and a number of other countries, such as Ireland and Australia, have passed freedom of information legislation and regulations. Unlike the Aarhus Convention, these apply to a wide range of types of information. But like the Aarhus Convention, they apply to public bodies alone. In addition to information on national security matters, these acts also tend to exclude trade secrets and 'information likely to prejudice commercial interests'. The UK Act (UK Legislature, 2000) provides for a series of exemptions from the obligation to disclose information; however, these may be subject to a 'public interest test', which, although it is undefined in the Act, provides that the exemption be considered in the light of the public interest. The public interest test may therefore, in principle, favour either disclosure or concealment.

The Environmental Information Regulations in the UK (UK Legislature, 2004) specifically exclude from the obligation to disclose information which might adversely affect intellectual property rights or 'commercial or industrial confidentiality [...] to protect a legitimate economic interest'. However, information relating to emissions to the environment may not be withheld on grounds of commercial confidentiality. In 1970, the US established the Environmental Protection Agency, an independent body charged with the implementation of federal laws designed to protect the environment. One of its main achievements has been the Toxic Release Inventory, which records the emissions of certain chemicals to the environment.

In summary, there is a reasonable right to know about environmental issues, at least in the UK. The public right to know about other issues is much more limited – particularly by commercial interests.

TRUTH, LIES AND OBLIGATION

If the right to know is circumscribed, what about the obligation to disclose? As we shall see in Chapter 7 when discussing reporting, there are also strict limits on what companies have to say about their activities. However, the critical question remains as to whether we presume that when companies do talk about their activities, they have to tell the truth.

It may seem an odd question to ask: telling lies is clearly not an option in regulated financial reporting and no company would admit to lying about anything. However, it does happen. The most famous case is perhaps Enron in 2001, but there are other contenders, including the mis-statement of Shell's oil reserves in 2004. Shell admitted that it had 'over-stated' its oil reserves by 20 per cent. On the face of it, it is good that the company corrected its own error. However, Lynn Turner, a former SEC chief accountant, said the revision looked like more than a mistake:

> *A 20 per cent restatement of proven reserves is a humungous error [...] For a company like Shell to have missed its proven reserves by that much is not an oversight. It's an intentional misapplication of the SEC's rules.* (SMH, 2004)

Yet clearly these examples, if they are cases of untruthfulness, are well-known because they are exceptions. It follows that most corporate communications are fair and truthful.

Marc Kasky thought otherwise when he read Nike's claim that it paid 'on average, double the minimum wage' in overseas countries, for example, and that its workers 'are protected from physical and sexual abuse.' (Kanzer and Williams, 2003) He sued Nike in 1998 for these statements, which appeared in Nike's social report concerning the situation of workers employed in overseas factories making Nike products. The case put a damper on social reporting in the US for several years. It was only resolved in September 2003 by mutual agreement and not by court ruling (Nike, 2003), despite having worked its way through most of the California state legal system.

What is interesting about this case was the argument that Nike used that such statements in their social report were political speech and thus protected by the US Constitution's First Amendment. This provides that there shall be 'no law [...] abridging the freedom of speech, or of the press' (US Bill of Rights, 1791). Nike was claiming the right to free speech for its assertions about worker conditions. One might have thought that the First Amendment was framed rather more with the idea of political freedom of individuals in mind. At any rate Marc Kasky thought that Nike's statement in this regard should be governed by the conventions concerning 'commercial speech' and should there- fore be accurate, as required by Nike's commercial stakeholders.

The peculiar nature of Nike's arguments can be seen if we were to apply them to a scientific article. If the author of an article, having been challenged on the accuracy of its contents, were to argue that they had a perfect right to say what they pleased, it would seem a very odd response. Surely the point of the article was to assert that something was true, rather than to be able to avoid blame if it turns out otherwise. Of course what Nike was really trying to do was to limit or remove its liability, rather than preserve its integrity. In the end, perhaps that was just what it achieved.

Similar arguments concerning the freedom of speech of companies have been made in Europe also. BAT appealed to its human rights when it argued in 2004 that UK Government regulations restricting point of sale (POS) adver- tisement of tobacco were:

> *disproportionate to the aim of promoting health because they allow so limited an amount of advertisement at POS as to impair the 'very essence' of commercial free speech. Accordingly, the Regulations infringe art 10 of the European Convention on Human Rights and are unlawful by virtue of s 6(1) of the Human Rights Act 1998.* (R v. Secretary of State for Health, 2004)

One area in which companies in practice acknowledge that they must be open in their communication concerns announcements to the Stock Exchange. The *Financial Services Authority's Handbook* attempts to 'promote prompt and fair disclosure of relevant information to the market' and in particular to ensure that 'inside information' is made public as soon as possible. Inside information is defined as information that will have a significant effect on price 'if and only if it is information of that kind which a reasonable investor would be likely to use as part of the basis of his investment decisions' (FSA, 2006). Transparency over company practices has, of course, to be carefully controlled, or rather subject to a systematic discipline, to ensure that no one potential investor is favoured over others.

What is interesting with regard to transparency over social and environmental issues is that these are hardly ever the subject of such regulatory announcements. Environmental matters may occasionally fall into this category, but social matters very rarely do. This means, first, that such issues are not thought to be significant or material enough to affect the commercial prospects of a company. It also suggests that attempts to prepare a business case for ethical behaviour are doomed always to be of marginal significance. At any rate, no reasonable investor, of the type recognized by the FSA, is likely to have regard to ethical issues in considering their investment.

In conclusion, there is currently no defined legal human right which imposes a general duty of transparency on companies. However, the interest of some companies in information about individuals prejudices their moral claim to their own privacy. It can also be argued that the practical achievement of rights other than transparency demands that companies are transparent wherever their power and impact on their stakeholders affect the achievement of their stakeholders' recognized human rights.

6

The Ethics of Personal Transparency

What do the moral issues of transparency mean for those – often a very large number of people – employed by a company? How should transparency operate on a personal level? How should an individual employee behave in a corporate context when they have doubts about the integrity of the organization – or of others working within it? Is there a duty to be a whistleblower?

At times, perhaps all of us feel that we know what we want to do at work and we know what is expected of us. We may be clear about the goals of the organization we work for and even enjoy achieving them. And we may have no doubt that we can call on the support of sympathetic ears when the path is not so clear. These times are the sunlit uplands of working life.

For all other times, we need integrity or honesty. One of those times occurs when the values of our employer are different from our own. The case study about the desire of mobile phone companies for sex is an example. In this case, the values of some employees may make them feel uncomfortable about developing products which include pornography. In other cases, some employees may also have values which would lead them to more adventurous behaviour than the company will officially permit. How should these issues be resolved?

If there is any systematic resolution, then there clearly has to be compromise. How is this to be achieved? At the level of the individual, this will involve preserving integrity and personal dignity, in a sense close to that which Kant defined:

> *What is related to general human inclinations and needs has a market price* [...] *but that which constitutes the condition under which alone something can be an end in itself has not merely a relative worth, that is, a price, but an inner worth, that is, a dignity.*
> (Kant, 1785)

Kant's remarks, and the idea of the intrinsic worth of people, are central to his conception of morality. They suggest that everyone already has an intrinsic worth and that, in this sense, there is nothing which people have to do to deserve their dignity. The preservation of dignity at work is of course the subject of many human, and particularly labour, rights which cover gross violations of dignity, such as forced labour. However, there may well be things people or companies might do which appear to take away from it. In a business context, as elsewhere, those behaviours which detract from human dignity involve a loss of integrity.

This chapter looks at how the integrity of our work at an individual level can be preserved in a business context in those cases where the violation of rights may be less direct or where the issue is how to react to the violation of others' rights. It focuses first on the formal regulation of integrity in terms of 'doing the right thing' and then turns to the other meaning of integrity: honesty, interpreted as personal transparency. It concludes with an acknowledgement of the difficulty of maintaining integrity at work.

ENCODING INTEGRITY

One way of maintaining integrity might seem to be to work within an agreed code of conduct. Codes of conduct developed by companies themselves are becoming increasingly popular in large organizations. They ostensibly seek to ensure that employees – and therefore also the company as a whole – behave properly. Yet there is a degree of confusion about what such codes can achieve, and there are also several areas in which there is a conflict between individual ethical behaviour and the interests of the company.

There are two key issues:

1   To whom does the code apply? A particular code may apply to the company or to its individual employees.
2   Who developed the code? Codes may be developed by a company for its own use, by one or more individuals within it or by a third party.

These two issues interact to determine the legitimacy and likely effectiveness of a code. A code developed by an external party and imposed on others will have less legitimacy and effectiveness. Conversely, a code developed with the individuals to which it applies can expect greater legitimacy and to be taken more seriously.

Taking a broad view of the term 'code of conduct', the entire system of law may be regarded as a 'code of conduct', applying to society as a whole and, in different ways, to the various components of society, including individuals and companies. Yet even where laws have democratic legitimacy, this legal corpus is scarcely readily available to either companies or ordinary people in trying to make day-to-day decisions. However, the law does cover many of the situations which are also covered by codes of conduct, and, as we shall see, codes of conduct typically refer to the law directly.

Outside the field of such 'hard law', there have been calls for codes to regulate the conduct of multinational companies since the 1960s, although, again, the practical usefulness of such codes (even when they do exist) can be extremely limited. These have varying status and are often described by the term 'soft law'. Examples include the OECD Guidelines (OECD, 2000) which cover issues such as bribery and corruption, and bear quite directly on the behaviour of employees. However, this is not the same as a code concerning the behaviour of employees directly. What such codes should do is to ensure that a company's management in turn ensures that bribery, for example, is not practised by its employees.

Another example of a code which applies to companies themselves, but has also been developed through a process which includes companies, is the Fair Labor Association, whose code of conduct prescribes acceptable behaviour in relation to the following issues (FLA, 2005):

- forced labour;
- child labour
- harassment or abuse;
- nondiscrimination;
- health and safety;
- freedom of association and collective bargaining;
- wages and benefits;
- hours of work; and
- overtime compensation.

What is noteworthy is that this code has been derived from ILO Conventions and explicitly covers the behaviour of the company towards its employees. This is a crucial factor in enabling individuals to maintain their dignity.

Other codes may be developed by different kinds of organization. The widespread codes developed by professional associations provide another example. Almost all professional associations, from doctors and lawyers to engineers, estate agents and even politicians, now have codes of ethics. These describe with practical examples what is considered ethical conduct, unethical conduct and (usually) how to deal with doubtful cases. These are perhaps more relevant to individuals' decisions at work, rather than to the conditions under which they work. The principal reason why such codes are so common is that the alternative to self-regulation is regulation by the law and the passing of control of the profession concerned from the hands of its practitioners.

In the spectrum running from codes developed by third parties and imposed or applied to organizations to those codes developed by individuals, professional codes occupy an intermediate position in several respects. They are developed by individuals acting collectively. 'Professions' are not organizations; profession-als are individuals who practise a profession. Their codes of conduct typically describe not only ethical rectitude, but also technical competence. This is appropriate as technical incompetence is likely to damage clients and practi-tioners alike. But such codes are not usually appropriate to the conduct of employees in general or to the behaviour of professionals within general employ-ment and operating outside their direct professional sphere.

There are also codes of conduct developed by individuals for themselves. Although this is not the place to discuss individuals' personal morality in any detail, it may be observed that the strength (as well, perhaps, as the weakness) of the way individuals express their moral views is that their moral judgements are highly context-specific and appropriate to a given situation. They are rarely codified and written down, unless taken directly from a religion. In consequence, the essence of personal moral judgement is not really to be found as a compilation of answers to questions such as 'Would you ever lie to your boss?'

How do corporate codes of conduct found in many companies work in relation to individual integrity? The position is surprisingly unclear, both as to whether the code applies to companies or to individuals and also as to who has or should develop the code. At first glance, the content of many corporate codes seems directly concerned with the behaviour of its individual employees. Yet the avowed reason the code exists is usually to ensure the corporation as a whole behaves with integrity. Of course, the existence of such 'higher'-level codes, or at least corporate integrity, is important. As Jamison and Steare have observed, 'personal integrity cannot flourish outside a context of corporate integrity.' (Jamison and Steare, 2003). However, can a corporate code be in any way a substitute for a personal code or personal integrity?

The difficulty over exactly to whom the code belongs is evident in the following quote from BP's website:

> Our code of conduct is the cornerstone of our commitment to integrity. As Lord Browne, the group chief executive, affirms: 'Our reputation, and therefore our future as a business, depends on each of us, everywhere, every day, taking personal responsibility for the conduct of BP's business'. The new BP code of conduct is an essential tool to help our people meet this aspiration. The code summarizes our standards for the way we behave. All our employees must follow the code of conduct. It clearly defines what we expect of our business and our people, regardless of location and background. Ultimately it is about helping BP people to do the right thing. (BP, 2006a)

It is a brave thing to dictate what should be expected of people 'regardless of location and background'. This is not just because individual morality varies in important respects with culture, but also, as we have seen, because an individual's 'code of conduct' is rarely of the explicitly articulated form in which a corporate code usually has to be.

This is perhaps one of the reasons why corporate codes of conduct are usually greeted with such cynicism by employees. No-one really believes them and, in general, the financial interests of the company are thought to come first. Most people would suspect that only the most egregious cases could ever really justify pushing sales targets into second place. There is thus a paradoxical effect whereby the active management of morality may be counter-productive. This may partly explain the findings of a survey of the impact of 'ethics officers' a few years ago that while ethical commitment made a positive difference to financial performance, a formal commitment to ethics management systems was not important (Verschoor, 1999).

So while it may be useful for both companies and their employees to have moral codes, it is not possible for one sort to fill in for the other. However, it may be possible for the personal and corporate codes to interact. When they do, both may benefit. One way to think about this is to consider how corporate codes come into existence. There are many possible ways: some may be developed by a group of interested mid-level or senior managers; alternatively, a third party may be consulted to develop something apparently suitable; a further possibility is that the code is developed as a result of discovering what staff think is important. It is fairly predictable that codes which are developed without staff involvement are not recognized by the staff as their own. It follows that such codes are far less likely to be adhered to with any rigour.

Conversely, those codes developed in conjunction with staff are more likely to be taken seriously. This has another implication: given that the turnover of staff for many organizations is rising, it follows that codes of conduct need to be constantly re-developed if they are to continue to remain relevant. The nature of a corporate code is thus a proper subject for stakeholder dialogue.

What do corporate codes of conduct cover? From the perspective of the kinds of issues which are included, BP's code of conduct referred to above covers a number of different stakeholder areas: health and safety, security, the environment, employees, business partners (including suppliers), governments, communities, and company assets and financial integrity. It makes clear, for example, that employees are expected neither to offer nor to take bribes and should use personal information about other employees only as it was originally intended to be used.

Yet from another perspective, there are only two sorts of things to be found in BP's guide: temptation and confusion. More precisely, the code covers what should be avoided and what to do when it is not clear what to do. The list of things to be avoided is of course closely connected to the list of issues set out above, including issues such as financial integrity. What to do about those things which are not clear is much more limited, but essentially involves asking for advice. The code concludes with the following: 'Ask if you are ever unsure what is the right thing to do. Keep asking until you get an answer with which you are comfortable.' (BP, 2006a)

This is an optimistic note on which to end the code, as it presupposes that it is possible for a troubled employee to find someone who can supply a satisfying answer. Even, or perhaps especially, in a large company, it cannot be presumed that the values and interests of an employee will necessarily coincide with those of the company as a whole.

So corporate codes on the one hand appear to be quite paternalistic in the way in which they try to regulate individual behaviour. On the other, they assume a high level of personal moral development of individuals.

PERSONAL REVELATION

Honesty, or personal transparency, is at one level a good example of an area that codes of conduct are intended to regulate. Yet personal transparency can also greatly facilitate the ethical behaviour that codes attempt to achieve through articulation, external imposition and compliance. When transparency is a personal commitment it can promote ethical behaviour.

At a personal level transparency is challenging. Transparency over one's own personal behaviour opens us to scrutiny from others and potentially to their judgement. The fear of judgement, when it is too strong, may inhibit any transparency at all – but when it is less overwhelming, it will work positively.

So what is the proper role and extent of transparency in delivering personal integrity in a work context? Or put another way, how far should we expect ourselves, and others, to be open with each other when working for a company?

It is of course necessary to acknowledge that there are limits to transparency. Ibsen's play *The Wild Duck* reminds us that transparency can be a destructive force, if not simply embarrassing, when pursued without any thought for the consequences. Yet most of the time the problem is not too much transparency, but too little. At any rate, the exercise of transparency itself requires judgement. The remainder of this section will explore what that judgement might entail.

The culture of a company will have a profound effect on whether personal transparency can flourish. In a very supportive culture, in which staff in general and management in particular are genuinely concerned for employees, it will naturally be easier for individuals to be open with each other. On the other hand, in a combative culture, transparency will be inhibited. For example, in one company there was huge competition to demonstrate commitment among the sales force. A key sign of commitment was the hour at which salesmen arrived in the morning, the evidence for which was the presence of their cars in the car park. Of course, the sales manager came in extremely early in the morning. So in order to demonstrate commitment (without actually making it) some of the sales staff took to leaving their cars in the car park over night and travelling by other means. The sales manager became suspicious and started checking the temperature of the cars' bonnets on his way into work.

Now this is obviously a pathological situation in which fear is inhibiting transparency. And the consequences of such behaviour extend well beyond the apparently trivial area described here. Knowing of this situation, it would be hard to trust any sales figures produced by this sales team. The adverse business consequences of a lack of transparency are never far away.

The appropriateness of the level of individual transparency varies according to the context. There are three main sorts of situation, involving:

1   employee–individual relationships;
2   employee–third party relationships; and
3   employee–company relationships.

While it is not acceptable for anyone to *demand* transparency within private relationships, some companies seek to foster communication between staff in the hope that a benefit may emerge. Many companies seek to harness the energy of personal relationships (at least within management) in order to tap into the intellectual capital of their staff. They encourage an informal 'water-cooler culture' in which ideas are freely floated and shared. The benefits of this approach are considered to greatly outweigh any commercially 'unproductive' exchange of gossip with which it may be accompanied.

It may seem obvious that what two people say to each other, whether employees or not, is not the business of anyone else: privacy is a basic right and should be respected. The level of transparency within that relationship is a matter for the individuals concerned. However, if another party is adversely affected, the situation becomes more complex and those affected may claim that they are entitled to know what has been said and even to control the level of transparency.

The BP code states that:

> Consistent with its respect for employee privacy, BP does not normally take an interest in personal conduct outside of work – unless such conduct impairs the employee's work performance or affects the reputation or legitimate business interests of BP. (BP, 2006a, p24)

BP appears to believe that it has a right to know – and perhaps interfere – in its employees' private lives if it is in its interest to do so. This is at best troubling and, while it may accurately capture what BP does, it is hard to see why this statement should be part of any *ethical* code.

What a member of staff may say to outside third parties presents companies with quite difficult issues. In general, companies do not very actively encourage transparency in such cases. This may sometimes be justified on the grounds of commercial confidentiality, but this is usually a rather thin veil for fears over company reputation. The BP Code of Conduct says in relation to external speaking engagements:

> Even where the venue is informal, such as a trade association event, if possible, seek review of your presentation by your line manager **and in all cases take care not to cause any harm to the reputation of the BP group.** (BP, 2006a, p52 emphasis added)

Yet there are many subtleties here: it would seem entirely reasonable for a member of staff to be completely open about issues at work with their families, if they so wished. This would apply whatever the nature of the issues about which they chose to be open. It would not, for example, be claimed that an employee who divulged fraud to her husband had done wrong. By extension, it would be hard to claim that a similar disclosure to a friend would be wrong.

If the individual to whom an employee speaks is not a family member or friend, but a reporter, then the policy of most companies is sharply different and typically tightly controlled.

Do reporters, and the wider public to whom they 'report', deserve an employee's transparency? Is there a right to hear the whistle blown? This depends on the validity of the public interest. It should also be borne in mind that reporters are more than sympathetic ears and can be rather treacherous friends. They are typically people acting for another company, and their job is to discover information that can be sold. Thus they promote transparency as long as this supports their commercial ends. Despite these issues, a fairly common maxim is to advise staff to do nothing they would not like to see reported in the papers.

Finally, what sort of transparency should one expect between an individual and a company itself? To an extent companies clearly need to know information about their employees, yet they must also respect an individual's privacy. Of course, if the company knows something about an individual, in almost every case so will another individual within the company, such as a personnel officer. There is therefore a need to underline the privacy of the relationship and protect that information from inappropriate disclosure. For BP, this means:

> *Those with access to personal employee data must only use it for the purpose for which it was collected and adhere to the highest standards of confidentiality in using it. Never provide personal employee data to anyone inside or outside of BP without proper authorization. Personal data must not be held longer than necessary to meet the legal or business reason for which authorization was given.* (BP, 2006a, p24)

KEEPING A SENSE OF PROPORTION

As well as meaning honesty, integrity also means 'whole' and has the same root as 'integer'. This suggests that it is not possible to separate one aspect of integrity from another. If you expect integrity in honestly maintaining the company's records, then you must expect it when an employee speaks to the outside world – whether or not that is in the company's direct interests. Some companies recognize this, in that they have a whistleblower policy, whereby staff who report unethical behaviour are protected, particularly while their claim is being investigated. However, such policies rarely extend to support for staff that go to the press in combating unethical behaviour.

Of course, one reason companies have codes of behaviour and ethics is that they cannot rely on a well-developed moral sense in all their employees. But codes, as we have seen, are both general in application and inflexible in their nature. In contrast, the nature of the moral sense which individuals develop is both flexible and very highly context-specific. Whistleblowing policies are partially a response to this situation: particularly when a moral breach is sufficiently serious, they permit an individual's moral sense to be exercised appropriately.

What is a rational approach to this situation which preserves the dignity of the individual? Ethical codes are a management response to the problem. The essence of most management solutions is to set up a system which can 'run by itself'. While this may seem rational, it is simply not possible – or at least advisable – for moral codes. In practice, moral codes require interpretation. The nature of and approach to interpretation is crucial. This is important in two senses: first, it preserves the moral capacity of those who undertake the interpretation, acknowledging their contribution to the resolution of the issue in question. And second, it allows the specific circumstances of the issue more fully to be taken into account in a way in which the rigid or unthinking application of a rule could not do.

This is hard work. It would be much easier simply to follow (someone else's) rules without question. And to acknowledge the inherently unfinished nature of ethical codes may not seem 'rational' in the usual sense of that word. Yet it is true to the original meaning of the term, which has the same root as the word 'ratio', meaning the balancing of one consideration against another. If we can keep our sense of proportion, we can go a long way to preserving the dignity of people at work.

7

Reporting:
Talking Your Walk

Overview

Many of those who work in CSR assume that transparency and reporting amount to much the same thing, or perhaps even that CSR is somehow the same as reporting. But transparency is not the same as reporting: there is more to be transparent about than is typically reported and there are other ways to be transparent than reporting. So the problem is not so much whether a company is 'walking the talk' (Holliday et al, 2002), that is doing what it says it is, but whether that company is 'talking the walk', that is disclosing what it is actually doing.

Transparency can, of course, partly be achieved by reporting. This chapter assesses how companies actually report and how transparent they are in other ways. It chronicles the slow advance of transparency over power, covering financial reporting, non-financial reporting, auditing and the spectrum of regulation and standards for corporate transparency.

As far as reporting goes, the critical issues are what is reported, to whom and the appropriateness of the reporting. The vast majority of company reporting has historically been, and continues to be, financial reporting. This has, technically, been addressed to the shareholder. So this chapter begins with a review of the history of financial reporting. Financial reporting shows clearly how the actual level of transparency achieved at any stage reflects the balance between the need of a stakeholder to know and the desire of a corporation for privacy. The overt justification for privacy is typically founded on arguments based on the need for commercial confidentiality and on the projected cost of transparency. The result is that the position of shareholders should perhaps be regarded as something of a Pyrrhic victory, as Edwards has observed: 'accounting statements have a comforting appearance of complete accuracy because precise figures are given [...] the economic reality is very different' (Edwards, 1989).

Other stakeholders have enjoyed rather more patchy success, even though non-financial reporting has become much more common, at least from large companies in the last 15 years. But what should be reported, and to an extent to whom it should be reported, is still undecided. There is a particular discrepancy between the scope of the stakeholders covered by reports (such as consumers) and those to whom such reports are addressed (typically 'opinion formers'). Non-financial reporting has had a somewhat ragged beginning and halting development as a result. The consequence is that non-financial reporting appears to have lost credibility with some key corporate stakeholders.

Auditing is meant to address the question of trust – for both financial as well as non-financial reports. Unfortunately the practice of auditing for non-financial reports, particularly when based uncritically on the model of financial auditing, is beset with problems.

There are, however, considerable areas of reporting and information disclosure quite outside the current scope of most non-financial reports. Much of this is prescribed in (non-accounting) legislation. In addition, there has recently been an increase in regulation for non-financial reporting and a spectrum of attempts to agree standards which fall short of legislation.

FINANCIAL REPORTING

The development of financial accounting in the UK has been very influential on accounting practices throughout the world. Yet the growth of financial reporting in the UK over the last 250 years has been a hard fought battle driven mainly by the growing separation of the owners of a company (the shareholders) from those who run it on a day-to-day basis. As Adam Smith observed of stock corporations in 1776:

> The directors of such companies, being the managers rather of other people's money than their own, it cannot be well expected that they should watch over it with the same anxious vigilance with which the partners in a private copartnery frequently watch over their own. [...] Negligence and confusion, therefore, must always prevail, more or less, in the management of the affairs of such a company. (Smith, [1776] 1999, p330)

Financial reporting, the most common expression of financial transparency, has grown and developed with the development of joint stock companies and its changing role in society. What seems entirely natural today, such as an audited profit and loss account, took nearly 100 years to be accepted by the accounting profession, as Aranya and Edey have documented (Aranya, 1979; Edey, 1979).

In the UK, joint stock companies were formed as early as 1553, with the best known company from that era being the East India Company, formed in 1599. These early companies could be formed by the grant of a Royal Charter or a special Act of Parliament – both expensive and protracted processes. Their formation was typically related to the provision of some public good or the need to bear an extraordinary risk. At that time social and financial ends were perhaps more closely connected. Professional institutions today are typically companies of this nature.

These early companies were legal entities, but their owners did not enjoy the benefits of transferable shares or limited liability. The individual owners were closely connected with the company and were strongly motivated to exercise control as a result of their personal liability. Public transparency was very limited, but was occasionally delivered through comprehensive investigations by parliamentary committees after a request by proprietors or creditors.

Following the 1844 Companies Act, it became possible to form companies by submitting details to a public register, which is still the dominant practice today. Knowing that a company exists, and who controls it, remains the most fundamental form of transparency applicable to companies. Yet still in the UK today there is no requirement for companies to register their subsidiaries (which may of course be overseas and so hard for stakeholders to track down) or even to include them all in their annual accounts.

At any rate, in addition to registration, the 1844 act also required companies to:

- keep books of accounts;
- present a 'full and fair' balance sheet to shareholders; and
- appoint auditors to report on the balance sheet.

In 1855, a further act permitted limited liability for registered companies. This set the stage for a dramatic growth in the number of companies as it provided much more clearly a suitable platform for profit-making objectives to be met at minimum risk to the shareholder.

At this time it was recognized that there was quite widespread abuse through the submission of misleading balance sheets. Nevertheless, this did not prevent a further act being passed in 1856 which *removed* all the compulsory accounting and auditing of the 1844 act. Robert Lowe justified this in parliament in this way:

> *having given them [limited companies] a pattern the state leaves them to manage their own affairs and has no desire to force on these little republics any particular constitution.* (Lowe, 1856)

Other than for financial sector companies, which have had requirements greater than other kinds of company for transparency since the mid-nineteenth century, there was no significant additional legislative requirement for regular corporate transparency in the UK until 1900. In that year a new Companies Act reinstated the annual audit of the balance sheet; in 1907 it was required that the accounts be filed – and thus publicly available.

The Institute of Chartered Accountants (ICAEW) was formed in 1880. It brought its influence to bear in the development of new legislation. For example, in the consultations preceding the 1928 Companies Act it lobbied *against* the introduction of mandatory profit and loss accounts or the disclosure of too much detail:

71

[That] there should be in addition a Profit and Loss account is considered likely to do more harm than good [...] if in some cases [directors] disclose in the published accounts less than some people desire, the absence of detail is in most cases wise and is generally supported by shareholders. To give in a balance sheet such detailed information as would afford full protection to creditors might mean the giving away of a mass of detail of material value to competitors. (ICAEW, 1925)

It is interesting that what is today regarded as an entirely routine form of transparency should have been resisted on the grounds of commercial confidentiality. Significant changes were nevertheless introduced in the Companies Acts of 1928 and 1929. It is ironic that measures to increase transparency which might have helped reduce speculation without foundation were introduced immediately before the biggest such bubble burst in 1929. The measures then introduced included:

- the disclosure in a prospectus for shares of past company performance;
- the recognition of consolidated accounts;
- the introduction of a profit and loss statement within the accounts – although this did not have to be audited; and
- the disclosure of directors' remuneration – although this excluded that of the managing director.

After 1945, investment became a more specialized business and therefore more demanding of information about companies. There were two reasons for this. First, large scale institutional investment became a much more significant force after World War II. These professional investors demanded a scale and quality of information which was new. The institutional funds' analysts got their information, but it has not always been through regulated reporting. Most large companies hold special meetings with groups of analysts to talk about their company. The information revealed at these meetings may well go beyond what is officially and publicly available, and even where it does not, the ability freely to ask questions of senior management appears to constitute an additional transparency for some shareholders.

Second, some investors had additional, ethically based reasons to seek further transparency. While the Methodist Church had been concerned since the 1920s about investing according to its moral principles and avoiding companies involved in alcohol and gambling, after World War II this practice grew. The Pax World Fund, for example, which was designed to avoid investment connected with the Vietnam War, was launched in 1971. Socially responsible investment (SRI) became increasingly significant thereafter. More developed strategies, rather than simple avoidance alone, dramatically increased the scope of information necessary to make investment decisions. SRI has since become much more sophisticated and is today based on:

- the positive selection of stocks;
- strategies for influencing companies; and
- the weighting, relative to the overall market, of stock holdings within portfolios.

In the Companies Act of 1948, the requirement to produce and file *audited* profit and loss accounts finally became law. However, there were still some significant developments which were vigorously contested, including the disclosure of sales figures and the method used to value assets. The London Stock Exchange called for the disclosure of sales figures in 1961. This was opposed by the Institute of Directors, which argued that sales figures should not be disclosed where this was likely to be misleading or harmful to the company.

Further acts followed from 1967 to 1985, gradually introducing disclosure of sales figures and providing for fuller current cost valuation. The acts also required some disclosure of issues affecting employees and a limited description of business prospects. A new regulatory regime was introduced, involving the Financial Reporting Council (FRC) and the Accounting Standards Board (ASB). The ASB reflects the views of accounting professionals and defines acceptable accounting practice, while the role of government through the FRC is confined to enforcement.

More recent developments include:

- the internationalization of accounting practice together with the increasingly obvious divergence between the accounting regime of the US and that of the rest of the world;
- the introduction of European Union legislation for accounting;
- increasing pressure for forward looking statements; and
- the debate over the inclusion of a wider range of stakeholders in company accounting.

While much of the world has reporting regulations based on the UK model, the general direction and control of accounting is being regulated on an increasingly international basis. The UK is progressively implementing European Directives and the international accounting profession is becoming more prominent. The exception, to some extent, is the US.

In the US, the main legislative framework for company law is still provided by the 1933 Securities Act. This was intended by its drafters to be modelled on the UK 1929 Companies Act (see Bush, 2005), which is oriented to the interests of share*holders*; however, a number of factors meant that it became oriented instead to share *traders*.

These included the fact that most public companies were incorporated in the state of Delaware, which has relatively weak shareholder protection. In addition, the federal nature of the US meant that it was not considered constitutional for federal law to dictate a stronger regulatory system within Delaware. What remained within the 1933 act was a regime particularly concerned with the trading of shares of public companies. The over-riding question became: Do the accounts provide adequate information to underpin efficient secondary markets for shares? One response to this situation has been the development of Generally Accepted Accounting Principles (GAAP).

A further development, in response to the spectacular corporate collapses of large companies, such as Enron, was the Sarbanes-Oxley Act of 2002. In addition to strict criminal penalties for altering documents, this requires that:

- senior management must personally certify and be accountable for their company's financial records and accounting;
- auditors must certify the underlying controls and processes that are used to compile the financial results of a company; and
- disclosures be made of any events that may affect a firm's stock price or financial performance within a 48 hour period.

There has certainly been a significant increase in the volume of financial reporting over the past century. Yet most of what is produced, however technically accurate it may or may not be, is extremely inaccessible to the average stakeholder. The highly impenetrable language and hundreds of pages of an annual report and accounts are only read in any detail by the analysts employed by institutional investors.

Social, Economic and Environmental Reporting

The scope of transparency: Social, economic and environmental issues

In 1962 Rachel Carson wrote *Silent Spring* (Carson, 1962) about the devastating effect of pesticides on the American countryside. The environment then became 'an issue'. From the point of view of corporate transparency this meant that it was something with which a company's stakeholders would be concerned. Since then, the analysis of environmental issues has been greatly developed and a wide range of social issues have been added to the areas on which transparency is demanded of companies. Together, this range of issues is often described as those relevant to 'sustainability'.

The range of issues which are deemed to be relevant to sustainability is reflected in the transparency requested of companies. While there is no fully defined framework for analysing sustainability issues as there is for financial issues, one of the most interesting ways in which the impacts of companies may be set out is through the concept of the 'triple bottom line' originally developed by John Elkington (Elkington, 1997) as comprising economic prosperity, environmental quality and social justice. However, as I have suggested elsewhere (Henriques, 2004), it is important not to push the analogy with financial accounting too far, as information and transparency will be lost if issues are netted off against each other in the manner of profits and losses. Also, since the economic impacts of a company include (but are far wider than) its financial

---

BOX 7.1 THE BREADTH OF SUSTAINABILITY ISSUES

energy use
material use
water use
emissions to air
emissions to water
solid waste and pollution
transport
product impacts
land impacts
corporate governance
public perception
human rights – staff
human rights – local community

animal rights
supply chain impacts
demand chain (client/consumer)
impacts
commercial practices
leadership
health and safety
regulation observance
financial performance
intangible assets
innovation
taxes
employment

Source: Henriques (2001)

---

profitability, the reduction or 'collapse' of an economic bottom line onto a financial one should be avoided.

The list of issues with which stakeholders may be concerned is a long one, and it can never be finalized: new issues continually arise. The list in Box 7.1, while by no means exhaustive, is intended to show the breadth of such issues which can be relevant today.

The degree of transparency which a company exhibits can be measured partly by the coverage of relevant issues and stakeholders for the company. As transparency clearly requires that those to whom the issues matter are acknowledged, a simple index of this will be the range of stakeholders that is acknowledged.

For large companies, there are also technical issues with the boundary of their reporting. Clearly a holding company, for example, has a responsibility for the transparency of all wholly owned subsidiaries. If subsidiaries are only partly owned, however, the situation is less clear cut. In addition, companies will have much greater practical influence over some issues than others. The Global Reporting Initiative (GRI) has developed a protocol (GRI, 2006) to help with the resolution of some of these issues.

The following sections will describe something of how transparency over this large range of issues has in practice developed.

Early attempts

The term 'social audit', used in the broad sense to include a review of corporate performance, was introduced by Thomas Kreps in the 1940s in the US. There is some evidence that large companies voluntarily published information on their social impacts in the 1950s. In the UK, George Goyder declared in 1961 that more was required of companies than a financial audit:

[the financial audit] is a one-sided state of affairs and belongs to the days when companies were small and public accountability was secured. [...] In an economy of big business [...] there is clearly as much need for a social as for a financial audit. (Goyder, 1961)

Goyder saw no reason why social audits should not be undertaken voluntarily by companies. However, the practice was clearly an exception – most companies saw no reason to publish social or environmental reports.

Later, in the early 1970s, the Social Audit Ltd company, headed by Charles Medawar, was established with the mission of providing an independent view of companies' impacts. Since then the company has produced a series of critical reviews of the pharmaceutical industry. This can be seen as part of a long and continuing tradition of public or civil society organizations producing critical reports of companies and government.

One of the interesting aspects of social auditing was the suggestion that companies themselves should be transparent or disclose information, rather than respond to outside pressure. In the US, in the winter of 1989, for example, Ben & Jerry's, at that time an independent manufacturer and retailer of ice cream, produced a social report and asked an employee of the Council for Economic Priorities (CEP) to review it.

These early initiatives by companies were paralleled by further reports generated by NGOs and other organizations about companies and their impacts. In the UK one of the earliest of these was the Consumers' Association (now Which?). Established in 1957, the Consumers' Association independently tested and reported, initially with some trepidation as to the legal consequences, on the features and quality of everyday consumer products such as washing machines.

Just over a decade later, in 1971, Friends of the Earth was formed. Its first protest was 'a mass "bottle-drop" outside the offices of Schweppes to protest against their plans to start selling drinks in non-returnable plastic bottles' (FoE, 2005). Within a year of its launch the group had 2000 members and about 50 local campaigning groups:

Over the years, Friends of the Earth and other green groups have fought countless campaigns against companies over specific issues [...] We and other campaign groups have been able to expose the worst examples of corporate behaviour and indicate what kind of behaviour might be better. (FoE, 2005)

However, it would not be until the 1990s that the management of companies in general, and of their reporting and transparency in particular, became a central object of NGO campaigns.

In the mid-1990s a number of think-tanks and socially oriented enterprises combined to explore 'social auditing' and to develop a systematic methodology for it. These included the New Economics Foundation, a think-tank with expertise in indicators and participative community development, the BodyShop, founded to sell and campaign for animal cruelty-free cosmetics, and Traidcraft, a combined charity and trading company concerned with 'fair trade'. Traidcraft published its first social report in 1993 and the BodyShop's was published in 1996. From the late 1990s a number of socially oriented enterprises, including housing associations and a few charities, have published social reports (Raynard and Murphy, 2000).

The rise of CSR

The turning point for transparency, as well as for the involvement of the mainstream companies in the wider issues of sustainability, was provided by Shell. In 1995, the activities of Shell in disposing of the Brent Spar oil platform in the North Sea and its inactivity in the face of the indictment and subsequent execution of Ken Saro Wiwa, a human rights activist concerned with the impact of oil extraction in Nigeria, provoked a very big reaction from NGOs and the media. Shell later said that the challenge had prompted a major change of heart, taking it from a position of saying 'trust me' to one of listening to its stakeholders' demands to 'tell me' and eventually to 'show me'. In other words, there was a willingness to be more transparent. A few years later Shell and BP started to produce reports covering environmental and social issues.

Other sectors, such as manufacturers of footwear and sportswear, responded to campaigns against their activities in the same way, and the number of reports began to grow quite strongly, as Figure 7.1 shows.

CSR has, in fact, come to be identified with reporting. The major task of most CSR managers is to prepare for and publish the annual social or sustainability report.

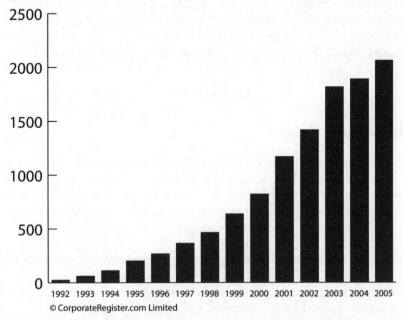

© CorporateRegister.com Limited

Figure 7.1 *The global trend in non-financial reporting*

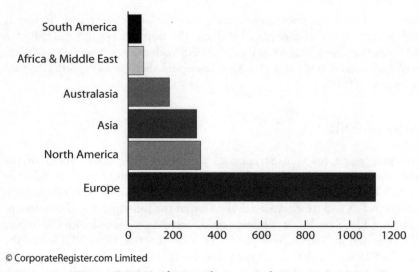

© CorporateRegister.com Limited

Figure 7.2 *Non-financial reporters by region in 2005*

By numbers alone, the growth of non-financial reporting at first sight looks phenomenal. From the handful produced in 1992, there are now approaching 1800 produced each year. In the UK, some 83 per cent of the FTSE100 produced some form of non-financial report in 2005.

Meanwhile, the production of 'counter-reports' has also continued and is perhaps becoming more common. Examples include reports on Rio Tinto (ICEM, 1998) by a mining union, on Shell by Friends of the Earth (FoE, 2002) and on Caterpillar by War on Want (WoW, 2005). Perhaps the major reason for the increase in such reports is disillusionment with the quality of the information and honesty of the corporate exercises in transparency. It is now a common view among NGOs that the voluntary approach to reporting has failed.

AUDITING

Establishing credibility

Who believes company reports? Doubt as to what companies are likely to say about themselves, as we have seen, is almost as old as company reporting itself. The response for financial reports has been formal auditing by a third party. For the recent spate of non-financial reporting, a wider set of possibilities has been explored. These include, in addition to formal auditing:

- self-certification by the reporting company, for example, for GRI reports;
- ad hoc commentary, by celebrities or well-known NGO figures;
- commentary by the external members of some form of advisory council or committee retained by the company; and
- statements about the company by some of its stakeholders.

Yet auditors are caught in a dilemma. If they are not paid (presumably by the company), how can any external party afford the time to thoroughly check a company report and go behind the scenes to see what might justify any particular claim? But if they are paid, how can they be trusted not to follow the company line? The traditional resolution to this dilemma was the adoption of auditing standards, which, if followed, would underpin the quality and credibility of the auditor's work.

Financial auditing

The development of financial auditing has been very closely intertwined with that of accounting regulation. The formalization of the one required the professionalization of the other. Its purpose remains broadly the same as it was 150 years ago: shareholders commission audits so that they may find the appropriate level of credibility to grant the accounts. Today it is mandatory for the financial accounts of the very large majority of companies and of other kinds of organizations to be audited.

To audit means to 'listen' to the accounts. The name for the activity is subject to fashion and it sometimes goes under other names. Auditing, verification and assurance are terms that have been fashionable at different times to describe a serious, systematic attempt by a third party to ensure that a report (financial or non-financial) is trustworthy. There have been attempts to distinguish different activities by these different terms, and some have been more common for environmental reporting, say, rather than for financial reporting. But none of these distinctions has stuck, and the terms will be used interchangeably here. Nevertheless, it may be noted of the term currently most used, 'assurance', that it does seem to have the implication that a positive outcome of an audit is not really in doubt.

Auditing does not solve everything: financial scandal is perennial. The most recent notorious cases, such as Parmalat and Enron, demonstrate that auditing is by no means a panacea for shareholders. Indeed, in some scandals, the auditors have been implicated in wrongdoing. Yet even where the audit has been conducted with the utmost propriety, it is entirely possible that the most serious risks facing a company will remain unreported. One of the reasons for this results, paradoxically, from the tight regulation of the profession. Both the form and construction of the accounts and the auditor's opinion are carefully controlled. The prototype auditor's opinion, according to ISA 700, is prescribed as follows:

> In our opinion, the financial statements give a true and fair view of [or 'present fairly, in all material respects'] the financial position of ABC Company as of 31 December 20X1, and of its financial performance and its cash flows for the year then ended in accordance with International Financial Reporting Standards. (IFAC, 2005, p599)

Any lesser endorsement of the accounts is a 'qualification'. Yet the qualification of an opinion is unusual. When it does occur it is usually expressed in relation to specific details. In other words the shareholder gets the same opinion, followed by a clause of the form 'except for the accounts for…'. There is very little motivation for auditors to deviate from the prescribed standard, since, in the event of being sued, it would be harder to argue that they had acted professionally in formulating their opinion. In practice, this means that issues which do indeed affect the financial position of the company, but are not included within the standard form of accounts, will tend to be ignored in the audit report. This allows new and complex forms of financial instrument to be developed, and while these remain profitable they will remain hidden from the balance sheet, the audited accounts and the public. Should shareholders suffer dramatic losses, they may become more publicly visible. It may, nevertheless, take some time for accounting standards to reflect the issue appropriately. There is a never-ending race between the hare of financial engineering and the tortoise of regulation.

Non-financial auditing

Non-financial auditing is perhaps at the stage that financial auditing achieved 150 years ago: it is sometimes recognized that it is necessary (or at least a good idea), but it has not yet evolved into a well-formed professional activity. However, for financial auditors there is already a mandatory standard for the auditing of non-financial information, ISAE 3000. This standard continues the approach of financial auditing in that the format for the auditor's statement is tightly constrained. The two forms of opinion permitted by this standard are given below:

> In a reasonable assurance engagement, the conclusion should be expressed in the positive form: for example 'In our opinion internal control is effective, in all material respects, based on XYZ criteria.' […] In a limited assurance engagement, the conclusion should be expressed in the negative form: for example 'Based on our work described in this report, nothing has come to our attention that causes us to believe that internal control is not effective, in all material respects, based on XYZ criteria.' (IFAC, 2005, p924)

These statements represent very limited feedback indeed. The feedback which is appropriate to a rich and complex set of issues that might range from the impact of building a dam in Turkey to over-selling credit in the UK ought itself to be rich. In fairness to the audit reports which have been produced, such complex matters are usually excluded from the auditor's opinion, which might be confined, say, to matters such as the number of reportable accidents that have been reported. While such limitations of scope may preserve the technical integrity of audit opinions, they do not go very far towards building the credibility of the audit process.

What is really needed for auditing the complex material of sustainability reports is feedback which:

- describes how well the issues reported have been described;
- indicates what has not been reported that should have been; and
- offers an opinion on the organization's performance.

The tradition of environmental auditing has come nearest to fulfilling these conditions. Environmental audits often include an opinion on substantive performance, such as whether the observed reduction in CO_2 could have been greater. This has been despite, or perhaps because of, the absence of a specific standard for environmental auditing. There is also a standard which has been used by non-accountants (as well as accountants until the introduction of ISAE 3000) to assure sustainability reports, AA1000AS.

AA1000AS is based on the three principles of materiality, completeness and responsiveness. Materiality concerns the inclusion of 'material' issues, in other words what is important; completeness concerns the scope of the report (although this is expressed, somewhat confusingly, in terms of the organization's systems for reporting); and responsiveness concerns how well the organization is responding to its stakeholders.

The most important aspect of AA1000AS is its stakeholder orientation. While ISAE 3000 appears to permit the auditor to address any appropriate party, the temptation in practice has largely been to address the opinion to management. AA1000AS, on the other hand, explicitly embraces the ideas that:

- an organization's report is directed at its stakeholders;
- the auditor is reporting to its stakeholders;
- materiality is defined in terms of stakeholders' interests;
- completeness includes consideration of stakeholders' issues; and
- responsiveness expresses a stakeholder view of performance.

Yet all of this raises the question of how far you can trust the auditor. Apart from technical competence, the main concern here must be in whose interests the auditor is working. For the financial audit community this is described as 'independence' and is largely taken to mean the extent of non-audit work for the same organization and the individual auditor's personal financial interest in the organization – all underpinned by the credibility of the standard. In practice, while there may be great rigour in avoiding individual, personal financial conflicts of interest, there is very little transparency on the overall relationship between the audit firm and the organization being audited.

There is also the issue of the financial interest in the audit by auditors, assuming they are being paid for their work. For financial audits, the cost of the audit itself can be found in the accounts, which is not generally true of non-financial auditing. This may be because the cost of a financial audit, while probably not material for large companies, is certainly substantial. For non-financial audits it is very much lower, typically by a factor of 50 or more. Given the much wider scope of non-financial issues for almost any company, this overall situation must cast doubt on the integrity of the audit.

Where an audit report is not even addressed to stakeholders other than shareholders or management, there is no compelling reason to consider that the interests of other stakeholders have been taken into account. When a range of stakeholders is explicitly addressed by an auditor, then the more significant and complex issue of impartiality needs to be addressed. How far does the auditor favour one stakeholder over another? Which stakeholders' issues receive particular attention in their enquiries and why? These and related issues have barely been addressed by practitioners or theoreticians, although the issue of impartiality has been identified in the AA1000AS standard. How this can play out in practice is illustrated in Box 7.2.

In summary, auditing has, or should have, the tasks of ensuring that not only are the things in the report right, but that the right things are in the report. Elsewhere (Henriques, 2005c), I have identified that, from a stakeholder perspective, there are three 'paradoxes of assurance' which suggest that the interests of the management are in fact best served when the audit focuses on the interests of other stakeholders:

1   **the stakeholder case is the business case** – the value of assurance to management is proportional to its focus on stakeholders;
2   **bad is good** – within the assurance statement, positive credibility is built by negative comments; and
3   **absence is presence** – assurance statements are most useful when commenting on what is not there.

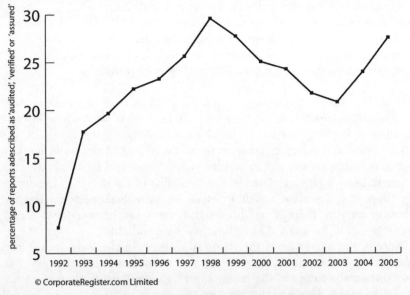

© CorporateRegister.com Limited

Figure 7.3 *Audited non-financial reports*

Box 7.2 Boundaries of completeness:
A case study in auditing

Background

Company X was a large, diversified utility company, historically based in the UK but with a significant international portfolio of businesses. As with many utility companies following privatization, Company X was looking for new business areas in order to maintain share price growth in a sector which had been confined to highly regulated and very mature markets. The auditors had worked with Company X for a number of years to provide assurance for their environmental and social report. Over time, both parties gradually worked towards a more transparent method of reporting and assurance. The approach was based initially on AA1000 and then on AA1000AS, following its introduction. One of the issues with which the audit process had to grapple was that of the appropriate boundary of reporting for Company X. Both in the UK and overseas, Company X had a number of subsidiaries in which the great majority of the business was conducted. However, none of these component businesses produced a social report; it was the group report which was subject to assurance.

Material issues

Clearly such a company has many material issues. Of these, two were concerned particularly with the boundary of reporting and therefore the completeness of the report. The first of these was connected to UK staff as a stakeholder; the second with the public and its connection to certain overseas operations. Within the UK, Company X worked through about six different subsidiary companies. For the audit, one of the problems was to ensure that the various companies and their brands were properly reflected in the report. In principle (and in practice) each component company had a full complement of stakeholders to whom the company was important. One of the issues which emerged was that of staff pay and remuneration. A key factor was that the differences in the (modal) average levels of pay between the different companies within the group was large: for some companies many of the employees received much less than a typical worker in some of the other group companies. However, the levels of pay in all these companies were separately comparable with market averages.

Overseas, Company X worked with partner organizations and formed joint ventures. These joint ventures supplied directly to the public, which was thus a crucial stakeholder. In addition, in some cases utilities had been taken out of state hands and privatized, with Company X being the first licensee. The whole issue of privatization was contentious and involved complex issues of practical availability of water in shanty town areas.

Working towards a resolution

Company X was reluctant to disclose the average levels of pay within its companies in the UK, as this would expose the significant differences between the companies within the group. The company had spent some time trying to establish itself in these new business areas and to build goodwill between staff throughout the group. To the auditors, it seemed important that as basic a fact as the relative levels of pay should be publicly reported. The auditors' view was that in the long run more good will would be generated by transparency than might be preserved by ignorance.

Over a number of years, the level of transparency in this area was gradually increased. In the first few years, the issue was set out in the audit statement. Subsequent movement towards greater disclosure was also acknowledged in later statements. Initially the report had included only the overall group numbers of staff and overall pay. The next step was to disclose the numbers in the component companies together with group average pay. Most recently, and with different auditors, Company X has slipped somewhat: now only overall staff numbers and (an undefined) group average pay are disclosed.

Overall there was considerable reluctance to include much about its overseas operations in the report. Part of this reluctance appeared to stem from the lack of interest to UK opinion formers – or perhaps a desire on the part of Company X management not to generate any more such interest. Yet in connection with a different company's similar operations in Columbia, which had resulted in public riots, the death of a demonstrator and ultimately the loss of the contract, this was not a trivial issue. The auditors were therefore concerned, first, that this was a material issue for the public and customers, given the sensitivity to privatization. Another issue was concern for shareholders. Given the sensitivity of Western companies taking over public utilities in the developing world, the situation should at least have been considered a financial risk, and reported as such.

In practical terms, some of the issues centred simply on how many customers the overseas operations actually had and who should acknowledge responsibility. The relationship with these companies was typically one of part-ownership: so for every million customers of the overseas venture, how many should be apportioned to Company X? Furthermore, the contracts were structured so that Company X did not own the assets, but only provided management and service delivery. There was initially an acknowledgement of some of these issues in the report, followed by a gradual increase in the level of information disclosed. One strategy was to do a 'feature' in the report on a given overseas operation each year. While helpful, this approach did not facilitate a systematic picture being established.

More recently, Company X's reports have included very little information on their overseas operations. One reason for this is that the proportion of these ventures which Company X owns has declined. The overseas operations merit only a few paragraphs in recent reports and the current auditors have not commented on the lack of coverage of the issue.

REGULATION AND STANDARDS

The principal focus of this chapter so far has been on legislation bearing directly on company reporting to shareholders and on voluntary reporting on non-financial matters. There are, however, other laws and standards, considered as a set of rules, which tend to increase the level of disclosure by companies of non-financial issues.

Such rules can be roughly classified into three categories, according to the level of enforcement with which it is supported:

1   **hard law**, which can be defined as laws passed by national legislatures, with enforcement procedures in place and defined sanctions;
2   **soft law**, which comprises sets of rules which businesses in practice have to observe, but which may not be backed by sanctions of the same legal force as hard laws; and
3   **self-regulation**, which can take many forms and, although there may be few real sanctions other than loss of reputation attached to ignoring them, can significantly affect business behaviour.

Hard law

In France, Denmark, the Netherlands, Norway, Sweden, Belgium and Australia, there are laws requiring companies to disclose at least some of their impacts. While this has often concentrated on environmental impacts, this is not universally the case, as for example in France, which requires companies to also report on their social performance.

In the UK, recent legislation on the management of pension funds requires fund trustees to disclose the extent (if at all) to which they take into account social and environmental factors in the management of their funds. A number of other countries, such as Australia and Germany, have similar laws.

In many countries environmental monitoring bodies have been established to gather information on environmental performance, including that of companies. The Environmental Protection Agency in the US, and particularly its Toxic Release Inventory, is an example. However, such monitoring, while it may include information on instances of the performance of specific companies, does not make it straightforward to gain an overview of the performance of a given company. Other statutory bodies, such as the Low Pay Commission in the UK, provide only isolated examples or case studies on elements of the social performance of individual companies.

More generally, the constitution or national law of the UK, US and many other countries, from Albania to South Korea, provides for 'freedom of information'. According to Privacy International:

> *Over fifty countries around the world have now adopted comprehensive freedom of information acts to facilitate access to records held by government bodies and over thirty more have pending efforts.* (Banisar, 2004)

These acts are designed to allow citizens to request information on the activities of government; however, since many government activities involve relationships with companies, it is a potential source of information about company activities too. In general, these laws facilitate disclosure around specific issues, rather than specific companies. To build up a picture of the activities of a given company, even confined to its government dealings, is therefore laborious.

Over and above national law governing corporate disclosure, there are a set of international conventions (here taken to include 'treaties', 'protocols' and

85

other international instruments) to which many governments have subscribed. These include conventions such as the Basel Convention on hazardous wastes, CITES on endangered species, the ILO Conventions and the Montreal Protocol. All these agreements were made between nation states, although some, such as the ILO Conventions, systematically include other parties in their governance, development and monitoring.

From a transparency perspective, the critical feature is that each of these conventions includes provision for some level of monitoring and reporting of the performance of the member nations. It follows that where companies have contributed to the performance monitored by the Convention, the national government will need to implement regulations requiring companies to submit the relevant information to them. However, just as with the national efforts at monitoring, it is not easy to derive the contribution of any given company to the issues covered by the Convention.

Soft law

The EU's Eco-Management and Audit Scheme (EMAS) has been available, at least for certain European companies, since 1995. In fact, EMAS covers the European Economic Area, which adds Norway, Iceland and Lichtenstein to the list of EU participating countries. In addition, some international companies apply EMAS to non-European sites across the world. Its objectives, beyond complying with all relevant environmental legislation, include 'the provision of information on environmental performance and an open dialogue with the public and other interested parties' (EMAS, 2001). Companies managing their environmental performance through EMAS must produce a statement of their achievements and plans for improvement. This scheme is voluntary, but provides recognition of successful participants through permission to use an official label. At the end of 2005 there were some 3200 organizations with about 4600 sites registered.

Standards produced by the International Organization for Standardization (ISO) have, potentially, a much greater reach than Europe. In particular, ISO standards appear to be privileged from the perspective of the World Trade Organization (WTO), in that national legislation based on them is unlikely to fall foul of the WTO's anti-competition views. The ISO has agreed ISO 14000, a series of management system standards. Unfortunately, while EMAS and ISO 14000 are in some respects quite similar, ISO 14000 does not cover reporting (except for greenhouse gases). The ISO is also developing a standard for social responsibility, ISO 26000, which is likely to include guidance on reporting.

The OECD, whose member countries include most of the developed and Western world, has published guidelines for multinational companies. While the implementation of the guidelines has been disappointing, in addition to reporting on risk, the guidelines include the following text:

> Enterprises are encouraged to communicate additional information that could include:

a) *Value statements or statements of business conduct intended for public disclosure including information on the social, ethical and environmental policies of the enterprise and other codes of conduct to which the company subscribes. In addition, the date of adoption, the countries and entities to which such statements apply and its performance in relation to these statements may be communicated.*
b) *Information on systems for managing risks and complying with laws, and on statements or codes of business conduct.*
c) *Information on relationships with employees and other stake-holders.* (OECD, 2000, p20)

The London Stock Exchange listing rules require companies listed on that exchange to abide by the Combined Code on Corporate Governance (FRC, 2003). For listed companies, therefore, compliance with the relevant stock exchange listing rules is effectively mandatory. The Combined Code includes the Turnbull Guidance, which suggests that companies should report on significant risks and further suggests that significant risks would include not only market, credit, liquidity, technological and legal issues, but could also include health, safety, environmental and reputation issues.

Self-regulation

One of the innovations accompanying the development of CSR has been the idea of self-regulation. A number of standards have been developed by civil society or in response to the demands of civil society and the rising social aspirations of industry itself. In either case participation is voluntary, although when such standards have been widely adopted by industry the pressure to conform may be stronger. Where civil society is directly involved, the legitimacy and credibility of the standards so developed can be high.

However, standards for corporate responsibility are not the same as standards for *reporting* corporate responsibility. In general, standards for corporate responsibility can be classified into three groups:

1 **Substantive** performance in relation to social, environmental or economic issues covers actual results, for example, the level of staff diversity, tons of CO_2 emitted or profit levels. The Global Compact principles are an example of this type of standard.
2 The **management** of performance of social, environmental or economic issues. Most ISO standards are of this nature; ISO14001 for environmental management systems is a typical example.
3 The **reporting** of corporate activity concerned with social, environmental or economic issues includes reporting of either the management or performance outcomes. The GRI is an example of this type.

In practice, few standards are clearly of one of these types only. The Business in the Community approach, for example, covers management, substantive performance and reporting in its Corporate Responsibility Index. The AA1000 Framework Standard includes reporting as part of the stakeholder management process. The Global Compact requires regular 'communications on progress' to be produced. The SA8000 Standard for labour conditions includes both substantive performance along with an assessment of how these issues are managed.

Much self-regulation has been concerned with specific standards of performance, rather than with disclosure and reporting. However, even where the major focus is on performance, there is often a disclosure element. The Forest Stewardship Council (FSC), for example, arranges for the certification of timber and timber products on the basis of the sustainability of the forest of origin. However, FSC-certified products carry a label, which can be regarded as a limited form of disclosure. Similarly, SA 8000, a standard concerning labour conditions, supports reporting of the conditions at certified sites.

However, by far the most significant of self-regulated reporting standards is the GRI. The GRI has systematically developed principles for sustainability reporting and indicators for reports. The GRI began as a project of CERES, an NGO which developed reporting as a response to the Exxon Valdez environmental disaster in 1989. In 2002, the GRI became an independent organization and an official collaborating centre of the United Nations Environment Programme (UNEP). In mid-2006 there were about 800 organizations which had declared that they were using the GRI Guidelines in some way, the majority of these being large or multinational companies.

Of course, this does not mean that 800 organizations have applied the Guidelines in their full rigour; many say simply that they have 'referred to' or 'considered' the guidelines in preparing their reports. In general, corporate reporting is piecemeal and fragmentary at best. All of this leaves actual, current reporting practice rather confused, incomplete and, for most stakeholders, inappropriate and unsatisfying. The next chapter describes what companies currently actually do in more detail, and how far it is technically possible to improve the quality and scope of their reporting and to integrate it in the name of sustainability.

8

Reporting Challenges

AN ASSESSMENT OF CURRENT PRACTICE

The transparency actually delivered by companies is dominated by financial reporting, which is tightly regulated. On financial matters, companies rarely report more than they are required to. The information which has to be disclosed today has achieved that status as a result of long-term pressure from the stakeholders most concerned, the shareholders. In addition, some non-financial information also has to be disclosed by law, at least to some parties such as regulators, if not publicly. Again, this is historically the result of considerable pressure and does not often go beyond what is required.

More recently, companies have begun voluntarily to disclose more information about non-financial issues. We have seen that of the UK FTSE100 companies, over 80 per cent produce some kind of non-financial report in addition to their financial report, according to Corporate Register (CR, 2006). Reporting has also assumed a large role in CSR – to the extent that just producing a report tends to be seen as the discharge of responsibility.

Yet the global total of some 1800 reports a year is still a very small number considering the colossal number of companies worldwide. Furthermore, while the number of large companies which produce non-financial reports is significant in Europe, the global proportion of non-financial reporting companies is vanishingly small, at less than 0.01 per cent of the total number of companies worldwide. In addition, the global production of reports is largely skewed to the Western world (apart from environmental reports, which are slightly more evenly spread). Moreover, the production of such reports is almost entirely undertaken by large multinational companies along with some smaller companies with a significant public brand.

Moreover, while the rise in non-financial reporting is a welcome development, the reports produced tend either to be very high level with very little detail, or else very specific 'case studies'. In either case, it is hard to gain a systematic picture of the company's impacts. There is also a very strong temptation for companies to report only on beneficial impacts. It is hard for companies (as indeed for anyone) to do otherwise. Yet 'admitting only to perfection' leads to allegations of greenwashing and corporate spin.

Nevertheless, there is currently a great deal of experimentation in the reporting of non-financial information. In addition to new forms of auditing and the use of the internet, this has led to two conflicting trends: convergence of issue reporting and divergence of stakeholder reporting. Convergence of issue reporting is reflected in the move towards producing sustainability reports rather than separate environmental and social or community reports. Content that may have been reported separately may now be combined in a single 'sustainability' report. Whereas in 1992 some 80 per cent of non-financial reports were environmental in nature, the proportion that are still labelled simply as environmental reports is now down below 20 per cent. This is, however, more a reflection of the labelling, rather than of a reduction in environmental content. Along with employee and community issues, environmental content is still one of the most dominant components of non-financial reporting, although it is now often labelled 'sustainability' or 'corporate responsibility' reporting.

The trend towards stakeholder divergence of reporting results from the running of large companies requiring extensive communication with a wide range of stakeholders, including shareholders and many others. Since the communication needs of stakeholders differ, some large companies are now reproducing the same basic material in different formats for these different stakeholders. While there will be one sustainability report for opinion formers there may, for example, be another version, containing the same basic information, prepared especially for staff. It is important to bear in mind that only certain stakeholders will receive such treatment – very few companies produce reports specifically aimed at suppliers, for example. The overall reporting picture can therefore be quite complex, as Box 8.1 shows for a fictional company, 'Reportalot plc'.

BOX 8.1 REPORTALOT PLC

Reportalot plc, a typical large company, produces the reports listed below. Most are available both online and in print form.

Shareholder reports

Annual report – 150 pages
Form 20-F – 60 pages
Annual review – 25 pages
Interim results – 30 pages

Reports for other stakeholders

Sustainability report – 60 pages
Country CSR reports – 40 pages per country
Community report – 30 pages
Customer brochure – 8 pages
Special issues reports – 15 pages
Regulators' returns – 120 pages

Another noticeable trend is that towards auditing or assurance, as was noted in the last chapter. While still only a minority of non-financial reports are reviewed by a third party, the numbers involved are rising. However, by far the most common form of such review is of the correctness of the numbers involved in the report. In only a minority of cases is the overall appropriateness of the content of the report something within the purview of reviewers.

Finally, the growing importance in the use of the internet is important. There has been much experimentation with the internet and attempts to use it in different ways; sustainability reports, for example, may be available interactively. But perhaps the most common and the most important use is simply as a location from which an electronic copy of the non-financial (and indeed financial) report may be obtained. In the UK the regulations introduced as part of the Companies Act (2006) provide for the delivery of financial reports and other communications in electronic form. However, the internet can also be used to make more detailed information available than can sensibly be incorporated in a reasonably sized report. This has sometimes resulted in the provision of a deluge of information (in some case over 1500 pages) which actually makes a clear picture of corporate performance harder to obtain. This is the so-called 'databombing' or white noise effect, as documented by Ann Florini (Florini, 1999).

The history of the fictional reporting company Reportalot plc might run as follows. For the last 15 years, perhaps since 1990, the company may have been declaring the funds it had been giving to charity, in accordance with the 1985 Companies Act. This reporting gradually grew in extent because it was considered good publicity for the company. In the late 1990s, a separate community report was published, and a few years later an environmental report was produced. These were soon combined, without significant change in scope, as a CSR report. In 2003, with the addition of some information on staff activities, which still focused particularly on voluntary activities, the report was re-badged as a 'sustainability' report. The report is not, however, subject to any audit.

The consequences of this kind of history are that:

- financial results, together with community and environmental activities are predominant; and
- other than financial analysts, reports are addressed to two groups: regulators and 'opinion-formers' and the issues with which they may be concerned, rather than to the main stakeholders involved with the company.

Perhaps the most sensitive issue for those responsible for preparing non-regulated reports today is that it is not at all clear who, if anyone, reads them. In contrast to the number of reports distributed, the number read in any detail is probably very small. This is one of the more paradoxical consequences of the orientation of reports to opinion formers rather than to their main stakeholders. Pressure groups, at least, are concerned that companies address their main impacts, and one sign of this is the way they are reported on. Pressure groups, however, do not have the resources to follow every detail of every company's performance relating to an issue. So for companies to orient their reports to pressure groups is unlikely to bear the fruit of readership. Conversely, to address stakeholders directly in reports would make them more relevant and possibly more widely read.

The main legacy for most companies is therefore a rather fragmented set of reports which do not appear to serve the interests of many stakeholders (often including shareholders) very well. Companies face a number of conflicting demands:

- to produce reports of a greater stakeholder relevance: stakeholder reporting;
- to economize on the profusion of reports produced and to integrate reporting; and
- to resolve the conflict between the legal risk of transparency and legitimate stakeholder interest.

STAKEHOLDER REPORTING

As a large multinational with perhaps 150,000 staff operating in subsidiaries within maybe 70 countries across the world, how can you produce a report of your social and environmental impacts in less than 50 pages? The only way to do this is to be so selective that the information conveyed can no longer give a systematic picture of overall impact. It is worth bearing in mind that the report dedicated to just one stakeholder, the shareholder, for such large companies often runs to several hundred pages. It does not seem feasible to cater adequately for more stakeholders in a shorter report, and the solution which more companies are in fact coming to is to produce separate national reports in addition to a group report. Diageo, for example, produces global, regional and country reports. While this still does not solve the problem of what to put into the group report, it can in theory provide more suitable communication to most stakeholder groups.

While regulated shareholder reports are far from perfect, the rules for consolidating group accounts do make it possible for shareholders, at least those professionally involved, to manage their relationships and decisions with respect to the company. This is far from the case for, say, the consumer element of a sustainability report. There is a considerable overlap between the information which a chief executive actually uses to manage shareholder interests and what is reported in the financial accounts. But it would be simply embarrassing if a chief executive were to try to manage the company's consumer relations on the basis of the consumer section of a sustainability report. If that is so, how can consumers (or even their professional interest groups) be expected to manage their relationship with the company on the same basis? The situation is the same for most other stakeholder groups.

One response might be to produce stakeholder-specific reports for each stakeholder, with the main issues of concern to that stakeholder and the company's progress in dealing with them as the main part of the content. At the moment, while there are a few stakeholder-specific reports, there are very few of a quality which can make the stakeholder take them seriously.

Stakeholder-specific reporting, however stakeholder-friendly it might be, cannot be the whole answer. From the company's perspective, multiplying reports tends to multiply costs, and from the stakeholder perspective, without a company-wide report, it is very hard to get an overview of the company's impact. Beyond that, many stakeholders actually have interests in the company's relationship with other stakeholders. This may arise from an ethical orientation, as a result of which the customers or shareholders of a fair-trading company, for example, may wish to protect the interests of suppliers. However, it may also arise from more pragmatic motives: those affected by pollution may want to know if the company's success has been predicated on that pollution – and shareholders may wish to know the same thing in order to understand any potential liability.

So a complex picture emerges: in addition to the challenges of reporting on the impacts of a multinational company, there are multiple stakeholders, each with a number of issues. Furthermore, the interests of different stakeholders may conflict and different issues may turn out to be connected and so not readily reportable in isolation.

It is precisely here, in the interaction between different stakeholders and their interests, that the need for transparency emerges most strongly. The way the needs of different stakeholders are managed and balanced reflects the balance of power between them. It is therefore an issue of justice and morality, and squarely within the scope of what needs to be made transparent: where there is power, there should be transparency.

To take another example, mobile phone companies need to ensure that there is adequate coverage by phone masts in order to operate. The issues raised by these masts affect a range of stakeholders:

- consumers want as many masts as give universally good signal coverage;
- residents may be worried about radiation effects from masts;
- visitors to the countryside may be concerned about the visual impact of masts; and
- regulators may be trying to encourage the sharing of masts.

In reporting terms, one response has been to produce reports relating to these specific issues (GreenAlliance, 2001) – or at least sections within the overall non-financial report (VodafoneUK, 2005) addressing these concerns directly.

Taking another example, a large retailing or manufacturing company may manufacture its products in a number of places around the world. Parts may be produced in China, assembled in Germany and sold in the US, for example. Labour conditions in the supply chain may be a particular issue in China; the assembly and sale of the end product will require the transportation of the parts across the world at an environmental, as well as financial, cost. However, none of this would be happening if it were not deemed the most financially efficient way to do business. The analysis and reporting of this set of issues is complex and cannot easily be confined to one stakeholder group or type of issue (such as environmental impact) alone.

The complexity of these issues does not permit a reporting solution which responds neatly to the demands of corporate public relations. No all-purpose shrink-wrapped company position is likely to be satisfying to any one group. When it comes to reporting, to take advantage of economies of scale is fraught with the danger of diminished moral responsibility.

INTEGRATED REPORTING

As we have seen, the two main strands of current company reporting are reporting for shareholders and the financial community, and reporting for other stakeholders. The idea of 'integrated reporting' suggests combining, to some extent, the communication needs of these two groups. How far is this possible? And what might integrated reporting look like? To answer this question it is important to be clear about:

- the nature of the legal and regulatory constraints on financial reporting; and
- the potential content and structure of an integrated report beyond that required by law.

There are many requirements on company directors regarding reporting. The Companies Act (2006), following EU Directives, defines a number of different reports which directors must prepare, place on their website and send to shareholders. The most significant are:

- the company accounts;
- the directors' report, including a business review; and
- the directors' remuneration report.

However, these various reports are in fact separate requirements. They do not have to be produced as one document. It would, therefore, theoretically be possible to publish them separately. But historically they have usually been combined by most companies into a single report: the 'report and accounts'. Under certain conditions (as determined by the Secretary of State), shareholders may be sent only a summary financial review. This must contain a summary of the accounts and the directors' remuneration report. It need not contain elements of the directors' report, but it must say whether or not it does so. The law, and also the rules of the accounting profession, ensure that the content, and in certain respects the precise layout of the company accounts is carefully controlled.

Coverage of extra-financial issues within financial reporting

The consultations over the Company Law Reform Bill resulted in the development of the reporting standard RS1 (ASB, 2001) from the Accounting Standards Board (ASB). While this standard was developed with the now

Box 8.2 What the directors' report should cover

The business review must contain –
(a) a fair review of the company's business; and
(b) a description of the principal risks and uncertainties facing the company.

The review required is a balanced and comprehensive analysis of –
(a) the development and performance of the company's business during the financial year; and
(b) the position of the company's business at the end of that year,
consistent with the size and complexity of the business.

In the case of a quoted company the business review must, to the extent necessary for an understanding of the development, performance or position of the company's business, include –
(a) the main trends and factors likely to affect the future development, performance and position of the company's business;
(b) information about –
(i) environmental matters (including the impact of the company's business on the environment);
(ii) the company's employees; and
(iii) social and community issues, including information about any policies of the company in relation to such matters and the effectiveness of such policies; and
(c) [...], information about persons with whom the company has contractual or other arrangements which are essential to the business of the company.
If the review does not contain information of each kind mentioned in paragraphs (b)(i), (ii) and (iii) and (c), it must state which of those kinds of information it does not contain.

The review must, to the extent necessary for an understanding of the development, performance or position of the company's business, include –
(a) analysis using financial key performance indicators; and
(b) where appropriate, analysis using other key performance indicators, including information relating to environmental matters and employee matters.

Source: UK Legislature (2006), s 417

abandoned Operating and Financial Review in mind, the ASB believes that RS1 still stands as best practice reporting. The expectations set in RS1 are therefore important. The standard purports to cover the full range of issues which may be of interest to shareholders. This obviously includes financial performance, but also a range of factors which may affect financial performance in the future. This includes 'risks and uncertainties' and issues likely to affect the company's reputation, considered in the longer term. RS1 also suggests a range of key performance indicators and defines these with a rigour which, while customary for traditional financial indicators, is new to the reporting of non-financial matters.

In addition to indicators such as return on capital employed (ROCE), economic profit and market share, the range of factors recommended in RS1 for consideration includes:

- customer churn;
- environmental spillage;
- CO_2 emissions;
- waste;
- employee morale;
- employee health & safety;
- social risks in the supply chain; and
- noise infringements.

Social and environmental issues are therefore firmly on the agenda of emerging practice in shareholder reporting. But is that enough? What else might be required by those who demand more from companies' sustainability reports? Before outlining standards which have been proposed and used for non-financial reporting, it is important to bear in mind that even RS1 only requires consideration of extra-financial issues where these have relevance for shareholders. If they are unlikely to impact shareholders, then there is no need to report them.

For powerful stakeholders that can affect financial performance, perhaps through adverse effects on reputation, that is fine. Poor customer service is an obvious example of an issue that needs to be addressed and reported on as it must, in the long run, affect company performance. But for those who may be very vulnerable, this may not work. Consider the need of a company to reflect the impact it may have on poor communities in developing countries, for example. Unless perhaps their plight draws the attention of the Western media, there is no compelling reason under RS1 why a company would have to report its impact on them.

Integration and the GRI Guidelines

The GRI is particularly relevant for integrated reporting, as it not only focuses specifically and directly on reporting, but, in the words of Dr Klaus Töpfer, Executive Director of UNEP:

> [it] has an ambitious and innovative vision [...] an increasing number of stakeholders, including the investment community, share the goal of the GRI to raise the practice of corporate sustainability reporting to the level of rigour, credibility, comparability and verifiability of financial reporting. (GRI, 2002)

The GRI Guidelines have been developed from a wide-ranging and continuing consultation process involving many different stakeholder groups as well as companies themselves.

The underlying approach the GRI Guidelines take to sustainability reporting is an analysis of sustainability as a set of social, environmental and economic issues. A key part of the content of a GRI report consists of reporting against a set of indicators for each of the social, environmental and economic issues identified within the guidelines. If financial reporting can be integrated with sustainability reporting, it is an interesting question how far the requirements of financial reporting might make use of the GRI. This question can be addressed in two parts: first, how the GRI deals with the 'economic' dimension of sustainability; and second, how far a fully compliant GRI report might address the current financial reporting regulatory requirements.

The treatment of the economic dimension of sustainability within the GRI encompasses several aspects:

- an outline of the financial profile of an organization characterized, for example, by net sales and capitalization figures;
- a statement of the cash flows experienced by major stakeholder groups in a form similar to a value-added statement; and
- a series of indicators intended to capture the impact of the organization on the economic capacity of its stakeholders. The level of staff training is an example of an indicator of this type.

The most significant point here is that the GRI's view of economic reporting is significantly greater in scope than that of financial reporting. However, it is also true that there is nothing in current financial reporting practice which would be out of place in, or beyond the scope of, a GRI report.

In relation to the question how far a GRI report would satisfy financial reporting requirements, the picture is mixed. The GRI Guidelines, wisely, make no attempt to incorporate the technical details of regulated financial reporting, or even to require that the financial figures are derived from audited accounts. The reporting of environmental expenditures (and presumably liabilities) falls outside the economic section of the indicators. While the guidelines permit the structure of a sustainability report to reflect that of the financial report of a group of companies, they do not call for any significant cross-referencing to relevant international accounting standards.

The GRI Guidelines identify issues for reporting, in the sections on 'vision and strategy' and 'structure and governance', which are broadly equivalent to significant parts of the business review and directors' remuneration report. Overall, therefore, there is an important potential for making use of a GRI report to satisfy financial reporting requirements. Currently, a few financial reports refer readers to sustainability reports for further detail. It should also be possible, with careful presentation, to do the reverse: to produce a GRI report as the primary communication for all stakeholders and refer the shareholders among them to the audited financial reports provided as appendices to the document.

TRANSPARENCY AND LEGAL LIABILITY

If the scope of what should be reported includes those areas in which a company has power, and for which it should therefore admit responsibility, then transparency must include both positive and negative impacts. An important question for companies which may wish to do this is that of legal liability. If they admit to negative impacts, what are the consequences from a legal perspective? Box 8.3 reproduces an extract from Rio Tinto's website. It is part of a disclaimer which appears to be accessible from every single page of their website, including those related to financial and sustainability reporting. Any large company's website could have been used for this purpose, as there is nothing unusual about Rio Tinto in this respect.

Put into slightly more user-friendly language, the main thrust of Rio Tinto's disclaimer is that:

- the material on the website is 'for information only', in other words it is not intended to be acted on;
- the company has tried to ensure the information is accurate, but it may not be (note there is no suggestion that the company has tried to ensure that the information is *complete*);
- the company will not be liable for the consequences of anyone making use of this information or for the fact that it may not be accurate or complete;

BOX 8.3 CONDITIONS OF USE OF THE RIO TINTO WEBSITE

All information on this website is provided for information only.

Rio Tinto has made reasonable efforts to ensure that information provided on Rio Tinto's website on the internet is accurate at the time of inclusion. However, there may be inadvertent and occasional errors for which Rio Tinto apologises.

Rio Tinto makes no representations or warranties of any kind about the information provided on its website or via hypertext links or any other item used either directly or indirectly from Rio Tinto's website and reserves the right to make changes and corrections at any time, without notice. By accessing this website, you agree that Rio Tinto will not be liable for any inaccuracies or omissions or any direct, special, indirect or consequential damages or losses, or any other damages or losses of whatsoever kind resulting from whatever cause through the use of any information obtained either directly or indirectly from or through Rio Tinto's website and any decisions based on such information are the sole responsibility of the visitor.

No information contained in Rio Tinto's website constitutes or shall be deemed to constitute an invitation or inducement to invest or otherwise deal in the shares or any other securities of Rio Tinto plc, Rio Tinto Limited, any other member of the Rio Tinto Group, any other person, or to engage in any investment activity, and must not be relied upon in connection with any investment decision.

The above exclusions and limitations apply only to the extent permitted by law.

Source: Rio Tinto (2005)

- the company is not trying to sell its shares using this information, and no-one should invest on the basis of it anyway; and
- if anything in the disclaimer is not lawful, the company takes it back.

Such disclaimers may or may not have a great deal of force in law, but they do detract from the credibility of the website as a whole – and therefore also from the reputation of the company.

If this level of distancing is placed on the reporting of the largely positive aspects of the company and its impacts that are to be found on the website, it is perhaps not so surprising that negative impacts are not mentioned. A more serious legal problem with doing so is that to be transparent about negative impacts may be to admit liability for them. It may be possible to admit responsibility for negative impacts in cases where there may be moral fault, but no material harm done; however, if someone has suffered harm and there is a legal remedy enforceable through the courts, then the admission of liability could put the company in a worse position than it would have been in without such admission.

It is therefore not too surprising, from a legal point of view, that there is little or no disclosure of negative impacts. During the Kasky case, discussed in Chapter 5, Nike initially stopped producing social reports, fearing the consequences if it misreported the situation in its supply chain. It should perhaps be regarded as an achievement when companies report any negative impacts of their activities at all, even where these are commonplace and not very damaging.

What transparency may then be hoped for concerning the more serious impacts of a company? The chapters to follow will address some of these more difficult issues, from taxation to corruption, for which companies may be responsible. They will attempt to set out what transparency is needed, what is now typically delivered and what could be delivered. In general, companies need to develop a coherent strategy for transparency.

Towards a Transparency Strategy

One such strategy would be to avoid transparency altogether. Some companies have suggested that the demands of Sarbanes-Oxley and other regulations have led them to consider de-listing their shares and operating with the greater freedom and privacy of a private company.

For those companies that remain interested in 'writing their wrongs', there is a need to bring a thought-through strategy to bear. This should above all avoid box-ticking. Transparency should be treated as an exercise in communication with stakeholders, not a formal demand for compliance.

Such a strategy should cover:

- **an overall commitment to transparency**. There should be a presumption of transparency, rather than of concealment. Areas of confidentiality should be well defined and their existence should itself be disclosed in some way;

- **the relationship of staff communications to public communications.** The nature of this relationship should be articulated. This should bear in mind that for most large companies, staff communication is, in practice, effectively public communication, but is rarely treated as such; and
- **the role of specific communications vehicles.** In addition to the financial report, one such vehicle is the 'traditional' non-financial report. In addition, the use of the internet as a repository to support more formal reports should be clear. Finally, the diversity and availability of other kinds of disclosure, such as regulatory returns, should itself be disclosed.

9

The Story of the Media and the Honest Truth

People don't actually read newspapers. They step into them every morning like a hot bath. (Marshall McLuhan)

The media, as an industrial sector, is about communication: a central aspect of transparency. The very word 'media' means something in the middle, or in between. But what is the sector in between? And how much does it get in the way? The answers to these questions will determine how far the sector can be said to be transparent. If the media has a crucial role to play in delivering transparency in a modern society, how can this role be assessed and how effective is the industry in that role?

The media industry today comprises a diverse range of organizations that can be analysed and segmented in a number of ways. One way to analyse it is in terms of the delivery channels. The key channels, according to KPMG (KPMG, 2004) are broadcast, hardcopy and online. Another way to segment the industry is in terms of content, which would separate news and factual content from entertainment in particular, although clearly a great deal more analysis of each of these categories is possible. It can, of course, also be questioned how far it is possible to make such a clean distinction between fact and fiction in this way at all. Yet another way to analyse the industry is through its stakeholder structure. This would encompass shareholders, audiences, advertisers, staff and the subjects of news stories, among many others.

This chapter is not intended to provide a systematic overview of the complete set of responsibilities of the media or of its actual transparency. The central concern will be factual or news content and what transparency means and how it may be measured for this type of content. From this perspective, the differences between delivery channels, while important, are not central to the power relationships between the more powerful, traditional media organizations and their stakeholders.

Drawing on the US experience, Noam Chomsky set out five 'filters' which news has to pass before seeing the light of day:

1   *the size, concentrated ownership, owner wealth and profit orien-
    tation of the dominant mass-media firms;*
2   *advertising as the primary income source of the mass media;*
3   *the reliance of the media on information provided by govern-
    ment, business and 'experts' funded and approved by these
    primary sources and agents of power;*
4   *'flak' as a means of disciplining the media; and*
5   *'anticommunism' as a national religion and control mechanism.*
    (Chomsky, 1995)

These five filters in effect express some of the main interests of different
stakeholders of a news organization. As a way to be clear about the various
power relationships within the industry, the next section will therefore look at
its stakeholders and their issues. This will be followed by a discussion of the
critical issue of editorial propriety. The chapter concludes with suggestions for
some appropriate measurements of the achievement of transparency in this
sector.

MEDIA STAKEHOLDER ISSUES

Of media organization stakeholders particularly important for the transparency
of the news, perhaps the most significant are the public and those in the news,
in other words the 'news subjects', advertisers and shareholders.

Interested subjects

A vast number of subjects are covered by the spectrum of newspapers each day.
Within that spectrum there are two groups of special significance for transparency: politicians and celebrities. Because politicians are engaged in
responding to issues which may affect all of us, it is reasonably clear why they
are 'in the news'. Some celebrities are famous because they have achieved
something remarkable; others are famous because they have been in the news:
they are 'famous for being famous'. Probably all politicians and most celebrities
(certainly the famous for being famous sort) want publicity, which the TV, radio,
newspapers and magazines can provide. However, the sort of publicity they
want is 'good publicity'. They want fame rather than notoriety.

The media, however, want good stories, rather than stories of good things,
where these are not the same thing, as is usually the case. As a result, stories
about arguments, conflict and indiscretion, especially of a financial or sexual
nature are highly prized by the media. Thus a story about a sportsman's or politician's infidelity to their spouse will receive more attention than a policy
(perhaps about climate change) the politician may have been trying to
champion. News organizations appear to have great difficulty assessing the
relative significance of what they report. The *News of the World*, the UK's most
successful Sunday tabloid, for example, proudly says that:

[their] first edition [of 1 October 1843] [...] proclaimed: 'Our motto is truth. Our practice is the fearless advocacy of the truth.' Since that day, we've become world-renowned for breaking the biggest stories and fighting the hardest-hitting campaigns. (NotW, 2006)

Yet it also proudly says that:

Last year, we won Newspaper of the Year, Scoop of the Year for our revelation of David Beckham's affair with his PA Rebecca Loos [...]

In their defence, there is an argument that if politicians are to represent the public, then their integrity must be paramount. Since integrity is of a piece, the argument would go, then it is in the public interest to make any failure of integrity known. This argument only applies to politicians, of course. It cannot really apply to celebrities, for whom integrity might be a bonus but is not generally a requirement.

In any case, those in the news in fact appeal to privacy as the reason why negative stories, and sometimes any stories at all, should not be told. Whether justified or not, those in the news regard positive coverage as welcome and negative coverage as an intrusion. In practice, to court publicity is to court all publicity and raise the risk of negative publicity, but the appeal to privacy is an appeal to a basic human right, as we have seen. It may also result, in the UK, in an appeal to the Press Complaints Commission (PCC). The PCC is an example of self-regulation – its board is substantially composed of members of the press. The PCC administers its Code, which contains a series of clauses restricting the freedom of the press to report on issues which might intrude on privacy, involving an individual's home life, victims of crime and children, for example. However, many of the restrictions are subject to a public interest exemption, and the 'public interest':

includes, but is not confined to:
1 *detecting or exposing crime or serious impropriety;*
2 *protecting public health and safety; and*
3 *preventing the public from being misled by an action or statement of an individual or organization.* (PCC, 2006)

This broad interpretation of the public interest means that almost anything can be reported, particularly since the PCC also declares that there is a public interest in freedom of expression itself.

Interestingly, the PCC does not appear to have consulted the public on the nature of their interests. The public interest therefore appears to be something anyone, including a news editor, can decide. So the public interest, much like the concept of the national interest discussed in Chapter 5, is very poorly defined. It confuses the idea of something which the public might *like* to know and something which the public *ought* to know because it affects them.

More generally, the public has a real interest in being kept informed of events beyond their immediate community. The media, in its various forms, has among its basic products the delivery of information to citizens, if not the delivery of informed citizens. How far can this be accomplished when trivia dominates the 'news'? As Jackie Ashley wrote on the eve of the second Iraq war:

> with a few notable exceptions, the newspapers have lost their critical faculties [...] consider the difference between a looming war, that could kill huge numbers of people and destabilize the world's most sensitive region, and the question of the PM's wife's beautician's boyfriend's involvement in buying a couple of flats in Bristol.
> (Ashley, 2002)

The media does, of course, also report non-trivial news. However, much of this serious news is, in effect, provided by the government and the corporate sector. Both government and the corporate sector are keen to try to control the way they are reported by the media. This means, as Chomsky pointed out, that a relatively small number of organizations are controlling, or at least attempting to control, the serious issues which do manage to reach the public domain.

Advertising

There is an argument that advertising informs consumers and potential consumers, enabling them to enjoy choice, which is often held up as the principal benefit of a capitalist economy. Of course this does assume that choice, or at least the quantity of it that consumers typically need to make, is indeed a benefit rather than a burden. At any rate, for those media companies wholly in the commercial sector, advertising receipts dominate their overall income. For most of those in television and radio it is overwhelmingly the main source of income. This means that advertising space has to be regarded as the principal product of most media companies. Yet, of course, advertising space can only exist if there is also demand from consumers for the space in between the advertisements. So while media organizations cannot afford to neglect their consumers, they are in an unusual position of having two key stakeholders directly interested in the delivery of their products.

Whichever side of this ambiguous stakeholder *Gestalt* is taken to be the main customer, advertisers have tremendous power over their media companies. This first of all imposes a transparency requirement on the advertisers themselves. However, it also demands that the media companies should be transparent as to how the power of advertisers affects them.

Advertisers can demand advance knowledge of magazine coverage in order to determine whether to advertise. But how far does this influence the content or nature of news stories actually published? How often are stories pulled because they might offend advertisers' interests? Advertisements can also offend one section of an audience at the same time as they appeal to others, illustrating that commercial decisions are the result of a negotiation between the interests of different stakeholder groups. A 2005 *Guardian* social audit (Guardian, 2005) discussed the paper's decision to stop accepting advertising from providers of sex services as these were greatly disliked by a section of their readers. The paper had the courage to forego the annual £350,000 these brought in. Yet although the majority of readers agreed with the decision, subsequently 9 per cent of readers thought it was unnecessary censorship.

Shareholders

If you own a newspaper company, you can make it say anything legal. The only practical constraint might be whether the public wanted to hear what it was you were saying. If not, you might lose business. Still, this is a powerful position to be in. On the other hand, the broadcast media can reach right into homes with no purchase decision necessary at the time of consumption. This is generally considered so powerful a position that, particularly where they are not directly owned by the state, there is usually some obligation on media organizations to provide 'balance'. This is explicitly the case in the UK through regulations such as the requirement on broadcasters to deliver fairness by ensuring that all interested parties have been offered an opportunity to contribute.

In the US, the regulations appear to work the other way round, prohibiting deliberate falsification but allowing the free market (although not necessarily any individual programme) to arrive at the truth. According to the Federal Communications Commission:

> As a public trustee, the broadcaster may not engage in intentional and deliberate falsification (distorting, slanting, rigging, staging) of the news [...] the drafters of the First Amendment to our Constitution knew that the way to preserve truth was not through government surveillance or censorship (for in that, government may also be wrong), but by giving all persons with views the freedoms to express them. From this 'market place of ideas', they believed, the truth would ultimately emerge – for every citizen would have the freedom to judge the truth of a thought or idea for himself. Therefore, the policy of the First Amendment to foster what the courts have termed 'robust, wide-open debate' certainly permits the analysis of any one spokesman to be one-sided. (FCC, 1997)

This approach appears to trade the fact that no one person can convey all points of view for permission for a company to confine itself to a single point of view.

Unfortunately, the market place of ideas is not especially healthy, as its ownership is becoming increasingly concentrated. In the US, five companies control some 75 per cent of the production of primetime television (SustainAbility and WWF, 2004) and worldwide six groups, including Bertelsmann and News Corporation are becoming increasingly dominant. This reduces the diversity of opinion. As Anthony Sampson points out, 'When

America and Britain prepared for war in Iraq in 2003 nearly all his [Rupert Murdoch's] 175 editors across the world echoed his support for the war.' (Sampson, 2004, p234) According to the Pew Research Centre (Pew, 2000), 35 per cent of 300 US broadcast journalists surveyed admitted that they commonly or sometimes avoided news stories which might hurt the financial interests of their broadcasting organization, and 29 per cent of all journalists avoided stories which might damage advertisers' interests.

Against all this some argue that the broadcast media, and the media as a whole, merely reflect the demands of the public – indeed, that they have to in order to survive. This ignores the fact that the media have an influence on the public and change what the public is interested in. Indeed, the press deliberately set out to do this through their editorial comment and campaigns. The active selection of stories is also crucial to shaping the news. Radio and television news programmes talk of 'setting the agenda' for the day's news through the first broadcasts in the morning, a tactic unavailable to the press.

EDITING THE TRUTH

The central task in reporting the news is perhaps reporting it transparently. But what does this mean in practice? And how do conflicts *between* media company stakeholders affect the process of editing the news?

One important part of the answer to what transparency means is accuracy, and the application of all the tests for truth outlined in Chapter 3. Yet what most editors and journalists seem most concerned with is the issue of the freedom of the press. It is relatively clear what the need for this is in countries with governments that exert direct control over the media. It would be helpful, therefore, to discover whether it is possible to measure it. Freedom of the press is obviously not sensibly measured by counting the number of times government claims are simply contradicted, since government claims can be correct.

In practice, the cry from journalism is usually for 'editorial independence'. Given the pressures to select the news exerted by the various stakeholders discussed above, this might seem a reasonable ambition. Unfortunately, it is not at all clear how it is possible for an editor (or a journalist) not to be dependent on any of a media organization's stakeholders. Editors are the focal point of stakeholder interest in the news and are, in reality, beholden to their owners and advertisers, just as are journalists to their editors, and all parties to the whims of the public. So it has to be admitted that what a paper publishes or a broadcasting organization broadcasts as the news is likely to be dependent on a range of stakeholders and to be influenced by them. Independence is impossible.

A different approach is to consider impartiality, in other words the extent to which one stakeholder is *preferred* above another. This is far more realistic in theory, but still, in practice, exceedingly difficult to measure.

Yet another approach is to encourage *diversity*. Where a diversity of views is reported, a diversity of interests will be represented. This might at first sight seem like a wasteful approach, but any redundancy is amply compensated for by a much greater likelihood of the achievement of impartiality.

To properly deliver diversity requires a radical approach, which means that the more aspects in which diversity is encouraged, the better. In other words, it is not sufficient to ensure that a diversity of, say, reporters gather the news, although that is necessary. It is also important to have a diversity of sources, of viewpoints, of audiences and of as many other aspects of news production as possible.

The reason that diversity is so important is not so much that it automatically provides balance, although it will tend to do so, but that it maximizes the chances of material evading the various Chomskyan filters. Diversity also has a special relationship to sustainability (Henriques, 2004). Just as particular biological species ensure the survival of their genes, despite natural selection, through natural fecundity, 'editorial diversity' ensures that the function of journalism as a whole can deliver despite the pressures of stakeholder selection.

Implementing diversity will mean that any given newspaper will contain inconsistent or contradictory accounts of the same issue. Yet consistency was one of the tests of truth, so this seems to suggest that diversity could actually reduce the truthfulness of media coverage. However, the tests for truth were designed to assess the validity of a single view or voice. Just as in the legal process in the courts, the overall trustworthiness of the outcome is strengthened by the contest between the defence and the prosecution, yet it remains a legitimate tactic for the defence or the prosecution to show that a given piece of testimony is not coherent.

The freedom of the press is also interpreted to mean the freedom to campaign and to comment on issues. Unlike the broadcast media, the press, both in the US and the UK take strong positions, run campaigns and ceaselessly comment on 'the news'. The US approach to separating news from the paper's views is to put them into different sections of the paper, typically with separate editors. However it is done, as Alan Rusbridger, editor of the *Guardian*, puts it:

> *The important thing is that the reader knows what they're getting. If something looks like a straight news story and reads like a straight news story, that's what it should be. It shouldn't be laced with opinion. There's plenty of room for opinion in the paper – including, on occasions, in the news pages. It just needs labelling or signalling. (Guardian, 2006, p9)*

In relation to the reporting of corporate issues, which is of course much wider than simply the 'business news', an important question is how far a particular media organization reflects the major impacts the corporate sector has on the rest of society and the environment. These issues are now increasingly appearing in the media (SustainAbility and UNEP, 2002). However, the very scale of these issues, together with their apparently slow onset, means that they are not inherently amenable to sensationalist news reporting. In the words of Fran Allen, 'these stories don't break, they ooze' (SustainAbility and UNEP, 2002, p34).

Nevertheless, because these issues are of such major global importance, new ways need to be found to alert the global public to their impact. Diversity is again a part of the answer: if the issues are not amenable to the usual pattern of story, new patterns must be found. No doubt this will include the use of new media such as the internet.

Telling tales

Journalism, as the 'first draft of history', has a powerful influence on all the others. In the modern world journalism is often the first public attempt to make sense of what is happening and of how the many power relationships in society, including the activities of politicians, are playing out. The public also expects that one of the deliverables of journalism is 'the truth', in other words a transparent view of what is happening. To tell the first true story of power relationships is a big responsibility.

How well do – or can – journalists do this? The view of the public seems to be 'not very well', according to a MORI poll (Worcester, 2003) in which only 18 per cent of the public said they trusted journalists to tell the truth, compared with the top score of 91 per cent for doctors (NB the British Medical Association commissioned the poll) and 53 per cent for the 'ordinary man/woman in the street'. For journalists, this is the same level of trust enjoyed by politicians, which is at least consistent with the fact that the prime source of information about politicians is journalists.

The public has a point. What we get are simple, short, negative stories about events, rather than in-depth coverage of complex issues, however much more significant they may be. There are some profound reasons, however, why the job is actually nearly impossible for reasons connected to, but going beyond, the filters imposed by the stakeholder structure of the industry described above. These are:

- the need to construct a story;
- the pressure to deliver to deadlines; and
- the role of the journalist in 'making news'.

'Stories' need to be constructed in order to make the news interesting enough to sell. As Andrew Marr has pointed out:

> *What is a news story?* [...] *We are perpetually intrigued by the extreme, the gruesome, the outlandish* [...] *so journalists learn to take less extraordinary things and fashion them into words that will make them seem like news instead* [...] *journalists reshape real life, cutting away details, simplifying events, 'improving' ordinary speech, sometimes inventing quotes, to create a narrative which will work.* [...] *Journalism is the industrialisation of gossip.* (Marr, 2005)

Only what is interesting makes the news, where 'interesting' is defined by the power to sell papers. And to make something interesting is an art which also involves putting something personal in the foreground.

Providing context is what moves journalism beyond telling stories. A two-page spread provides not only more facts, but a more secure foundation for beliefs than a six inch headline. But how far towards providing context and the full transcripts of interviews can journalists or newspapers realistically go?

> *In a presentation to his senior editors, Rusbridger [the editor of the Guardian at that time] introduced his vision for the paper's journalism, saying that it was not realistic to be completely objective, but that we should strive to be fair: 'There are such things as verifiable objective facts; they are the building blocks of any story. Beyond that, there are numerous complications of the sort they teach in the better sort of journalism school. We accept that, from the moment reporters write an intro, they are introducing an element of subjectivity into an article.* (Guardian, 2006)

So a story is something which connects the subjectivity of the writer or of the news subject with that of the reader. It appeals to the subjectivity of the audience. It is not an accident that facts are described as 'cold' and 'hard', the sort of things that on their own do not make a story. A list of 'verifiable objective facts', if it were read at all, would either make no sense, or more likely suggest many possible stories or interpretations. So subjectivity is not only needed to motivate someone to read a story, it is perhaps also necessary to some extent for them to make sense of it at all. And, ironically, one of the features which can make something interesting is very often a lack of transparency on the part of the people in the news.

Not only do stories have to be constructed, they have to be constructed very rapidly. In order to deliver interest to the pressure of fixed deadlines, the evidence is sometimes obtained in what might be considered unethical ways. These can include purchasing it from criminals or the police, or perhaps simply making it up. The saga of the faked pictures published by the UK's *Daily Mail* in May 2004, which purported to show a glittering stream of urine falling on Iraqi prisoners, is an example. Subsequent, non-faked stories of the same general nature show that even if the fabricated events are in some sense true to the general situation, in that they could have happened, they are not regarded as valid journalism.

More profoundly, in order to make a story, journalists do not just register facts and write copy, they actively participate in events. Politicians court journalists and journalists bait politicians. The performance of politicians in this dance is itself the material of many news stories. And of course at a personal level, journalists have an agenda in all this. No doubt this results from the story journalists tell themselves – that, like the *News of the World*, they are fearlessly seeking the truth.

What are the conclusions to draw from all these obstacles to transparency? In relation to the practice of journalism, it suggests there are two sorts of constraints on full transparency, these are:

1 structural constraints, which make subjectivity an essential component in any 'story' or account of reality; and
2 the fact that journalists are active participants in making news: sometimes deliberately directing the attention of the public, often caught up in events, but never merely passive vehicles for the truth to reveal itself.

This suggests that news reporting will always be subject to an irreducible quantum of uncertainty that will be a constraint on transparency. This uncertainty results from the relative power of the reporter and the reported, and also from the political momentum of the events in question. So the truth to be expected from a fast-moving, weighty event is low. Similarly, the more powerful the subjects of the news become, the less transparency may be delivered.

WHAT MIGHT MEDIA TRANSPARENCY LOOK LIKE?

The implications of this analysis of transparency for non-media companies is that considerable caution should be exercised in mimicking the reporting model of transparency. Companies which couch the accounts of their impacts as 'stories' or 'case studies' are courting a lack of transparency as well as readers. Yet the news model for corporate reports is a deliberate strategy. It is no accident, for example, that PR agencies are becoming increasingly involved in the production of 'CSR reports', while more systematic accounts are more likely to give a more rounded and reliable picture of affairs.

Among media organizations, the more 'serious' UK papers as well as ITV and the BBC have produced corporate responsibility reports, which address some of their routine organizational impacts. Some of the major US television channels also say something on their social impacts on their websites. Only the social reports of the *Guardian* newspaper, however, even begin to address the central questions of the editorial function and the purpose of a media organization in any depth. How should such organizations be transparent about those social impacts which they have and which can shape the societies in which they operate?

The most important such measures, and the ones hardest to implement, would be those which actually captured the social impact of the paper. Such broad social outcome measures are hard to develop and evaluate because outcomes result from a range of influences and not only from the activities of a given media organization. For example, a series of stories on environmental damage to a particular river may obviously contribute to action eventually being taken to address it. But other factors contributing to the eventual outcome might be the concern of local residents expressed directly to councillors. So how far can the newspaper running its stories claim credit?

Possibly more practical would be measures concerning the extent to which individuals were influenced by the media organization. This, of course, does not necessarily translate into social impact, but it would capture a key part of the difference which a media organization was making. The idea of a 'brainprint' suggested by SustainAbility and the WWF (SustainAbility and WWF, 2004) aims to capture this, but no way to measure it was described.

It is unlikely that there is any easily constructed measure which will yield the desired brainprint. It could, however, be measured in two ways. The first would be to analyse the extent to which a group of individuals' ideas had been changed by reading, listening or watching media output. However, this would be a difficult social science exercise, albeit a theoretically possible one. Moreover, from the point of view of practically capturing the impact of a given organization over time, this approach suffers from requiring continuing, detailed and no doubt expensive research.

Somewhat easier to implement would be a measure which captured the total time which the media organization occupies for its audience. This measure of brainprint loses the ability to trace the impact of a given idea, but gains the important feature that it is far more easily measurable. It is also possible to see how 'exposure time' relates to overall social impact and to sustainability (Henriques, 2006). Yet given the importance of diversity described above, the principal measure of the transparency of a media organization must be the extent to which, and respects in which, it embraces diversity.

10

The Certainty of Tax

In this world nothing can be said to be certain, except death and taxes. (Franklin, 1789)

Tax has never been a popular subject. For the many people whose income is taxed at source, tax seems both unfortunate and inescapable. However, for companies and rich individuals this is not the case. For them, tax can appear to be optional. Very few enjoy paying their taxes but, perhaps for this very reason, there is a sense of outrage when people or companies seem to be escaping them. The following news stories illustrate something of the nature of the problem.

> *Media tycoon Rupert Murdoch may run one of the most profitable businesses in the UK, but it appears that he has somehow managed to avoid running up a tax bill over the past 11 years. According to* The Economist, *Mr Murdoch has saved at least £350m in tax – enough to pay for seven new hospitals, 50 secondary schools or 300 primary schools. How he has done it remains a mystery – and News Corporation is certainly loath to give away any financial secrets. But it appears that Mr Murdoch's tax accountants have surpassed themselves – making full use of tax loopholes to protect profits in offshore havens.* (BBC, 2006)

> *The Rolling Stones have paid just 1.6 per cent tax on their earnings of £242 million over the past 20 years, it has emerged. Documents published in Holland show that Sir Mick Jagger, Charlie Watts and Keith Richards used offshore trusts and companies to ensure tax breaks. Of the fortune they have accumulated since 1986 for royalties, they have paid just £3.9 million in taxes.* (Hind, 2006)

But how much tax should be paid? Companies present a confusing picture in their disclosures: on the one hand they are keen to appear to be law abiding and dutiful 'citizens'; on the other, they don't want to appear to shareholders to be paying more than necessary. McAlpine, in its 2005 Corporate Responsibility Report, says:

*Group underlying profit before tax rose by 12 per cent to £37.4m
(2004: £33.4m) on revenues increased by 12 per cent to £1038.8m
(2004: £930.7m). [...] Our tax charge continues to benefit from
prudent planning and brought forward losses. Our effective underlying tax rate remained at 19 per cent during 2005 and we expect
that we will benefit from a similar rate this year.* (Alfred McAlpine,
2006)

Bearing in mind that corporation tax is levied at some 30 per cent, the message
appears to be that there is virtue in keeping tax paid down.

This raises the question as to why companies are so keen to reduce the
tax they pay. This may seem an absurd question, since everyone is bound to
want to reduce their costs. Yet companies are not ordinary people and, from
an accounting perspective, tax is not a cost to them. Tax is actually considered a distribution which should be viewed in a similar manner to that other
distribution companies make – shareholder dividends. Yet companies treat
tax as a cost and as a result they argue that in their role as custodian of shareholders' funds, they have a duty to minimize it. Of course, if it is accepted
that tax is a cost, then the benefit represented by avoiding it might itself be
taxable!

Apart from being unpopular, taxation is also a complex subject, involving
transfer pricing, tax havens and complex regulation. This chapter will attempt
to unravel what is going on with tax with a view to understanding:

- why there is outrage when people escape tax;
- how escaping tax on a large scale is possible; and
- what it is reasonable to disclose.

WHY TAX MATTERS

Tax has a clear moral dimension – and corporate performance in relation to tax
is therefore an issue for which transparency matters.

Taxes are funds collected by governments to pay for government expenditures. The precise things which a government should do and pay for is of course
one of the central and abiding questions of democratic politics. But that governments should collect taxes to pay for at least some things is only challenged by
the most conservative of libertarians.

Orthodox economic theory acknowledges that some things are 'public
goods', in other words 'commodities for which the cost of extending the service
to an additional person is zero and which it is impossible to exclude individuals
from enjoying' (Samuelson et al, 1995, p32). The classic example of a public
good is the public road. More generally, taxes are useful to finance positive
externalities – those beneficial things which you do not pay for by transaction,
but get anyway.

Typically taxes are used to pay for at least part of the basic infrastructure of
society, from physical communications, like roads, to basic research and educa-

tion, healthcare, waste disposal, policing and defence. This is important for developed economies; it is even more important for developing economies, as the extent and quality of infrastructure is one of the most critical factors in development.

In very general terms, taxes are collected in most places where money changes hands, whether the hands are individual or corporate. And corporations and individuals may seek to *escape* taxes through either legal or illegal means. If there is a systematic escape from tax, then others in that society will have to shoulder the burden of funding public goods, or else those goods may no longer be provided. There is therefore potential for those who escape tax, but still enjoy the various public goods which society provides, to become free riders on the rest of society.

As we will see, many corporations and wealthy individuals do in fact systematically escape tax. Some companies, especially smaller ones, pay more than the nominal rate of tax, but for the majority, actual payment rates vary from the nominal rate downwards to zero. The proportion of government revenue contributed by corporations in the US and the UK is now about 20 per cent. This represents a fall of about half since the Second World War, which means that ordinary individuals are being asked to pay more tax. And since people do not like to pay taxes, there is increasing pressure to reduce expenditure on public goods, which will tend to cause a deterioration in social and economic infrastructure. The argument that 'the market' (in other words private companies) will fill the gap may work for some of those things which governments fund, but for truly public goods it cannot be economic. This is a further reason why paying or escaping tax has a moral dimension.

WHAT THE LAW EXPECTS

Corporations pay many sorts of tax. These include not only corporation tax paid on declared profits, but also local taxes, employment taxes in respect of staff, customs duties and other fees. Companies also collect value added tax on behalf of government in many parts of the world; typically this will be recovered through sales, but if not, companies will have to pay this tax too. Although it costs companies effort to calculate and pay the various taxes due, for a local (in other words up to national scale) company, the situation seems relatively straightforward.

Of course it is, and always has been, illegal to *evade* tax. Tax evasion would arise if, for example, a false set of accounts were prepared which rendered a transaction apparently liable to less tax than would be indicated by a true set of accounts. However, in 1936 the Duke of Westminster, in the UK, wished to *avoid* paying surcharge tax by paying his staff in the form of covenants. In the courts this practice was challenged, but it was ruled by Lord Tomlin (Inland Revenue *v.* Duke of Westminster, 1936) that 'every man is entitled to arrange his affairs so that the tax attaching under the appropriate Acts is less than it could be.' This established the rule that there is no compulsion to pay as much tax as possible and that it is lawful to avoid some of it.

Ever since, there has been much 'arranging of affairs'. Over the years more and more arrangements were made to reduce tax liability, and tax laws have been gradually adjusted and added to in consequence, making the precise legal position difficult to state. In general terms, following the 'Ramsay Principle' (Ramsay *v.* Inland Revenue, 1982), the approach now is that it is not lawful to conduct a transaction wholly to avoid tax. On the other hand, if a series of transactions has a strong commercial motive as well as happening to reduce tax, that may be lawful.

It is permissible to plan to reduce tax for a transaction or series of transactions which you were going to do anyway for commercial reasons. It is therefore lawful to *avoid* tax, as long as that is not the only thing that you intend to do by a transaction or series of transactions. This is not straightforward to demonstrate, however, and so there is a grey area. As a result there is a very active tax industry of lawyers, accountants and professionals within companies – all working on ways to minimize tax legally. From time to time there is also talk of introducing a general anti-avoidance rule, as exists in Canada and some other jurisdictions, which would clarify the situation once and for all. But this has not happened, at least in the UK.

GLOBALIZING TAX

What companies can and should do becomes much more complicated when the international dimensions of tax are considered, and globalization means that this perspective is relevant to an ever-increasing number of companies. Two of the many features of globalization relevant to tax issues are the extending geographic reach of companies and the greater freedom of movement of capital between countries. Both of these factors have led to a growing mismatch between the established approach to global and state governance and economic governance. In practice, economies have globalized but political governance has not. Sol Piciotto writes that 'international regulatory avoidance entails exploiting disjunctures in the interaction of the regulatory systems of different states' (Piciotto, 1999).

The traditional approach to state governance is based on territory, with the residency approach of many laws applicable to tax being an example. International or world governance to date has largely been a poor relation of state power, being based on treaties made between states as the key actors and so reliant on their acceptance of these treaties. Certainly international agreements on tax have not progressed very far in ensuring the collection of tax revenues from companies with operations spanning a number of different state boundaries and its subsequent allocation in an equitable manner.

The freedom of movement of capital is a shorthand way of describing the huge quantities of money which can be moved across the world almost instantly in search of high returns or to avoid risks. The tax system (or perhaps, on a global scale, the lack of one) is a key enabler of such flows since it reduces the tax distributions companies pay in connection with major capital flows. These flows, over which countries appear to have no power, can have severe consequences on states of almost any size. The collapse of the Thai currency in the mid 1990s is one example: this caused an annual regional inflow of US$93 billion to become a net outflow of US$12 billion, with 13 million people losing their jobs. In general, the mobility of capital undermines the advantages which a free market system might be expected to bring. As John Gray puts it, 'both in theory and in practice the effect of global capital mobility is to nullify the Ricardian doctrine of comparative advantage' (Gray, 1998, p82).

Corporate strategies for dealing with the new features of a globalizing world are varied; strategies for 'tax planning' are, however, a crucial component. The various devices for dealing with tax are both a cause and a consequence of globalization – and it is not necessary to establish the precise history here. Nevertheless, the corporate interest in minimizing tax has given rise to many of the anomalies concerning tax described below, particularly including the possibility of escaping it altogether.

How do companies extend their power and influence into other countries? LargeCompany Inc from the US, for example, will have only limited power to act in the UK. The national laws of any given country provide protection mainly for 'residents' of that country. As a consequence, LargeCompany Inc will set up a subsidiary in the UK (LittleCompany Ltd) if it wishes to do business there. One of the meanings of subsidiary is that LittleCompany Ltd will usually be wholly owned by LargeCompany Inc; this means that LittleCompany Ltd is effectively an extension of LargeCompany Inc and does what it is told. Does LittleCompany Ltd pay tax? Of course it should, but how much is a vexed question that raises the question of transfer pricing – how much one company in a group should pay another company in the group (in other words owned by the same holding company). Bearing in mind that it is commonly thought that some 60 per cent of all world trade consists of such intra-company transactions, this is a crucial question.

There are some legitimate problems in determining how much tax one subsidiary should pay rather than another, as the following makes clear:

> Take the example of a French bicycle manufacturer that distributes its bikes through a subsidiary in the Netherlands. The bicycle costs €900 to make and it costs the Dutch company €100 to distribute it. The company sets a transfer price of €1000 and the Dutch unit retails the bike at €1100 in the Netherlands. Overall, the company has thus made €100 in profit, on which it expects to pay tax. [...] But when the Dutch company is audited by the Dutch tax administration they notice that the distributor itself is not showing any profit: the €1000 transfer price plus the Dutch unit's €100 distribution costs are exactly equal to the €1100 retail price. The Dutch tax administration wants the transfer price to be shown as €900 so that the Dutch unit shows the group's €100 profit that would be liable for tax. But this poses a problem for the French company, as it is already paying tax in France on the €100 profit per bicycle shown in its accounts. Since it is a group it is liable for tax in the countries where it operates and in dealing with two different tax

authorities it cannot just cancel one out against the other. Nor should it pay the tax twice. (Neighbour, 2002)

As well as sorting out such technical aspects, dealing with transfer pricing also has unfortunate consequences for the overall management attitude of a business. Philip Gillett, Group Tax Controller for ICI, was quoted in *The Economist* as follows:

> *Commercially, transfer pricing makes no sense. It forces us to spend a lot of time doing things that are pointless from a business point of view. We have to waste time trying to price unfinished goods being 'sold' from one plant to another. It is like asking Ford to value a camshaft half-way along the production line: a nonsense. Businesses want to organize as if there were a single global or regional product market. Instead, tax is determining how they organize themselves. It makes local managers think more territorially, to start looking after their own particular country issues. The tax system promotes parochial thinking.* (*The Economist*, 2000)

The OECD has recognized at least part of this problem, and in its Tax Convention (OECD, 2003) it has recommended how it should be tackled. Essentially, the Convention attempts to introduce the 'arm's length principle', under which transactions between subsidiaries are priced as if they were operated wholly commercially. This would have the important effect that the tax liability in a given country would be broadly in line with the value produced there. This seems entirely reasonable; however, exactly how it can be applied is a matter of continuing debate. Of course, it also only applies to transactions between subsidiaries located within the OECD. It also assumes that all parties are acting in good faith and are willing to cooperate with the various tax authorities in this spirit. This may not always be the case.

THE WORK-AROUND FOR TAX

The OECD Tax Convention, assuming it can be implemented properly, is also based on the assumption that a country will wish to maximize the tax it receives. While this may be true for OECD countries, and many others, the 'business model' of tax havens and other offshore financial centres is quite different. Although the UK is often accused of being a tax haven, because of the Egyptian Delta Land case (see Chapter 4) and its treatment of Eurobonds, the countries usually thought of as operating as tax havens are shown in Table 10.1.

Tax havens are usually small countries. They are supported by facilitating companies (and rich individuals) in escaping taxes imposed elsewhere. Their own tax rates are very low indeed. But because of the volume of their tax-related business, and the lack of an extensive economy or population, this business model is possible. They provide laws, regulations and other devices to

Table 10.1 *Offshore financial centres*

The Americas	Europe	Africa and the Middle East	Asia	Pacific
Anguilla	Cyprus	Bahrain	Hong Kong (China)	Cook Islands
Antigua and Barbuda	Gibraltar	Lebanon	Labuan (Malaysia)	Marshall Islands
Aruba	Guernsey	Liberia	Macau (China)	Nauru
Bahamas	Alderney	Mauritius	Philippines	Niue
Barbados	Sark	Madeira (Portugal)	Singapore	Samoa
Belize	Ireland	Sao Tome & Principe	Thailand	Vanuatu
Bermuda	Isle of Man	Seychelles		
British Virgin Islands	Jersey	Tunisia		
Cayman Islands	Liechtenstein	United Arab Emirates		
Costa Rica	Luxembourg			
Dominica	Malta			
Grenada	Monaco			
Montserrat	Northern Cyprus			
Netherlands Antilles	Switzerland			
Panama				
St Kitts & Nevis (St Kitts; Nevis)				
St Lucia				
St Vincent & the Grenadines				
Turks and Caicos				
Uruguay				

Source: USDoS (2000)

support the establishment of companies – and also trusts, foundations and other vehicles – which can be used to escape tax.

The system works as follows: a multinational sets up a subsidiary company in a tax haven to which it sells its goods; the subsidiary sells them on to a subsidiary in the country in which they will be sold. The transfer prices are adjusted so that no profit (or a loss) is made in the countries of manufacture or sale; all significant profit is made in the tax haven, on which taxes are negligible. It is also worth noting that the goods will never travel through the tax haven: they go directly from the country of manufacture to the country of sale. This process is illustrated in Table 10.2.

It might seem as if the series of transactions by which companies escape tax using tax havens are contrived entirely to avoid tax and thus should not be lawful under the Ramsay Principle. And that is entirely correct. However, the transactions concerned do not all take place within the jurisdiction of the UK. All transactions are lawful in the jurisdictions in which they take place. So the global reach of companies and its mismatch with the powers of countries enables tax to be escaped.

Table 10.2 *Operating with a tax haven*

Parent Co. Country A		Subsidiary Dummy Co. Tax Haven B		Subsidiary Sales Co. Country C	
Production Costs	$1000				
Selling Price	$1000 →	Buying Price	$1000		
		Selling Price	$2000 →	Buying Price	$2000
				Selling Price	$1500
Profits	$0	Profits	$1000	Profit (Loss)	(–$500)
Taxes	$0	Taxes	Negligible	Taxes (Offset/loss)	C/F

Source: Baker (2005, p137)

In addition to the tax advantages of offshore financial centres, the other major advantage of doing business there is privacy. This is provided in a number of ways:

- protection of the identity of depositors and shareholders;
- absent or very relaxed auditing and reporting requirements; and
- failure to cooperate with international law enforcement agencies.

Companies are not usually forthcoming about the nature of their tax arrangements. However, some light was thrown (*The Economist*, 1999) on the Murdoch tax strategy illustrated above. In the 12 years to 1999, the main British Murdoch holding company had made £1.4 billion profit but, through entirely legal arrangements, had paid no tax at all. Through the 1990s, the most profitable of the 101 subsidiaries was 'News Publishers', registered in Bermuda, which in the seven years to June 1996 made £1.6 billion profit, despite not having any employees and trading only with other News International companies. This suggests precisely the tax escape strategy set out above.

The sectors which make particular use of tax havens are the extractive, finance, aviation, shipping, communications, pharmaceutical, media, traded commodities and arms sectors (Christensen and Murphy, 2004). But it is not necessary to be a company to take advantage of tax havens, just to have access to gross income (in other words, income before tax). This can then be used in exactly the same process as that used by multinationals. This is the route which rich individuals use and gives rise to the stories reported at the beginning of this chapter. It is also behind the famous pronouncement by Leona Helmsley:

> *'We don't pay taxes', the 'hotel queen' of New York told one of her abused servants at the end of the eighties. 'Only little people pay taxes.' Helmsley's pride was followed by a fall which made a satisfying morality tale. She was true to Dickensian aesthetics: she looked vulgar and selfish and was vulgar and selfish. She claimed everything from her bras to the refurbishment of her $11 million mansion as business expenses. 'Naked greed' drove you, said the judge as he sent her down for four years.* (Cohen, 2002)

Tax departments in large companies, assisted by the accountancy firms, expend a lot of effort to make such arrangements work, often operating at the margins of lawfulness. From the company's perspective, these arrangements are a calculated risk, the corresponding reward being an ability not only to pay much less tax, but also to manage far more closely the declared profits from year to year. Of course, the management of tax, although it is material to shareholders, is not adding value in any real sense. So it is ironic that one of the key measures of corporate success, the P/E (price to earnings) ratio, makes use of earnings after tax. In other words, this measure of a stock's value depends significantly on the ability of a company to manage its tax, rather than on its ability to create value.

How aggressively are companies pursuing such tax strategies? Henderson Global Investors surveyed 335 of the FTSE350 companies. Of those, 162 responded in some way and 49 per cent of these said that they had no formal tax policy. One per cent admitted to being aggressive in their approach to risk, implying perhaps that they sought every opportunity to minimize tax, while 45 per cent said they were conservative in their approach. Some 22 per cent declined to respond to that question at all. An interesting response from one respondent was that:

> *Where there are grey areas in tax legislation and its application, we are prepared to be challenging when we judge this to be in the interest of our shareholders.* (Henderson, 2005)

However, in responses to questions on the likelihood of being challenged on their use of transfer pricing, tax havens or tax avoidance schemes generally, this was judged to be 'low' by at least 60 per cent of respondents.

THE SCALE AND CONSEQUENCES OF ESCAPING TAX

The scale of this activity is huge. Wealthy individuals focus on escaping taxes on investment income, rather than minimizing corporation tax. They seem to hold about a third of their assets, some $8.5 trillion, in offshore centres, which is probably a majority of the total assets worldwide held offshore (Baker, 2005; Christensen and Murphy, 2004).

For most companies, on the other hand, trade is the main route to escape tax. Although accurate figures are hard to find, it is commonly estimated that 60 per cent of world trade consists of intra-company transactions, requiring transfer pricing of some sort. Dominique Strauss-Kahn, the French Finance Minister in 1999, is reported to have estimated that at least half of world trade passes through tax havens. Yet overall, tax havens account for only 1.2 per cent of world population and 3 per cent of world GDP.

In addition to the immediate loss of tax to governments, an additional consequence of such tax arrangements is that they put in train a global competition between governments to try to lower tax rates as far as possible. This particularly affects developing countries. The economies of the developed world currently still have some advantages, such as developed legal systems, that are attractive to multinationals and enable them to some extent to resist the continual pressure for lowering taxes; this may not be the case for developing countries. As a result, the governments of developing countries are more likely to increase government debt in an effort to develop.

It is important to be clear that the 'competition' between states to reduce tax rates is not an economic competition which might improve markets in some way. Economic competition requires producers and consumers within a market context; the struggle for the favours of large companies is not of this nature. It follows that there is no reason to suspect that consumers, that is the citizens of the states engaging in this struggle, will benefit from it. Clearly large companies benefit from lower tax rates in that they can manage their affairs more easily. So it is not always clear what benefits governments hope to extract from lowering taxes or the other aspects of globalization which they have embraced.

Tax havens do not happen by accident. At the very least they require the tolerant support of major economies. In fact tax havens, while sometimes situated in 'small island economies' such as the Bahamas, are not just tolerated but almost always *established* by major economies like the UK. The UK has used a number of dependent territories, such as the Isle of Man and the Channel Islands, for this purpose. Tax havens can also be significant economies in their own right, Switzerland being an example. Moreover, tax havens are only part of a larger pattern including 'special economic zones' and the system of flags of convenience which is designed to provide considerable freedom for companies from regulation.

Furthermore, the effort and resources to operate through tax havens is a negligible expense for large multinational companies, whereas for small, local companies, again particularly in developing countries, it is much less feasible to make use of them. The market is therefore tilted in favour of large companies and away from smaller companies within developing countries.

It is estimated that the UK government fails to collect about £20 billion annually as a result of these arrangements (Davies, 2002). Oxfam has estimated that tax havens have contributed to losses to developing countries of at least US$50 billion annually:

> to put this figure in context, it is roughly equivalent to annual aid flows to developing countries. We stress that the estimate is a conservative one. It is derived from the effects of tax competition and the non-payment of tax on flight capital. It does not take into account outright tax evasion, corporate practices such as transfer pricing, or the use of havens to under-report profit. (Oxfam, 2000)

Finally, it is important to note that these same mechanisms of tax havens and offshore banking that are available quite legally to companies and wealthy individuals are also used by criminal and terrorist organizations to support their far from legal activities. A serious blow to international organized crime and terrorism would be dealt by removing tax havens. It may be conjectured that some of the resistance to the removal of tax havens is coming from the corporate community.

TRANSPARENCY OVER TAX

The ultimate goal must be to align the collection of tax with the jurisdictions in which value-producing activity takes place. Where trade passes through tax havens, the connection between the collection of tax and economic activity is broken and tax collected can fall to zero. But to remedy some aspects of the international tax regime will require international cooperation, and this, as can be seen from the slow progress of the OECD initiative, will take time. Nevertheless, a key part of the need here is for transparency, not secrecy, from the tax haven authorities over:

• the nature of their regulation and treaties; and
• the beneficial ownership of all entities (companies, trusts and foundations) registered in their jurisdiction.

However, transparency from multinational companies could be implemented more quickly than this, if they chose to do so. Clearly transparency alone will not alter the practice of using tax havens. There is no need for companies to change their behaviour simply on account of transparency – at least if their use of tax havens is entirely legal. What transparency over taxation would do is enable all parties to understand how the international financial system is being used by companies. This would support a consensus on how international tax regimes can be globally regulated.

How could such corporate transparency operate? Richard Murphy has pointed out (Murphy, 2004) that the 60 per cent of international trade which passes through tax havens is not reflected in corporate accounts because current accounting standards require consolidated accounts to be prepared. Of course, it is important to disclose an overall view of a company's financial affairs; but it is also important to disclose how such figures are derived. This will enable, for all stakeholders, a much fuller picture of the risk a company is running to be seen.

Such an approach also has advantages for financial stakeholders in particular. It would allow financial stakeholders to make a much more realistic assessment of the prospects which a company is facing. The experience of Enron and other companies shows that this can be very important. Other advantages include greater investor certainty and insight into company cashflows.

The information which needs to be reported is very largely already available to international companies, as it is already required to prepare consolidated accounts. Murphy (Murphy, 2004) suggests that the information which should be reported includes:

1   the name of the state in which it is located;
2   the names of the states in which each of its subsidiaries, branches or related companies are located;
3   in respect of each subsidiary, branch or related company it should disclose:
    • its name;
    • its principal trading activity; and
    • the means by which it is related and the proportion of the entity controlled by the holding company; and
4   the holding company should also be required to report in respect of itself and each subsidiary, branch or related company:
    • its turnover as reported in its own financial statements;
    • its turnover with third parties;
    • its turnover with related parties;
    • its purchases from related parties;
    • its labour costs and number of employees;
    • the value of natural resources included in turnover at sale price;
    • its profit before tax; and
    • its corporate taxes due in cash for the period as well as any deferred tax movement, identified separately.

In addition to these bare figures, a proper appreciation of a company's approach to tax would also require disclosure of the supporting policies and overall context in which the transactions take place. This should be supported by publishing company tax returns.

What about transparency over the tax affairs of individuals? Does the fact that a rich 'individual' is involved entitle them to a greater degree of privacy? The use of legal devices, such as trusts, foundations and companies, means that it is no longer merely individual privacy at stake, but that of legal fictions and devices. These devices should enjoy far less privacy than actual individuals. The use of legal devices by rich individuals should therefore be subject to the same scrutiny as any company. After all, the trusts, foundations and tax havens which rich individuals use are employed simply to avoid tax and to escape a moral and social obligation.

For the affairs of ordinary individuals, there is one country in which individuals have very little tax privacy. In Norway, for some time, the annual net taxable income, net taxable wealth and taxes paid by every citizen have been freely available. More recently this information is also being published on the internet. Other than a slightly more informed examination of the affairs of celebrities in the press, and possibly a slight pause in the national working day when the figures are made available each year, this policy has produced no ill effects.

11

The Crisis in Confidence

The right of privacy was designed to protect ordinary individuals from unwillingly having to expose their personal and family life to the arbitrary inspection of others. Yet, because of the legal fiction of personality granted to companies, it applies to corporate entities as well. The routine operation of many companies is regarded as their private business. This means that even where their activities have adverse impacts on others, there is no automatic right to know what they are doing.

Yet free markets require free information. When market participants do not have full information on which to base their decisions about price and quality, the market will be inefficient, as buyers and sellers will, in a real sense, not know what they are doing. Despite this, modern commercial activity is full of secrets and commercial confidentiality is generally regarded as a right. Perhaps as a result, for most of the last 20 years, less than 30 per cent of the public have trusted business leaders to tell the truth (Worcester, 2003). Ironically, the word 'confidentiality' means 'with trust'.

Of course, this does not seem to be at all the same thing as lying, or deliberately saying things which are not true. There are many manifestations of 'not telling the truth', some of which can mislead, without anyone making formally erroneous statements. Exaggerated advertising claims and misleading or distorted product claims can be of this nature. What is not said, the material kept confidential, the product impacts which are concealed or downplayed can also mislead. This chapter particularly concerns commercial confidentiality and the extent to which, and the reasons why, things are not said.

One striking example of the truth not being told is US chemical manufacturer Monsanto's approach to marketing bovine growth hormone. This is a naturally occurring hormone found in the pituitary glands of cows. Monsanto developed a way to manufacture it in the laboratory using recombinant genetic techniques. The hormone Monsanto produces is therefore called recombinant bovine growth hormone, somatotropin or rBGH and was sold as POSILAC®. The virtue of rBGH is that it can increase milk production in cows by about 10 per cent. Given that in the West it costs about $30 to produce 100kg of milk (Hemme et al, 2005) and that the world market is around 600 million tonnes (FAO, 2004), the size of the opportunity for Monsanto is clear.

There are, however, concerns about the safety of rBGH. Some are concerned about the impact on the cows, which are already very intensively milked. Others are concerned for the possible impact on humans and the fact that there are differences between rBGH-produced milk and traditionally-produced milk. Monsanto says that the only difference is a raised level of Insulin-like Growth Factor 1 (IGF-1). However, high levels of IGF-1 have been associated with breast and prostate cancer in humans. After much controversy and a reference by the EU to the WTO, rBGH is now permitted in the US but banned in Canada and in parts of the EU.

During its marketing campaign, Monsanto prosecuted the Oakhurst Dairy in Maine in the US. Oakhurst Dairy did not use rBGH and they wanted to advertise this fact on their products and used a label which assured its customers that their milk did not use it. Monsanto wanted to stop Oakhurst Dairy from informing the public about this. Monsanto's aim was to:

> *prohibit Oakhurst from showing the statement 'Our Farmers' Pledge: No Artificial Growth Hormones', or any similar statement, on the labels of its milk or milk products, or in any other commercial advertising or promotion.* (Monsanto, 2003)

Monsanto argued that since, in their view, rBGH-produced milk was indistinguishable from traditionally-produced milk, the public were being deceived by such a label. The case was eventually settled with Oakhurst Dairy agreeing to add that 'FDA states: No significant difference in milk from cows treated with artificial growth hormone' to their existing label.

What is very striking here is that Monsanto did not want consumers to know what they were drinking. There may or may not be health issues, but the transparency issue is not whether or not rBGH was a health or animal risk, but that its use in milk production might be kept secret from the ordinary consumer. Monsanto's argument rested solely on whether or not there was in fact a difference in milk produced with and without rBGH. Even if there were no difference and the variation in IGF-1 levels were ignored, the difference in the production process could have (and, at least for those concerned with animal welfare, did have) an effect on consumer decisions. If Monsanto's interest in the case really was a concern that consumers should not be deceived, they must have been worried that this 'deceit' would lead to lower sales, as other dairies followed Oakhurst's lead. From a moral perspective what worsens Monsanto's position further is that they were seeking not simply to remain silent themselves, but to silence a completely different party that was not using its product.

Another example concerns the approach of Tesco, the UK supermarket chain, in attempting to set up a store in Sheringham, Norfolk. Large supermarket stores are controversial because they tend to drive smaller, locally owned stores out of business. In Sheringham, the local town was against the opening of a Tesco store, even though more shopping facilities were needed (Barkham, 2006). This is quite a common tale, but what was unusual is how democratically elected councillors found themselves behaving:

Tesco first purchased a site on the edge of the town. After John Prescott's Office of the Deputy Prime Minister halted out of town developments, Sheringham's boundaries were changed. 'It suddenly happened that the district council extended the town centre and then the Tesco application appeared for that area,' said Mr Grimes.

A 1500 square foot town centre Tesco was proposed on the site of the fire station and community centre. The supermarket offer to build a new fire station and community centre and 11 bungalows to replace a block of flats was narrowly approved by the planning committee in 2004. When the supermarket made no move to take up the application (the council imposed more than 20 conditions to protect traders), councillors turned against the supermarket. Last September Tesco's plans were rejected. As Tesco signalled it would appeal, the council discovered a legal agreement in the office of a retiring official. Lawyers advised councillors the contract prevented them from objecting to Tesco's proposals. After voting 20–0 against the supermarket in September, the council voted 10–2, with seven abstentions, in favour of Tesco's original application. (Barkham, 2006)

The councillors were also advised by their lawyers that they could not talk about the contract with Tesco, as they were bound by confidentiality. This sudden change in the voting together with a refusal to talk about the matter at all left many people assuming that Tesco had somehow forced the hand of the councillors and bound them to silence. A Tesco spokesperson later said that the contract was covered by 'normal' commercial confidentiality and that the existence of the contract was not itself confidential. The contract has subsequently been publicized. But what is alarming here is that the freedom of the public to run their lives seems to be threatened by commercial confidentiality.

SECRECY, TRUST AND CONFIDENTIALITY

What is behind the public lack of trust in business? Perhaps the tales of Tesco and Monsanto are exceptions. Perhaps we can trust business in general. As we go about our everyday lives we do in fact trust that the cereal we eat for breakfast, including the milk we put on it, will not poison us. Most of us also believe that we are not wholly embroiled in a web of conspiracies and suffering some kind of loss or harm as a result. But we are still deeply distrustful of most companies. One important driver of distrust is lack of knowledge, or rather the reluctance of most companies to be transparent about their activities. But in the end trust is induced by trustworthy behaviour, as Kieron O'Hara has pointed out (O'Hara, 2004). The much documented low level of trust in companies can therefore only partially be arrested by disclosure and transparency. However, when lack of transparency is combined with instances in which companies fail to perform honourably, then distrust is inevitable.

The corporate withholding of information has two aspects: secrecy and silence. William de Maria has made a distinction between these two terms as follows:

> *secrecy is the deliberate withholding of public interest information (data, reports, surveys, etc). Silence, on the other hand, is the forced or voluntary withholding of public interest voice (speeches, verbal declarations, oral evidence, conversations, etc).* (De Maria, 2006)

De Maria's concern was with the concealment of illegitimate wrongdoing. However, the distinction is also useful in understanding all forms of lack of transparency, both legitimate and illegitimate. For this purpose it is possible to re-phrase the distinction in this way: secrecy involves a deliberate, articulated plan to conceal information in the future; silence is less formal and involves the absence of disclosure in all forms (not only through speech) particularly in relation to past events. Secrecy attempts to create the conditions for silence in the future.

Transparency, secrecy and silence all have an important relationship with trust. Overall, for legitimate and legal behaviour, transparency will increase trust. But if there are to be secrets, then a number of conditions affect how far they will impair trust. If one person shares a secret with another, then if they both keep the secret, a kind of trust will develop between them. On the other hand, if other people know that something is being withheld, they will be inclined to distrust those who are keeping the secret. The trust of outsiders is diminished more seriously if the presence of the secret comes as a surprise, ambushing a pre-existing condition of trust. So in general there are three factors connected to secrets which particularly affect trust:

1   the existence of a secret;
2   how the existence of the secret is revealed; and
3   whether the existence of the secret is itself secret.

What is the legitimate role of secrecy for companies? Legally, companies are allowed to protect from disclosure commercially confidential information which is not already in the public domain anywhere in the world and which is genuinely related to their interests – provided of course that there is no overwhelming public interest in its disclosure or some other law would be broken by keeping it secret.

In practice, commercial confidentiality can be vital to a company's survival. The bidding process for major commercial licences, such as those for the UK national lottery or for 3G telecommunications licences fall into this category. In the case of the lottery the various bidders are particularly concerned that their plans for a contested licence should not fall into the hands of their competitors. This is especially important since in this type of business, product marketing plans may be the key (or indeed only) point of differentiation between bids. On the other hand, confidentiality may also be held to be in the public interest. In the bidding for telecommunications licences, the bidding authority will be concerned that a breach of confidentiality does not thereby reduce the level of competition between the bidding companies, as this could reduce the revenue received, which the authority will generally have a duty to maximize.

Silence also has other uses. All those who take out car insurance are advised what to do in the case of an accident. One of the principal pieces of advice is not to admit any error, even if you in fact believe the accident was entirely your fault. This can seem scarcely moral, although two things should be borne in mind. First, the advice is not to lie, but to maintain silence on the matter. And second, what is perhaps most needed in such situations is to acknowledge the feelings of the other party. This might be done partly by apportioning blame and admitting fault, but this is not necessarily the case.

Of course, there are also less legitimate uses of secrecy and silence, some of which have been described throughout this book. There are also occasions on which it is not clear whether or how secrecy and silence are legitimate strategies. This can happen when companies make a minor mistake and the company remains silent. This may not be because any serious commercial interest is at stake, but more because those acting for the company will simply be embarrassed at the particular details of disclosure.

GETTING TO KNOW THE STAKEHOLDERS

Irrespective of legitimacy, the list of things which companies typically want to keep private is extensive. There is, in general, a presumption of confidentiality, rather than a presumption of transparency. The information kept private falls into two categories: that concerning the company's stakeholders and that concerning the company itself. This section will deal with information about stakeholders, the next with the company itself.

Before dealing with what can or should be known about specific stakeholders, it is important to note that companies are generally poor at simply describing who their stakeholders are. Nevertheless, almost all companies have staff. Personal data on employees can be particularly sensitive, yet this information is required by companies in order to operate effectively and it is held largely with the permission of the employees concerned. The employees, as well as the company, will typically wish to keep the information confidential – and indeed the information is protected by laws on data protection.

Information on some other stakeholder groups is also readily available in many countries. It is usually possible to find out who is on a given company's share register, for example. This is a fairly basic form of transparency: it is clearly in the public interest to know who controls any given company. However, this facility has also been used by junk mailers to try to sell dubious share schemes to shareholders. Share registers have also been used to threaten shareholders by animal rights activists. The public availability of share registers has, for these reasons, been called into question (Willman, 2006). If there is a threat of violence, it appears already to be lawful in the UK for directors to remove their name from the public records available at Company's House.

Information on other stakeholder groups is less easy to find. Information on customers and on suppliers can be very difficult to get hold of. Relationships with these two central stakeholders is often regarded as 'commercially confidential'. Although at some times companies will proudly list their customers, at other times they will resist all efforts at such discovery. The reason usually given is that such disclosure would help their competitors. It is indeed a realistic fear, particularly in a consumer business, that competitors would benefit from a list of potential customers.

Information on suppliers is often withheld for the same reason, although here there may be somewhat less commercial justification. The history of concerns about labour conditions in the supply chain illustrates this point. When campaigners first drew attention to the poor conditions for workers who made big consumer brand products for companies such as Nike, Gap and Adidas, the companies at first refused to reveal the names and locations of the manufacturers who made their products. After some years of campaigning, which included demands for greater transparency, however, this information is being released, at least by some companies, such as Nike (Nike, 2004).

COMPANY PROPERTY AND INTERNAL AFFAIRS

While the moral case for disclosure about impacts on stakeholders is at times strong, the release of information about the company itself can be a different matter. A certain amount of information is released as a result of the disclosures required by law, as described in Chapter 7. Beyond that, however, it can be hard to get information. And the law generally protects a company's privacy and recognizes the concept of commercially confidential information.

Nevertheless, the principle and practice of confidential information run counter to the idea of market transparency. In addition to its impact on trust in the company, it is likely that when information about either stakeholders or internal company matters is withheld, it will mean that the market cannot operate efficiently. If a farmer, for example, is not made fully aware of the adverse effects of a particular pesticide, they are more likely to purchase the product – and may have to pay for this later in ways not foreseen. This is a clear distortion of the market which can only lead to inefficiency and waste. Yet it is precisely information such as this which may be withheld.

Much of the case for commercial confidentiality rests on the idea of private property. All persons, including corporate ones, have a right to own property individually and collectively. There is an enormous body of law stretching back centuries supporting this. But what counts as property when you are a company?

Things which a company owns, and can make money from, are assets. Things which are owed to other parties are liabilities. Before describing the different kinds of assets and the implications for transparency, it is important to begin with liabilities, or rather with capital. For a balanced business, assets and capital are related like this:

Assets = Liabilities + Shareholder Capital

In financial terms the capital on a company's books represents what shareholders have lent the business. What other stakeholders, such as banks, may have lent the business is a kind of liability, but is also called capital. The key point here is that capital is never something which the company owns. Financial capital does not belong to the company. This is the basic reason why companies must account for it and be transparent as to what they have done with it.

When social and environmental impacts are considered, metaphors such as the 'triple bottom line' (Elkington, 1997) and 'natural capital' (Hawken et al, 1999), which describe how businesses make use of natural resources, are drawing by analogy on the accounting treatment of money. Similarly, the idea of 'social capital' implies that companies can depend on social resources in order to run their business.

There are two important implications of this. The first is that there is a problem with common language such as 'the company's financial capital' or 'the company's social capital'. There is a sense in which it is obviously true that the capital which a company makes use of is 'connected' to the company in a very important way. It is also true that one company may be the shareholder in another company and so own the capital of that other company. However, it is very misleading to suggest that the capital on a company's balance sheet belongs to that same company. Similarly, neither the natural capital nor the social capital which a company makes use of belongs to that company. As Alex Wipperfürth has put it (Wipperfürth, 2005), brands (which are often described as part of social capital) don't belong to the company, but to the market.

The second implication is that the fact that the natural and social capital which a company employs do not belong to that company is the fundamental reason why the company should account for their use. However, while the ownership of financial capital is carefully defined in law, the owners of natural and social capital are not clearly defined. It may even be questioned whether natural or social capital should be subject to private ownership. Nevertheless, the question over ownership does not diminish the moral obligation to account for the use of something which you do *not* own.

One crucial corporate resource which cannot be regarded as an asset is the people who work for an organization. Despite the common pronouncement that 'staff are our greatest asset' or 'our people are our greatest asset', people cannot be owned. They therefore cannot appear on a balance sheet. What such statements mean is that the company greatly depends on its staff, and merely uttering them is intended to recognize the fact. However, it is unusual to compliment someone by telling them they are in fact owned by someone else!

The things which a company does own directly are its assets. Should greater privacy be expected for a company's assets? Assets are often divided into tangible and intangible. Tangible assets are those you can touch. The disclosure needed for tangible assets include their economic, financial, environmental and social impacts. In practice, transparency over tangible assets may not be easy, or easily forthcoming, but the issues are perhaps by now fairly well defined and some have been described in earlier chapters.

Intangible assets present a different, more complex picture. An item called 'goodwill' has to be entered as an asset on a balance sheet when a company's market value (the share price multiplied by the number of shares in issue) is more than the value of its tangible assets. Goodwill will therefore, in general, cover the list of intangible assets. Intangible assets increasingly form the majority of a balance sheet and are therefore of large and growing importance to companies. Companies that produce tangible products will certainly have intangible assets, but these may be a minor part of their balance sheet. Companies with intangible products will tend to have a much larger proportion of intangibles among their assets. For Microsoft, this proportion has been over 96 per cent. Coca-Cola, which is often cited as the owner of the most valuable brand in the world, has intangible assets and goodwill worth about US$1.87 billion (Coca-Cola, 2006).

Goodwill may be left unanalysed, in which case it must be assumed to be made up of the attitudes and behaviour of its stakeholders. The company will enjoy these but have no direct control over them. Where it is possible to define and protect intangible assets, this is what a company will try to do. Intangible assets which can be defined and protected include:

- intellectual property, which itself includes brands, patents, copyrights, designs and trademarks; and
- contracts.

Intellectual property

Intellectual property is unusual in that, although there are obviously material things which are instances or expressions of the asset, such as books or pictures under copyright, what is claimed by ownership is something both more and less. It is less than (all) the physical copies of a particular book, most of which will belong to those who purchase them. But it is also more, in that what is owned includes an aspect (something like the set of words it contains) of all possible copies of the book. Most intellectual property protection is of this nature and is directed at the protection of an idea as embodied in some physical way (for example, a design or trademark). However, patent protection is unusual in that it seeks to protect the idea itself.

How transparent should a company be regarding its intellectual property? There are two sorts of intellectual property to which different strategies apply: those which require other people to purchase instances of them and those which are needed to make the product but are not sold themselves. The latter are often trade secrets, the recipe for Coca-Cola being one of the more famous examples. Another example could be a proprietary production process for the manufacture of some kind of machinery. Here the secrecy of the intellectual property is regarded as essential to maintain commercial success. The courts and many regulations (for example, freedom of information legislation, as discussed in Chapter 7) usually respect this sort of commercial confidentiality.

When the result of the trade secret is harmless, then the system can work well. But as the associations with the phrase 'patent medicine' show, if the secret involves harm to others, or the product is sold on the basis of exaggerated claims as to the effectiveness of the secret, then the public interest is threatened. Unfortunately, as Petra Moser has pointed out (Moser, 2006), inventors generally consider secrecy to be preferable to formal legal protection because it actually offers better protection. The story of margarine is a case in point:

> The French inventor Hippolyte Mège-Mouriez, who invented margarine in 1870, blithely showed his invention to two Dutch entrepreneurs. Mr Mège-Mouriez, having received a patent, felt confident that his idea was protected. The Dutch entrepreneurs took the Frenchman's ideas, improved on them (keeping their improvements secret) and established a thriving margarine business that in the 20th century merged into the multinational conglomerate Unilever. Mr Mège-Mouriez died a pauper. (Riordan, 2003)

The intention of the modern patent industry is to provide better protection than M Mège-Mouriez received. However, its economic justification is usually given by companies as fostering innovation, by allowing the inventors time to profit from their invention and so making the investment in the invention worthwhile. This is the common argument which pharmaceutical companies give for the importance of patent rights. However, it also makes possible monopoly pricing, which in the pharmaceutical industry can have very serious adverse consequences for the public.

Yet the way patents actually work is to provide protection for an idea in return for public access to it. This is a transparency which cannot be acted upon commercially, but may be useful to protect the public interest. From a company's commercial perspective, taking out patents will increase the risk to the company unless the patent can be enforced. It requires both a well-functioning legal system and significant financial resources to pursue any breaches of the patent to be confident of protection. As a result, there is perhaps more evidence that patents bend the course of innovation to areas in which patenting is effective than that they increase the overall rate of innovation (Moser, 2005).

In general, the appropriate transparency protocol connected with the ownership of physical assets appears relatively clear. Other people have no right to know about what I own or what I have invented, unless it affects them or could affect them. If I have a collection of coloured toothbrushes, then it is really nobody's business but my own. However, if I collect lumps of radioactive metal which I like to keep on the boundary with my neighbour, then that neighbour has a right to know about it (and no doubt have it removed). A right to transparency exists where people are affected by things I own.

Where the assets in question are non-physical, the case is less clear. Of course it is still true that transparency is called for if corporate ownership of intellectual property affects others. This would apply to the public or private ownership of personal genetic information, for example. Does it also apply to the information collected by RFID (radio frequency identification)? RFID can enable people's movements to be tracked through monitoring the clothes they wear. This is clearly less personal information than an individual's genetic code, but even if it is argued that the collection of such information for marketing purposes does not constitute its misuse and does not harm the individual, the collection of such data does seem to infringe personal privacy. The point here is that if the collection of such information *feels* intrusive, then it *is* intrusive. Therefore, such information should not be collected and, if it is, then the use made of it should be disclosed.

Under the UK Data Protection Act, a person has to give their consent to the use of personal data about them. Data on their movements would presumably count as personal. However, the act appears to permit the use of such data where individuals are not identified; it does not preclude the statistical use of personal data, provided that the individual is not identified. Yet it is unclear whether to use that data to try to sell something to them would constitute 'identification'.

Contracts

Two people, corporate or otherwise, can enter into a contract or legally binding agreement. The variety of contracts is huge: from employment contracts to contracts of sale, contracts to supply goods or services, and many others. A contract is an inherently private agreement, so should any sort of transparency be expected?

In general, there will be a case for transparency if there is a significant impact of the contract on either party or on third parties or (which is largely the same condition) the contract has been imposed by one party on the other. From a legal perspective, when a contract is the result of 'undue influence' of one party to it on the other, it can be declared void. Yet if the contract has what we might call 'undue impact' on third parties, then, unless it violates a specific law, it may be unjust, but not unlawful.

Contracts can also be used somewhat manipulatively as a vehicle for an organization to place information in the public domain without delivering transparency. This can happen when a consumer contract is couched in very technical terms that are hard for anyone who is not a lawyer to understand. Many contracts and advertisements also contain 'small print', which is written literally in very small fonts or spoken very rapidly on the radio. As Onora O'Neill has pointed out (O'Neill, 2006), the intention in these cases is not to communicate, but at best to legitimate a claim to having disclosed something and thus to transfer risk from the company to the counterparty. Other examples include safety warnings on medication or the risks involved in financial products. Such manipulative strategies are common with consumer contracts and products, and it has taken repeated regulation, coupled with pressure from the Plain English Campaign and other campaigning groups, to begin to improve this situation for financial products.

For business to business contracts, different strategies are usually adopted, as each party will have access to a lawyer. These contracts almost invariably pay detailed attention to IPR (intellectual property rights) and to confidentiality. The issue with IPR is usually a concern by the dominant party that any IPR which arises as a result of delivering the contract is retained by the dominant party. The concern with confidentiality is that the other party will not put anything in the public domain which is not already there. An interesting question is whether the disclosure of the existence of the contract itself is permitted. There is an increasing trend for legal contracts to specifically prohibit the very existence of the contract and its terms from being disclosed.

It must be admitted that it is quite likely that few people will, in practice, be particularly interested in the numbers and quantities of apples which a supermarket might agree to buy from its suppliers. The contents of most contracts are not interesting to the public. It can also be argued that the terms of some contracts contain material which, if disclosed, would give a competitive advantage to the parties' competitors. And if the substance of the contract is indeed specifications to deliver apples, perhaps secrecy would not matter. If there are wider implications, however, then the situation may be different. When supermarkets, through entirely private transactions, progressively take over retailing premises in cities, this can profoundly affect the economic prospects of many small local businesses and change the social composition of a town.

In the situation involving Tesco described at the beginning of this chapter, the contract was with a public authority, but it still included strong confidentiality provisions. The Tesco contract included the following clause:

> *the terms of this Agreement are confidential to the parties both before and after Completion and neither party may make or permit or suffer the making of any announcement or publication of the information concerning any of those terms nor any comment or statement relating to them without the prior written consent of the other as to the form and content of any such announcement, publication, comment or statement.* (North Norfolk Council, 2006)

Tesco apparently told the council this clause was standard and included in all its contracts.

PRIVATIZING THE STATE OF TRUST

The role of the public sector is changing. Activities that were once, in the second half of the twentieth century, deemed to be a natural part of the function of the state are now being carried out by the private sector. Whether in health, education, transport or security, large parts of the job of the delivery of services paid for by the state are being delivered by private companies. Sometimes services are delivered by semi-autonomous organizations established by the government, but often they are simply contracted out directly to private sector organizations (and sometimes to voluntary organizations). Another variation on this is the 'public–private finance initiative', which involves public funding of private companies for public projects.

All this is significant from a transparency perspective as activities which were once wholly within the public sector and subject to a public sector transparency regime are now at least partly within the private sector. When an activity is conducted by the public sector, it is subject to freedom of information provisions. However, there are usually specific exemptions within such legislation concerning commercial confidentiality which can easily be invoked to remove any obligation of transparency from both the private company and also from its state counterpart. In the UK even direct requests by Members of Parliament for the costs of government contracts, for example, are typically refused on the grounds of commercial confidentiality.

The following evidence submitted to the Department of Trade and Industry Select Committee on the issue of the Nuclear Decommissioning Authority (NDA) sums up the issues in this area. After noting the transparency goals of the NDA, the submission sets out a revealing analysis of the actual situation:

> The NDA 'will be publicly accountable for its performance and operate on an open and transparent basis. It will be judged not only on its operational performance and cost effectiveness but also on its ability to command public confidence'. The experience to date on the level and transparency of information provided by the NDA has been less than encouraging, particularly in relation to Sellafield's commercial operations. Documents so far produced by the NDA for public consultation purposes have been woefully 'short on detail' on the financial aspects of reprocessing and MOX operations. The paucity of information in these fields is such as to prevent robust, detailed and well-considered responses being submitted by consultees. The NDA's reticence in providing information not only smacks of the historic over-use by British Nuclear Fuels plc (BNFL) of commercial confidentiality, but also prevents any accurate measurement of the cost-effectiveness of the new Authority. To many observers, this perpetuation of confidentiality has aligned the NDA more with its commercial contractors than with the taxpayer whose money is shoring up these commercial operations, and has done little to boost public confidence. (Cumbrians Opposed to a Radioactive Environment, 2006)

This is a worldwide phenomenon, as suggested by the work of De Maria (De Maria, 2001), who has documented similar restrictions on disclosure by the Australian authorities.

The use of privacy to restrict transparency from companies is widespread. It can sometimes be justified, although the interests of corporate stakeholders demand that each case should be independently justified in the context of the impact which the matters kept secret actually have. The onus for disclosure needs to be on the company, as otherwise a Kafkaesque situation could result in which disclosure might be accepted if shown to be necessary, but where the information to do so may itself be withheld.

12

Corruption

The word 'transparency' is often used as a synonym for the absence of corruption. Transparency is also thought of as a solution or vaccine against corruption. This is appropriate as corruption involves the misuse of power. This chapter sets out the issues relating to bribery and corruption, and describes what practical transparency can look like and what it can deliver.

There are perhaps two things about corruption on which there is widespread agreement: that its scale is huge and that it is very difficult to quantify. Its consequences are vast and severe not only economically but, indirectly, also socially and environmentally. It is therefore an important issue for the corporate sector to be transparent about. Yet, because it is both largely illegal and also highly ingrained in many large economic sectors, it is also very difficult to report on. Finally, the nature of corruption raises difficult questions about the responsibility of corporations, as opposed to that of individuals, for corruption, and therefore also for the necessary transparency.

THE NATURE OF CORRUPTION

Corruption is often defined as the misuse of public office for private gain. It is important to note that there is a perfectly legitimate use of public office for private gain: the official salary or wages paid. In general, any other income derived from a public office is regarded as a misuse. According to the United States Department of Agriculture, for example, (mis-)using public office for private gain means that:

> You may not use or permit the use of your position or title to induce or coerce someone to grant a benefit to yourself or another (for example don't call a subordinate and tell him/her that he/she has an application from your cousin and that you are most interested in the results of your subordinate's review of the application). You may not use or permit the use of your position or title to sanction or endorse the activities of any other person (for example don't make a television advertisement in which you identify your position and

title as a nutritionist for the Department and promote sales of a particular brand of margarine). Even when teaching, speaking or writing, you may refer to your official title or position only in the three limited ways permitted. (USDA, 2004)

The type of corruption which is most widely reported is the corruption of politicians, rather than of civil servants. Because they are elected and directly placed by the public in a position of trust, it is regarded as particularly scandalous if they abuse that position. Should politicians exert their legitimate influence in order to make money for themselves, that would be corruption. The allegations in 2006 that senior figures in the UK Labour Party were 'selling honours' in return for funding the party is perhaps less directly an example of corruption, since the individuals doing the selling were not gaining directly, although they certainly benefited indirectly through the improved fortunes of their party. On the other hand, through the corruption of President Suharto, the Suharto family at the height of its power controlled over 16 per cent of Indonesia's stock market (Claessens et al, 1999).

Corruption should, however, be interpreted more broadly as the misuse of *any* office for private gain. In other words an office can be abused not only in the public sector but also in the private sector. A position within any private company, if used to provide private gains other than the official remuneration, is corrupted. This raises questions as to what the *mis*-use, as opposed to the sanctioned use, of office may be. But the underlying issue is perhaps what the 'official remuneration' actually is. The response that the official remuneration is whatever it is declared to be is not quite as vacuous as it may at first seem. The reason it is actually quite a helpful answer is that what makes a remuneration 'official' is that it is *transparently declared.* In the public sector in many countries the salaries of most senior officials is a matter of public determination and record. Transparency is a key factor in legitimizing the use of public funds, including their payment to individuals. In the public sphere, the main defence for the receipt of money connected with public office is its declaration in some public way, such as through a register of interests.

In private companies the law generally requires that senior officials, and particularly directors, declare their income within the annual accounts. Unfortunately the actual remuneration packages of company directors are often very complex, so there is, in practice, rather limited transparency over their compensation. It further complicates the picture that within most large companies there are a large number of individuals with significant power, or who at least often act in the name of the large company, whose remuneration is not declared. Obviously this does not in itself make them corrupt, but it does broaden the potential scope for corruption. At any rate it does seem that the misuse of office of some kind is necessary for corruption. It follows that it is not possible for two individuals, say a householder and a builder operating as a sole-trader, to conduct a corrupt transaction. Of course it is possible for such transactions to be over-priced, but that is a different matter.

It is unlikely that companies themselves will be the recipients of bribes on their own account, rather than as a vehicle to channel money to an individual.

This is because companies do not usually hold an office, acting on behalf of others in a position of trust which can be abused. Companies can, of course, engage in wrongful and criminal behaviour. This may include anti-competitive practices of many kinds and rent-seeking behaviour designed to extract money without any productive economic advantage. These activities will often be associated with the corruption of government officials, in order, for example, to ensure that a cartel is not investigated by the government. In addition, companies may be induced to accept a situation (perhaps a loss of a contract) which is to their disadvantage through the payment of money. This may or may not be legal.

On the other hand, companies may initiate, or be complicit with, the corruption of others. This is one of the most common ways in which large companies are involved in corruption, and often happens in practice through the use of 'agents'. Particularly where companies are working overseas, agents are employed to facilitate business. Facilitation can mean using local knowledge and contacts to ensure business gets done. Unfortunately, this kind of practice shades imperceptibly into the deliberate or knowing use of agents to bribe others to secure business, which appears to be quite common practice.

Corruption has been described above largely in terms of payments of money. It should, however, be pointed out that payment may be made in kind rather than by paying money. This is not only true at the smaller end of the scale of corruption, where it is common, but can also characterize very large scale corruption involving complex transactions 'swapping' one kind of good for another or mis-pricing goods, services or contracts.

THE SCALE OF CORRUPTION

If you are corrupt, you are not going to volunteer how much money you have gained through your corruption. It is therefore difficult systematically to measure the total scale of corruption in its 'native units'. As it is so difficult to measure corruption in terms of the quantities of money involved, people's *perceptions* of corruption are measured instead.

According to Transparency International, an NGO and a leading authority on corruption, the most corrupt industrial sectors are seen to be public works and construction followed by arms trading, with the oil sector a considerable way behind them (TI, 2002). The three least corrupt countries are seen to be Iceland, Finland and New Zealand, the most corrupt Turkmenistan, Bangladesh and Chad. If Iceland ranks as number 1, the US ranks at number 17 and China at number 78 on this index (TI, 2005).

Although it is difficult to quantify overall, it is sometimes possible to measure the incidence of corruption in monetary terms. In the UK National Health Service, for example, the Counter Fraud Service has:

> detected and stopped corruption totalling more than £170 million
> since 1999, but this is only part of total financial benefits to the
> NHS of £675 million, which also includes recovery of monies lost

to fraud and reductions in measured losses due to CFS interven-
tion. (TI, 2006, p47)

Of course the problem is widespread globally: the Columbia/HCA hospital chain, America's single largest healthcare provider, for example, had fines of about US$1.7 billion levied against it in the decade to 2002.

Corruption takes place on a small scale as well. According to reporter Anna Adams, a culture of corruption is endemic in the UK estate agency business, for example:

> *The manager of a Chard estate agency branch in Fulham, west*
> *London, showed us round a flat worth more than £190,000. Yet if*
> *our developer was happy to grease his palm to the tune of £10,000,*
> *he'd tell the owner to take the offer of £140,000.* (Adams, 2006)

Corruption both large and small is a global problem and can make life miserable for large numbers of people:

> *Small-scale corruption is having to pay off individuals to get*
> *something done. The one most frequently mentioned across the*
> *continent [Africa] is paying a bribe to get a phone installed.*
> *Lengthy waiting lists simply breed this kind of petty corruption.*
> *One ICT business entrepreneur told us: 'There were several times*
> *when people sought a bribe from us and we only had to bribe the*
> *telephone engineer to get a line from [the incumbent telecom]. You*
> *were made to feel that it was the same as 'tipping' the person – an*
> *appreciation for his good work – and it was described as a facilita-*
> *tion fee in the accounts.* (Southwood, 2004)

CORRUPTION AND THE LEGAL MIND

In the UK (UK Legislature, 1906), as in most countries, it is a criminal offence for individuals to receive a bribe or to offer one, although the narrower defini-tion of corruption, relating to misuse of a public office, is used. Corruption is outlawed even if the act has taken place outside the UK (UK Legislature, 2001). In addition to national law, there are a number of international conventions on bribery, including those from the UN (UN, 2003a), the Organisation of American States (OAS, 1996) and the OECD (OECD, 1997). The Council of Europe Civil Law Convention on Corruption is another example and is notable because it provides in its Article 9 for whistleblower protection for employees:

> *Each Party shall provide in its internal law for appropriate protec-*
> *tion against any unjustified sanction for employees who have*
> *reasonable grounds to suspect corruption and who report in good*
> *faith their suspicion to responsible persons or authorities.* (CoE,
> 1999)

Despite these laws and conventions, however, very few prosecutions of multinational companies for paying bribes overseas are undertaken and even fewer are successful. Although perceived as fairly likely to be host to companies committing such offences, the US has successfully prosecuted more companies for this type of offence than any other state. One reason for this may be that, unlike many countries, in the US companies have vicarious liability for the acts of their employees acting on their behalf. Nevertheless, the most significant prosecution for corporate bribery remains that by the government of Lesotho of some 19 international companies for bribing the chief executive of the Lesotho Highlands Water Project.

Why is successful prosecution of bribery so rare? Making bribes is illegal in every jurisdiction, but what is required to make a successful prosecution varies (Unicorn, 2005). In some countries, bribery by companies is a criminal offence, in others it is an administrative offence. Germany, Greece, Italy and Sweden have regimes under which bribery can be established as a result of 'administrative liability'. In all other countries corporate bribery is a criminal offence.

The significance of bribery being a criminal offence is that it requires not only a specific behaviour (*actus reus*) but also a mental intent (*mens rea*). But as we have seen in earlier chapters, it is not easy to establish the mind of a company. The prevailing view of this issue by the courts is captured in the 'identification doctrine'. This holds that the conduct and state of mind of an individual may be regarded as the conduct and state of mind of the company itself. In practice, this means showing the same individual to be a 'controlling or directing mind' of the company. The individual concerned has therefore to be someone of sufficient seniority such as a director, company secretary or other formal officer of the company. One interesting exception to this type of criminal liability for companies is Australia, where the prevailing corporate culture alone is regarded as potentially providing sufficient evidence of liability.

This is one reason why when crimes of bribery are prosecuted, it is the individuals involved who are charged, rather than the company for whom those individuals worked – and it has even happened that the entire board of a company, but not the company itself, have been individually charged with an offence which the company was alleged to have committed.

THE ECONOMIC IMPACT OF CORRUPTION

For business, for government and for society, a market without corruption produces better outcomes. This is one area in which transparency is not only clearly in the public interest, but also in the long-term interest of companies themselves. Where corruption is endemic, such as in many resource rich countries, its economic impact can be devastating.

It is often argued that resource rich countries do not realize their economic potential because they suffer from the 'resource curse' (Ross, 2003) under which an economy is skewed towards its resource sector. In addition to such macro-economic effects, which it is the responsibility of the national government to address, abundant natural resources can also lead to adverse impacts on politics (Ross, 1999) and on the business climate. A significant part of the adverse effect on the business climate is played by corruption. Conversely, improving transparency is in the interests of all businesses; as Horst Köhler, Managing Director of the International Monetary Fund (IMF) put it, 'experience, as well as recent research at the IMF, shows that transparency is correlated with better investment and growth performance' (Köhler, 2003).

It may be obvious that transparency alone cannot create a perfect business climate; however, it should be seen as being in the long-term interests of businesses of all scales, from small local enterprises to larger companies and international corporations. The Extractive Industries Transparency Initiative (EITI) was formed to focus on transparency in relation to transactions between private companies and government over natural resource payments. For resource rich countries this is obviously the most pressing area on which to work; however, transparency is also relevant to a much wider range of transactions. It may be hoped that, through the leadership of senior figures in national economies, the implementation of the EITI will catalyse transparency at all levels within resource rich countries.

Terms of business

What is 'the business climate'? The term has no universally agreed definition and is taken to cover a wide spectrum of factors which positively or negatively affect the ability of companies to do business. It will be taken here to include the 'investment climate' or attractiveness of economies to investment. A positive business climate has three main aspects:

1 **Macro-economic conditions** include a greater propensity for foreign direct investment (FDI), more efficient markets, a lower cost of capital, higher growth and greater economic confidence.
2 **Infrastructure** includes both the human infrastructure, in terms of a better educated and healthier workforce, the institutional infrastructure, such as the effectiveness of the legal system, and the physical infrastructure, including more readily available utilities and communications.
3 **Operational conditions** include lower crime, political and economic stability, lower taxes and fewer costs of doing business.

Transparency itself is a key component of the business climate. A World Bank survey (World Bank, 2004) of 26,000 firms in 53 countries found that corruption was the issue most often ranked as the most severe obstacle to business; in 10 per cent of the countries it was the single most important issue. Overall, corruption distorts markets and depresses competition and so reduces competitiveness. There is a broad correlation between areas of high corruption and of low competitiveness

Combating corruption

While the paradigm of corruption is the abuse of public office for private gain, corruption often runs throughout an economy. Bribes may be requested by staff of private companies in their dealings with the public or with other companies. The depressive effect of corruption on the business climate can therefore extend throughout an economy. Conversely, the benefits of transparency may also be expected to run throughout an economy and not be confined to reducing the economically distorting effects of rent-seeking by public officials, significant though these may be.

Yet for an individual faced with the possibility of losing a contract, or of losing out to unscrupulous competition, the temptation to engage in corruption can be strong. Other than the immediate gain of a contract, one of the perceived advantages, especially in dealings with government, is often that of increased influence. However, the evidence (Faccio, 2003) shows that the more widespread the direct personal connections between owners of firms and politicians, the poorer the quality of a country's investment climate is likely to be.

Over the longer term, the consequences of corruption are likely to be fewer, not more, opportunities for business. To the individual firm it may nevertheless still seem that the advantages of securing a contract in the short term outweigh the apparently more abstract advantages of a better business climate in the future. However, there are more direct consequences for the company which seeks to secure influence in this way: a loss of competitiveness. The work of Desai (Desai and Mitra, 2004) shows that the consequences for the firms gaining influence in this way are that they are likely to become less innovative. Conversely, the shorter-term rewards for avoiding corruption will be enhanced reputation – for both the companies involved and government officials.

Worldwide, the pressure for transparency is growing (Florini, 1999). The policies of the World Bank, the International Monetary Fund and the aid policies of donor nations are all increasingly emphasizing the importance of transparency. This means that the transparency of the behaviour not only of governments but also of businesses will come under increasing scrutiny.

Macro-economic benefits of transparency

Transparency is a positive influence on the macro-economic components of the business climate. The positive economic experience of a number of countries is testament to this. Daisy Kohan has written that:

> *Chile's experience since 1990 suggests that its efforts to ensure a transparent business environment, combined with the country's strategy of international integration, have been key in attracting FDI, and that this has paid handsome dividends in terms of economic growth and advances in quality of life.* (Kohan, 2003)

Similarly, a study of Botswana's impressive economic performance comes to the following general conclusion:

> *if the country has good governance, particularly in terms of voice and accountability, government effectiveness, the quality of regulation, and anticorruption policies, resource wealth is conducive to economic development. Because this result is statistically robust, it can be concluded that resource abundance does not guarantee faster growth, but with proper government resource management, growth can be generated from resource richness.* (Iimi, 2006)

Investment is one of the key drivers of growth and so a crucial element of the business climate. As Jaques Loup has pointed out (Loup, 2000), aid, one of the traditional sources of development, has declined recently, whereas FDI has grown very significantly and is generally larger than aid flows. However, these flows are sensitive to corruption. One study concluded that 'high levels of non-transparency can greatly retard the amount of foreign investment that a country might otherwise expect' (Drabek and Payne, 2002). The same study estimated the size of the effect as a very considerable 40 per cent increase in FDI from a one point increase in transparency ranking.

In practice, investment can be realized in many ways, of which some are of more benefit to the recipient country than others. The World Investment Report of 2001 emphasized the importance of 'linkages' in relation to the effect of investment. In essence, when investment expenditure is spent locally, more of the benefit is retained:

> *A dense network of linkages can promote production efficiency, productivity growth, technological and managerial capabilities, and market diversification for the firms involved.* (UNCTAD, 2001)

In this context it should be noted that for the oil industry perhaps 80 per cent of initial investment involves construction activities, but that the majority of that is actually spent with multinationals, rather than locally. Greater transparency may be expected to facilitate the proportion that will be spent locally.

The presence of corruption will not only reduce growth, adversely affecting the business climate, but also distort the economy and particularly disadvantage smaller local companies. A study of the effect of discrimination over government contracts (Evenett and Hoekman, 2004) has pointed out that one of the effects of corruption is to shift demand to sectors prone to corruption, which will tend to reduce the economic diversity needed to avoid the resource curse. However, it also points out that corruption tends to exclude smaller companies from contracts, as they will rarely have the time and resources necessary to devote to oiling personal relationships with public officials.

Once corruption has taken place, the funds used to pay large bribes are also rarely spent locally. More often they are remitted abroad, so there is little local benefit. It has been estimated that the size of outflows may amount to about

10 per cent of aid inflows (Baker, 2005). Other than directly removing funds which could drive growth, this process also increases the unequal distribution of wealth both between and within countries. Such international inequality is a brake on growth: 'widening global disparities in turn may be harmful to growth itself' according to a recent World Economic and Social Survey (UN, 2006). Inequality within countries also has unfortunate consequences, as Nancy Birdsall has argued:

> *an unequal equilibrium trap is especially worrying for developing countries, to the extent that it is associated with destructive inequality – with inequality of opportunity that blocks the productive potential of the poor, undermining aggregate growth and perpetuating poverty.* (Birdsall, 2001)

Infrastructure

One way to understand the process of development is as the positive effect of economic growth on a country's institutional infrastructure. In this respect the importance of transparency in stimulating growth and supporting its appropriate application is clear. For the business climate, it is also important to understand the beneficial effect which robust institutions and infrastructure can exert on the economy. There is evidence that transparency is positively associated with a better business climate through this route.

One area in which this has been demonstrated is the efficiency of the capital markets. Rachel Glennerster and Yongseok Shin have shown (Glennerster and Shin, 2003) that transparency reduces market spreads on sovereign debt instruments. They report that 'the effect of increased transparency is economically large' having found that the average country experienced declines in spreads of between 4 and 17 per cent on the publication of reports on key economic and financial data.

Transparency can also lead to institutions which are more robust under difficult economic conditions. Under economic liberalization it has been shown (Mehrez and Kaufman, 2000) that there is pressure on the banking sector to lend to organizations about which it has little knowledge. However, where corruption is lower and transparency (taken to be the availability of information about likely project outcomes) is higher, the likelihood of a banking crisis is reduced.

On the basis of an empirical analysis of the Nigerian experience, Xavier Sala-i-Martin and Arvind Subramanian argue that the resource curse is realized in part through impairment of institutional quality by corruption. They conclude that:

> *in aggregate, some natural resources [minerals and oil] appear to have a strong, robust and negative effect on growth by impairing institutional quality.* (Sala-i-Martin and Subramanian, 2003)

However, they also found that when the influence of institutional quality on their results was taken into account, there was 'either very little effect of natural resources on growth or even a positive effect'. The implication is that transparency is a key determinant of institutional quality and has a major role to play in lifting the resource curse.

Business activity relies on the orderly and trustworthy performance of a variety of institutions. When the judiciary cannot be relied on (Begovic et al, 2004), when bank guarantees are worthless and when credit cannot be advanced, then business will tend to rely on advance payment. Such a strategy, which may be necessary if the business is not to go bankrupt, clearly limits the ability of the business to expand. The transparent performance of the basic institutions of an economy is necessary if the economy is to thrive.

The business climate also includes 'human infrastructure'. Transparency International has recently written (TI, 2006) that in both developed as well as developing countries perhaps 5 per cent of health budget revenues are lost to corruption before leaving central government departments. This will significantly affect health outcomes and, from a business perspective, lead to a less healthy workforce. This issue is of sufficient importance to some companies, including Ford, that they have implemented HIV programmes for their staff, including the provision of advice, counselling and access to treatment.

Operational conditions

The operational conditions under which businesses work have an immediate, practical effect on profits. A multitude of different factors comprise the operational conditions for any given business, although corruption may be regarded as the leading problem. The results of a survey of 100 businesses in Mozambique (Lanwehr, 2005) may be regarded as typical. The survey found that weaknesses in the overall business environment prove a more significant deterrent for international companies than for local companies; for national enterprises, corruption and crime are regarded as the most serious obstacles, with crime being far more of a problem than it is for international companies.

For both national and international companies, lack of stability or unpredictability characterize many of the issues which can undermine business confidence. The predictability of national policies, the incidence of taxes and the reliability of the judiciary are all dependent on transparency and the absence of corruption. In the extreme case, a lack of stability can become conflict, and the adverse effects of war on economic development are, of course, profound.

On top of the challenge of uncertainty, the direct costs of operational obstacles can also be high. According to the World Bank:

> [the] costs associated with weak contract enforcement, inadequate
> infrastructure, crime, corruption, and regulation can amount to
> over 25 per cent of sales – or more than three times what firms
> typically pay in taxes. (World Bank, 2004)

An issue of particular importance to smaller businesses is the appropriateness and simplicity of regulation. Here the differences between countries are profound:

> it takes 153 days to start a business in Maputo, but 2 days in Toronto. It costs $2042 or 126 per cent of the debt value to enforce a contract in Jakarta, but $1300 or 5.4 per cent of the debt value to do so in Seoul. It takes 21 procedures to register commercial property in Abuja, but 3 procedures in Helsinki. (World Bank, 2005)

It is important to realize that corruption is not just another component of difficult operating conditions, but a driving force. This is because the complexity of regulation provides increased opportunity for rent-seeking (Krueger, 1974). Once corruption is embedded, its impact on the business climate can also become important. When government revenues are diverted from their proper application, then taxes have to be higher than they might otherwise be. Similarly, the disposal of the proceeds of corruption can typically both involve and support further criminal activity, thus compounding the adverse economic consequences.

APPLYING TRANSPARENCY TO CORRUPTION

Companies do not instruct their staff to 'go forth and corrupt'. Yet they can be adept at ignoring corruption and are thus complicit in the abuse of the power of those who are corrupted. So should companies themselves be transparent about corruption, or should that somehow be left to the individuals concerned? As Professor James Gobert has pointed out (Unicorn, 2005), the individuals, in a sense, are not the problem. Companies create the context, provide the money, put pressure on individuals to deliver and fail to supervise or turn a blind eye to what the individual may actually do as a result. If this is the role of companies, beyond having a code of conduct, companies should also report on their performance in combating bribery. As we have seen, any extra expense resulting from additional disclosure will be amply justified by the improved economic climate that will result.

How then can a company be transparent on corruption? After all, bribery is illegal, so should companies open themselves to prosecution? And projects or transactions relying on corruption may be particularly profitable – should a company jeopardize its core business?

The current practice of most companies is to tread very lightly in reporting performance on this issue. Amec, a large construction company, for example, states in its 'guiding principles' that:

> We aim to be reliable, trustworthy and fair in all we do. We meet or exceed applicable legal standards, honour our contractual commitments and avoid conflicts of interest. We keep company data accurate, confidential and secure and avoid corrupt behaviour of any kind. We communicate in an open and transparent way, internally and externally. (Amec, 2005b, p5)

It also reports that there were 24 occasions on which employees or third parties brought alleged breaches of the guiding principles to management attention and suggests that this resulted in 2 cases in which 'action was taken' against individuals (Amec, 2005a). That is all from a major company operating in the most corrupt sector.

BP (BP, 2006b) and Shell (Shell, 2006b) provide very little more, although they do have much more developed, and publicly available, codes of conduct. However, their reporting against their codes in general, and on bribery and corruption in particular, is limited. Shell discloses, for example, that:

> we track the number of proven incidents of bribery, facilitation payments and fraud gathered by our internal incident reporting system and reported to the Audit Committee of the Board of Royal Dutch Shell plc. In 2005, 107 violations were reported. As a result, we ended our relationship with 175 staff and contractors. (Shell, 2006b, p34)

Shell also gives similar figures for its Nigerian operations.

Is this kind of reporting enough? Given the scale of the problem, it would seem that corruption needs to be reported far more systematically than this. First of all, whatever is reported should be reported uniformly and comparably across an organization in all its areas of operation. Particular care should be taken by companies operating in countries especially prone to corruption and by those in the arms and construction sectors, including those involved in major construction projects, which would include the oil sector, for example.

Second, it is important to know exactly what has happened. Dismissals and terminations of contract are good proxies for the existence of corruption. A further crucial indicator would be the number and nature of legal prosecutions, including those outstanding and the nature of any settled. In addition to such lagging indicators, it would also be useful to have some leading indicators. One such indicator would be the use of agents. It would be helpful to know where agents were employed and on what scale.

Third, it is helpful to understand how the issue is being managed. Policies against corruption are, of course, part of this. However, if stakeholders are to have confidence not only that a position has been taken but also that the issue is being actively managed, then there should also be disclosure of the procedures which have been put in place and how these are being implemented. Again, the procedures for managing agents should be disclosed.

Finally, reporting on whistleblowing is also vital. It is reasonably common for an organization to disclose that whistleblowing procedures are in place – but, at least in Europe, this is little more than what is required by law. Reporting should also cover how often whistleblowing procedures have been used and why. In this some care needs to be taken, not only to protect companies against malicious use of such procedures by employees, but also to protect *bona fide* whistleblowers. It is not justifiable to breach their privacy or security for the convenience of other stakeholders. Yet within these constraints it is entirely possible to disclose systematically how whistleblowing policies are being used.

13

Lobbying and Complicity

In recent years, in addition to their growing impact on their direct stakeholders, companies have been actively extending their spheres of influence. Lobbying usually refers to the practice of trying to influence one or more of the various branches of government. Much lobbying practice centres on attempts to influence the legislature and the framing of laws, but effort is also expended on the executive and the judiciary.

Lobbying and complicity are two sides of the same issue: benefiting from others' decisions. Whereas lobbying is active and involves influencing the decisions of others, complicity is passive and involves taking advantage of them. Both lobbying and complicity raise complex moral arguments. Neither can be said always to be 'bad' or always 'good'. This chapter deals first with lobbying and then with complicity.

LOBBYING IN PRACTICE

The classic function of lobbying is to influence specific legislation or regulation. In this respect effort is expended by companies over every stage of the legislative process, as Table 13.1 sets out.

In addition to all these activities, lobbying may continue with efforts to influence the way the judiciary will interpret legislation when (or before) it is finally in force. One way in which this may happen, quite legally, is for companies to sponsor meetings at which judges and other lawyers will be invited to

Table 13.1 *The goals of lobbying*

Stage of Influence	Main Goals
Policy climate	Prevent adverse issues surfacing
	Affect climate of opinion in favour of company
Policy formulation	Shape government policies
Legislation	Influence drafting of legislation
Implementation	Influence the manner of enforcement and timetable for implementation

discuss the legislation. These are often described in borrowed academic language as 'seminars'.

The practical techniques employed to influence the legislative process directly include:

- funding of political parties;
- meetings with politicians;
- meetings with civil servants;
- providing reasoned responses to official consultations;
- serving on consultation committees; and
- drafting legislation.

Donations to political parties can also be considered a part of lobbying, although there is much less control over the specific policies which may be supported as a result, as most parties campaign on the basis of a spectrum of policies, not all of which are relevant to business.

However, such 'traditional' lobbying must be considered within a wider context which aims to influence opinion, including legislation, indirectly. The legislative authorities, although crucial, are but one among the wide variety of stakeholders important to a company. From this wider perspective there are a number of other key stakeholders whose opinions count; and a company's attempts to influence these other stakeholders may be included under a broad interpretation of the term 'lobbying'. Perhaps the most significant of these attempts, for public-facing companies, are those directed at customers; for other kinds of companies, the media, the professions, NGOs and public opinion may be important. From the corporate perspective, the company functions, which at times may be involved in lobbying, in this wider sense may include marketing and sales, PR, corporate affairs, government affairs, regulatory affairs and research.

The main techniques used to influence the decisions of customers are simply the usual activities of advertising and promotion, with brand management as their fullest expression. Interestingly, although advertising probably has the furthest reach of any of the 'lobbying' techniques, it can seem the most legitimate. The reasons for this will emerge when the relationship of lobbying to transparency is considered later in the chapter.

To influence NGOs and public opinion generally, one of the main tools companies use is to publish reports. One of these is, of course, the 'CSR report' or 'sustainability report'. It is ironic to recall that these reports were originally conceived as mechanisms for companies to demonstrate that they were being influenced by their stakeholders, rather than vehicles for the opposite. However, to influence NGOs and professionals, the most effective route is usually a research report. One of the problems of CSR reports is that the NGO audience wants to see a 'research report' on the company, whereas the company wants to convey a public relations message. It can be difficult to reconcile these two aims. It is also sobering to realize that in this respect the ordinary company annual report, directed at shareholders, is conceived in much the same way, in other words as a way to *influence* shareholders.

THE ETHICS OF LOBBYING

The engineering of consent is the very essence of the democratic process, the freedom to persuade and suggest. (Bernays, 1947, p114)

Any consideration of the ethics of lobbying – at least in a democracy – must start from the justification on which it draws. It is usually claimed that this is provided by one or other of the fundamental texts granting rights to affect government. This includes Article 25 of the Covenant on Civil and Political Rights and Article 21 of the UNDHR, which refers to the right of citizens to 'take part in the government of their country, directly or through freely chosen representatives' (UN, 1948; UN, 1966a). The 1689 English Bill of Rights also asserts that 'it is the right of the subjects to petition the king' (English Bill of Rights, 1689) and the First Amendment to the US Constitution forbids any law which prevents the people from being able to 'petition the government for a redress of grievances' (US Bill of Rights, 1791).

These authorities for granting the right of access to government were clearly intended to apply to individuals; however, for the most part they also allow individuals access in combination, through those 'freely chosen representatives', for example. This would seem to cover both elected representatives and also organizations designed to influence government, acting on behalf of individuals. And this might seem to cover corporate lobbying. However, *corporate* lobbying takes this access to government one stage further as it involves companies, rather than organizations operating on behalf of individuals, influencing government. This is questionable – unless one takes the metaphor of corporate citizenship literally. So a key question seems to be 'On whose behalf do companies lobby?' If it is on their own behalf, the justification is much less clear than if it is on behalf of others. In the US, for example, companies clearly consider themselves a legitimate and actively participating element of the democratic process (Lascelles, 2005), so this issue is important.

Corporate lobbying is sometimes represented as being justified because it is essentially on behalf of the public. In this view (Woodstock, 2002), the public benefit of lobbying derives from educating legislators on specific issues. For such education to be acceptable, however, assumes that lobbyists always tell the truth. In practice, there is considerable pressure on lobbyists not to lie, since once discovered, their credibility will be destroyed. However, there is a difference between not telling lies and telling the whole truth. It is much less clear that lobbyists can be credited with this latter virtue as, by definition, they are working for their employers or their clients with a particular interest or goal in mind.

It is possible to argue that companies are lobbying on behalf of their stakeholders, rather than themselves. In that case, the question must be for which stakeholders companies are lobbying – and how that relates to the general public interest. The obvious answer to the first question is the shareholders. Yet even if lobbyists claimed to be working for the benefit of other stakeholders, a stake-

Table 13.2 *US lobbying expenditure*

Organization	US Lobbying expenditure (US$)
US Chamber of Commerce	193,582,839
Altria Group	125,274,200
Verizon Communications	105,426,174
General Electric	105,166,256
Edison Electric Institute	100,312,966
Northrop Grumman	92,958,937
PhRMA	92,582,135
Business Roundtable	90,376,500
Lockheed Martin	88,931,565
American Medical Association	84,000,000
AT&T	72,185,000
Freddie Mac (Federal Home Loan Mortgage Corporation)	71,975,000
SBC Communications	71,333,037
Boeing	71,075,810
National Association of Realtors	63,200,000
Microsoft	61,644,500
Fannie Mae (Federal National Mortgage Association)	60,397,000
ExxonMobil	60,270,242
Pfizer	54,845,520

Source: SustainAbility and WWF (2005)

holder is not, in most cases, the same as the public in general (possibly excepting consumers of basic utilities). In this regard, 'the public' can be defined as the entire population, considered as individuals capable of taking all possible stakeholder roles. Few lobbyists will have quite such a broad remit.

A further ethical issue for lobbying relates to the money spent on it. Table 13.2 shows the scale of such external expenditure in the US to influence decisions of the US Congress over the six years to 2004.

The point here is not simply the impressive scale of the absolute sums which large companies spend to influence government, it is the lack of other organizations which might spend comparable sums. This means that corporations have disproportionate access to government. Except in the unlikely event that companies lobby to represent the public interest, this means that the scale of the corporate lobby effort is acting *against* the public interest.

A final general ethical issue with lobbying is the nature of the issues which are lobbied. This is related to the previous point about the lack of balance overall, but goes beyond it. In addition to the impact of lobbying to lead to an imbalance in the issues which are put to government, it is also possible that companies lobby for causes which will cause actual harm to the public, whether or not there is any counter-balancing influence.

One such issue is climate change. It has been well-documented that the Global Climate Coalition, which was disbanded in 2002 and which described itself as an organization of trade associations (GCC, 2002), was supported by the oil industry, among the 'more than 6 million businesses, companies and corporations' that it claimed to represent. In order to protect the interests of US business, it publicized science which discredited climate change and the human role within it and campaigned for technology-led, voluntary solutions to climate change and against the Kyoto Protocol.

This point is directly relevant to the charge that campaigning NGOs are simply lobbying machines which don't sell anything, as opposed to companies which are lobbying machines that have something to sell. In other words, is there any ethical difference between the influence which NGOs exert and that exerted by companies? The lobbying techniques that can be used by NGOs are indeed virtually identical to those effective for companies (Dodds and Strauss, 2004). Yet although the techniques which NGOs use to influence legislation and the public are similar, there is a big difference in the transparency of the process. Above all, NGOs are much more open about what they are trying to do and why – in fact, the more people who know about it the better. This is not usually the case for companies' lobbying. The reason for this results from the nature of their mission: most NGOs are driven by a mission for some aspect of public benefit whereas most companies are directed towards shareholder benefit. The lobbying motives of the latter are therefore regarded as somehow deceptive, if not simply selfish.

Donations to political parties are sometimes seen to be fairly close to straightforward corruption. This connection has led to the practice being banned in France. Moreover, like philanthropic donations, if they are not effective in securing a more favourable business climate, they can be seen to be morally questionable from a shareholder perspective too. In the US the practice of companies supporting political parties through political action committees (PACs), which is now the largest source of political donations, also has its ethical problems. Companies do not themselves contribute to these funds, but facilitate the contributions of their employees and shareholders. Employees in particular may feel pressured to make such contributions. While this does not compromise the use of shareholders' funds, companies are usually tempted rather to misrepresent the total PAC contribution as deriving from their support – which is again similar to how companies present the activities of charitable trusts which they have helped to establish.

Another kind of ethical issue concerns the ethics of the lobbying industry itself. Although much lobbying is delivered by the activities of company employees, an increasing proportion is delivered through third parties. According to the Centre for Public Integrity, the top lobby firm is Interpublic Group of Companies, Inc. This organization reported some $293 million of lobbying fees between 1998 and 2004 (CPI, 2006).

While it emphasizes the importance of lobbying, the general ethical issues which this scale of activity raises are no different to those raised by any company lobbying activity, albeit with a greater emphasis, since lobbying is the core business of a lobbying organization. However, the alignment of the organization's individual lobbyists with the objectives of their clients presents an additional ethical issue. Such alignment, or the lack of it, can of course arise within any organization, but what particularly sharpens it for lobbyists is the potential contradiction between the interests of different clients. Professional lobbying thus raises ethical issues of conflict of interest for the lobbying organization and of personal integrity for the individual lobbyists.

The heart of the solution to such issues is to acknowledge them, in other words to be transparent.

THROUGH A GLASS DARKLY

If lobbying is legal, the first responsibility is to be transparent about the issues which are lobbied for. While companies might be at their most influential when attempting to persuade customers to buy their products, the sales pitch does not carry the moral undertone of other lobbying activities. The main reason for this is that a sales pitch is open and the potential customer knows what is going on and should know what is at stake. And provided this is indeed the case, there is nothing wrong in principle with selling something, which contrasts somewhat with the image some might have of lobbying, which involves secret deals being struck behind closed doors in dark, smoky rooms. Whatever the reality, a lack of transparency makes the innocent seem dubious and the unethical heinous.

The legislative support for transparency over lobbying is weak in many places. It is perhaps strongest in the US, where the principal law requiring transparency is the Lobbying Disclosure Act of 1995. This is not matched by similar legislation elsewhere – the figures for US lobbying expenditure reproduced above, for example, could not easily be prepared for any other country. UK legislation (the UK Political Parties, Elections and Referendums Act of 2000) only requires companies to declare their donations to political parties in their annual report. However, in both cases, the declarations required are confined to the country concerned – there is no disclosure for the majority of overseas countries in which subsidiaries might operate. Interestingly, the control of not-for-profit organizations' lobbying is achieved through more stringent controls, either on the use of government funds, as in the US or, in the case of the UK, on restrictions on the scope of charitable activities that charities are permitted to undertake.

Transparency on the part of those lobbied is also important. Official records of government consultations are typically published, painstakingly capturing every document which has formed part of a consultation exercise. Yet there is very rarely a routine obligation on government to declare the personal encounters they have had with company representatives, and it is often during such meetings that the real business is done. Without such transparency it is difficult to discern the pattern of influence to which government has been subject. It is sometimes possible to obtain information about such meetings by making use of freedom of information legislation, but of course this presupposes that the enquirer knows what to request.

The extent of voluntary disclosure of lobbying activities by *companies* is very limited, to the extent that currently it is rare to find any voluntary reporting on lobbying expenditure or activities. The most basic information here would be to provide an analysis of:

- those groups which have been funded, including a breakdown on expenditure on professional lobbying;
- the amount spent on each lobbying group; and
- the causes and issues supported through lobbying.

The ability to understand and analyse the various lobbying positions which companies take has been one of the recurring themes of NGO reports on corporate lobbying (SustainAbility, 2001; SustainAbility and WWF, 2005; Beloe et al, 2006). However, in the UK, for example, few organizations have followed the lead of Co-operative Financial Services (CFS). CFS has reported on the particular positions it has supported and, in recent years, also on its lobbying activities.

There are several important issues here. While, as we have seen, it could be argued that companies should have no influence on government, government itself is likely to want to know the effect of possible policies on companies, so will in fact solicit input from the corporate sector. What they will hear as a result will include the companies' attempts to influence the government.

Further, if lobbying of any kind is to be permissible, what issues are appropriate? One answer to this concerns the extent to which the issue relates to the company's core business impacts. If an issue is close to the heart of the business, it might be thought legitimate to lobby around it. However, the issues closest to a business are precisely those for which the interests of shareholders will be most apparent and pressing. On the other hand, if, for example, a telecommunications company is asked to support a campaign to save whales, which seems of very marginal relevance to its core business, how should it respond? If the response is that whales are just not relevant to telecommunications, then why is support for a philanthropic appeal, equally distant from the core business, a legitimate subject for support?

One of the most contentious issues in recent years has been the extent of consistency in corporate lobbying positions. Companies have been known publicly to support fashionable issues, while behind the scenes lobbying hard for contrary ends. The most well-known example of this was the simultaneous public positioning of some of the major oil companies in favour of action against climate change at the same time as they supported industry groups, such as the Global Climate Coalition, which were campaigning for the opposite end. Somewhat depressingly, one of the possible explanations for this was that one hand did not know what the other was doing. This is entirely credible within larger companies, each section of which can promote its own ends. However, it is much more likely to have been deliberate as a policy to back all possible outcomes of the issue. Companies frequently support opposing political parties so that whoever wins they can be seen as having provided support. This is no doubt a better position from the company perspective than being seen to have supported no-one.

One way in which such apparent double dealing often emerges is through industry associations. Within most sectors, industry associations provide support and combined lobbying services for an industry. However, the companies within a sector will have far from identical, albeit overlapping, issues. In consequence, most industry associations adopt the position most widely shared. This is

155

typically the most conservative one and has rarely included strong positions on sustainability, unless the link to the sector's core business is obvious. The Association of British Insurers, for example, has produced a number of publications detailing the likely consequences of climate change, such as the Financial Risks of Climate Change report (ABI, 2005).

Trade associations also have relatively privileged access to government, as officials are more likely to be protected from the charge of being beholden to an individual company if they consult sector-wide bodies. The consistency of lobbying positions is therefore a crucial indicator of responsibility, as the organization AccountAbility has pointed out (see, for example, AccountAbility, 2005b).

HIDDEN PERSUASION

Lobbying tactics in the earlier stages, intended to influence the policy climate and policy formation, can involve controversial techniques. One such technique, employed by the oil and pharmaceutical industries, is to sponsor and disseminate research. Pharmaceutical companies, as they often point out, spend large quantities of money on developing new drugs – $1 billion for one drug would be quite reasonable (Masia, 2006). Recouping that investment is therefore taken very seriously, quite apart from any issues about pricing. Yet in order to create demand, pharmaceutical companies may spend perhaps twice the research and development cost on marketing and advertising. (There are, however, restrictions on the advertising permitted to consumers; much marketing is directed at doctors.)

However, beyond this, and in order both to understand the effect of a drug and to affect the climate of opinion, pharmaceutical companies conduct research, often beyond that required directly for clinical trials. This is part of a growing trend in which an increasing proportion of research, which used to be conducted almost entirely by the academic community, is undertaken by commercial companies. The reason this is attractive to companies is that it leverages the idea of a privileged access to 'the truth' which science enjoys.

And it is possible, of course, to question the *bona fide* nature of such research, since it is paid for by those with an interest in the outcome. (Although to an extent it is also possible to level the same charge at the academic community, few of whose researchers now enjoy tenure.) Nevertheless, provided that the sponsoring organization declares its interest, the reader will know how to view the research appropriately and can judge it accordingly. This, of course, assumes that the readers, who often include prescribing professional doctors, have the skill and time to appraise it properly, and this is something that has been questioned by Richard Smith, a recent editor of one of the world's foremost medical journals, the *British Medical Journal*:

> this whole business of sending original research to doctors is kind of crazy. When you talk to ordinary doctors, they are not scientists and yet here we are sending them this mass of complicated infor-

mation that most of them are not equipped to critically appraise.
They haven't got the time. (Boseley, 2005)

Unfortunately, pharmaceutical companies have also placed articles describing research they or their subcontractors have conducted to be published under other names: the practice of ghost-writing. This further challenges transparency by misrepresenting the origins of a piece of research. As Michael Lynch has put it:

the normalization of 'ghost-writing' holds profound implications for
our conceptions of authorship, academic research and publication,
scientific community and, not least, editorship. (Lynch, 2004)

Occasionally, companies may think that sponsoring research or misrepresenting research findings overall is worthwhile – even if it is directed at conclusions which have been thoroughly discredited. Exxon, in particular, has been taken to task by the Royal Society in the UK in this regard:

I was very surprised to read the following passage from the section
on environmental performance [...] in the 'Corporate Citizenship
Report': 'While assessments such as those of the IPCC have
expressed growing confidence that recent warming can be attrib-
uted to increases in greenhouse gases, these conclusions rely on
expert judgment rather than objective, reproducible statistical
methods. Taken together, gaps in the scientific basis for theoretical
climate models and the interplay of significant natural variability
make it difficult to determine objectively the extent to which recent
climate changes might be the result of human actions.'
These statements are very misleading. The 'expert judgment' of
the Intergovernmental Panel on Climate Change was actually based
on objective and quantitative analyses and methods, including
advanced statistical appraisals, which carefully accounted for the
interplay of natural variability, and which have been independently
reproduced [...]
I have carried out an ad hoc survey on the websites of organi-
zations that are listed in the ExxonMobil 2005 Worldwide Giving
Report for 'public information and policy research', which is
published on your website. Of those organizations whose websites
feature information about climate change [...] 25 offered views
consistent with the scientific literature. However, some 39 organi-
zations were featuring information [...] that misrepresented the
science of climate change, by outright denial of evidence that green-
house gases are driving climate change, or by overstating the
amount and significance of uncertainty in knowledge, or by convey-
ing a misleading impression of the potential impacts of
anthropogenic change. My analysis indicates that Exxon Mobil last
year provided more than $2.9m to organizations in the US which
misinformed the public about climate change. (Ward, 2006)

ARE SMOKE-FILLED ROOMS A GOOD THING?

When company representatives are floating ideas or debating detailed proposals with government officials or ministers, what sort of transparency should be expected? The advice (written or spoken) which civil servants offer to ministers is exempted from UK freedom of information legislation, the rationale being that civil servants would feel constrained from free discussion if they were concerned that their arguments could become open to public scrutiny.

This raises a more general issue of the limits to transparency in situations where two or more parties are negotiating. Quite apart from any commercial considerations, arguments have often been made that the process of negotiation suffers if the negotiating exchanges are open to public scrutiny. One reason given is that to disclose the details of the process of negotiation can prevent negotiators from taking temporary tactical positions or floating ideas to elicit a response. Such positions may not be intended to go forward, and if they are unacceptable to the outside stakeholders whom the negotiators represent, then transparency may cause real difficulty. Another argument is that the complexity of ideas may not be appreciated by a wider, media-driven public, so the arguments actually presented may be distorted, thus ironically reducing transparency. Overall, 'decision-making space', as David Heald puts it (Heald, 2006a, p69), needs to be protected.

This idea has wide ramifications for many situations, from commercial lobbying to political decision making, international negotiations and conflict resolution. In some situations, especially conflict resolution, if there are any problems with the idea of protecting the decision space, they may be set against the urgency of a desirable outcome. But considered more broadly, while such protection will help those negotiating, the need to protect a decision space fundamentally works against wider participation and tends to preserve a somewhat distanced, 'professional' approach to stakeholder representation. More credit needs to be given to the public and a more mature approach needs to be taken by all sides. This will enable a more transparent approach to be taken.

COMPLICITY

'Partnership in an evil action' is how the dictionary explains the word 'complicity'. It is derived from words which mean to 'fold together'. It is interesting to note that the word 'complexity' is derived from similar words which mean to 'plait together' as hair is plaited. This is not surprising, perhaps, since complicity is a complex subject and one which most people prefer to avoid.

It was suggested at the start of this chapter that complicity should be seen as part of the same continuum as influencing or lobbying. In fact it should be seen as part of an even larger continuum, stretching from decisions over which a company has direct control, through those which they influence, to those over which they may have no control or influence but from which they still knowingly benefit.

The legal definition of complicity is much narrower. John Ruggie, in his Interim Report on human rights and transnational companies (Ruggie, 2006), declared that the best, and legally most widely accepted, definition of complicity was provided by a case brought in the US under the Alien Claims Tort Act. This defined a number of criteria for complicity, all of which have to be met, that:

1 the company should have given practical assistance to the actual perpetrator of a crime;
2 this assistance should have had a substantial effect on the commission of the criminal act; and
3 the company knew or should have known that its acts would result in a possible crime even if it did not intend for that crime to take place.

This legal definition probably supports the accusations levelled at Google and Yahoo of complicity in the Chinese government suppression of the internet and those using it to promote human rights. It also has the mildly paradoxical but technically correct consequence that if you directly perpetrate a crime, you are not complicit with it. However, especially in a corporate context, if the company or any of its officers are perpetrators, then most of those around them (including the company if it is not the perpetrator) are likely to be complicit.

The reasons why the strict legal definition of complicity is too narrow, and a wider one of greater moral relevance is necessary, are first, that a company's actions may be coherent with the actions of, for example, a government without necessarily facilitating them. In other words, there may be active, but non-essential, support from the company. Second, there may be no perpetrator! It makes perfect sense to say that a company is complicit with a market which invariably delivers economically or socially abusive outcomes. And thirdly, the company may have persuaded another party (possibly through lobbying) to commit an abuse.

The two examples in Box 13.1 are meant to illustrate what all this might mean in practice. They are drawn from an internal Amnesty discussion document (Marsden, 2006) concerning how companies should handle human rights abuses.

Of course, accusations of complicity are easy to make. If the web of complicity is to be spun wide, it is important to acknowledge different degrees of guilt, without allowing a marginal degree of complicity to be regarded as praiseworthy, rather than simply less blameworthy. Such a wide definition would suggest that all of us are to some degree complicit in the wrongs done in our name, for example by the state of which we may be citizens. Yet it does not require too unrealistic a degree of maturity to expect that anyone might acknowledge that they are not perfect – even companies.

Wherever the boundary is drawn, how far is transparency applicable? One answer is that it is important at least to be transparent as to where the boundary for actions relevant to complicity is being drawn. Currently, Dow Chemicals, which bought Union Carbide, states (Dow, undated) that the issue of the Bhopal disaster of 1984, which occurred at a Union Carbide site, has

---

Box 13.1 Practical complicity

Situation A

An oil company, at the insistence of the national government, employs the army to provide security for its plant and workers. It is aware that the army is likely to use its unofficial links with paramilitary groups to harass, torture and possibly kill local villagers which the army suspects to be harbouring dissident groups.

Steps the company should take

If the security forces commit abuses against local villagers, the company will be complicit in the abuses. The company should negotiate with the government, as stated in the Voluntary Principles on Security and Human Rights, for its own security standards and ensure that the army personnel guarding the plant are trained accordingly. The company should also let the government know that it is monitoring the behaviour of the army and paramilitaries in the area of its operations and will record and respond to credible allegations of human rights abuses.

Situation B

An internet company comes under pressure from a government to assist in repression of freedom of expression by providing information to the government about users of its services and censoring certain websites.

Steps the company should take

The company should avoid storing unnecessary information about users. If it is concerned about the nature of a government request for information it should first voice these concerns with the government and, if necessary, pursue all legal means to resist such a request. If information provided by the company leads to the arbitrary detention of a user, it should publicly raise concerns about the detention. The company should also adopt human rights policies, with particular concern for freedom of expression, preferably in conjunction with other internet companies operating in that country and in consultation with human rights experts.

Source: Marsden (2006)

---

been resolved. It wants to move on, saying that it has paid some US$560m into a trust fund, that the case has been legally settled and that before Dow bought Union Carbide, Union Carbide had itself sold its interest in the subsidiary which operated the plant at which the disaster took place.

However, NGOs describe the continued suffering of the local community resulting from the accident. The area is still contaminated. Can Dow 'move on'? Should Dow be regarded as complicit in the continuing suffering in Bhopal? If complicity does have such a broad definition, where are the boundaries? It is always possible to go back far enough in time to find something in which we, or a company, may be said to be complicit. This doesn't mean, however, that we are not complicit – it might instead simply indicate just how hard it is to bear guilt.

14

A Future for Integrity

The Limits of Transparency

The main claim of this book has been that power relationships require transparency. Transparency does not compensate for or negate power relationships, but it can improve the dignity of those living with them and provide the starting point for addressing the issues to which the power relationship relates. There should be a general presumption that transparency is in the public interest and in the interests of disadvantaged stakeholders in particular. Russell Stevenson has suggested (Stevenson, 1980) that there might be a corporate freedom of information act under which companies would be obliged to divulge information unless they could show that disclosure would not be in the public interest. This would encourage regular company disclosure and reporting to minimize the cost of ad hoc requests for information.

This does not mean, however, that there should never be limits to transparency. What it does mean is that the onus to establish their case should be on those who wish to deny transparency. In other words, the question should always be 'What can we say?' rather than the inhibiting 'What do we need to conceal?' A presumption in favour of transparency should result in the maximum possible transparency in practice, rather than the minimum.

Where transparency is curtailed, those responsible should be transparent about this fact. To hide the truth is bad enough, but to conceal the fact that you are hiding it is far worse.

The fundamental reason why there should be such a presumption of transparency is that transparency is a good in itself. This was one of the central messages of the film *The Truman Show*, in which the central character appeared to live a charmed life but did not realize that he was living inside a 'reality show'. The climax of the film comes when he forsakes his fake world for direct knowledge of the real one. In more general terms, other things being equal, it is always more desirable to have transparency than to be denied it.

Of course it would be very hard to claim that transparency is the only or supreme good; clearly the demands of transparency need to be weighed against other demands. However, if transparency is regarded only as an instrumental good, as David Heald believes (Heald, 2006a) – that is, valuable only for what

161

it brings about – then it becomes far easier to justify curtailing transparency. In fact, if transparency is only instrumental, then *any* disutility it brings would justify curtailing it. One such disutility is, of course, simple economic cost. It is rarely cost-free to be transparent. There can be real costs in collecting information and being able to prove that the information collected is correct, even though with access to the internet the costs associated with the distribution of information are now much less significant.

Beyond the financial cost argument, are there any other costs to which transparency might give rise? Some have argued that ignorance has a social function, which transparency undermines. Their argument is that society may function more smoothly and be less threatened if, at least in some circumstances, people do not know what is going on; transparency may lead to unrest. This position is an extension of the idea that decision-making space needs to be protected, and obviously has rather chilling political implications. Against the 'social functions of ignorance' it should be pointed out that if ignorance does sometimes succeed in preserving social equilibrium, then that equilibrium will be an unstable one, forever contingent on effort to maintain that ignorance.

This was illustrated when Ferenc Gyurcsany, the Hungarian Prime Minister inadvertently confessed to lying:

> *I almost died when I had to pretend for one and a half years [before April's elections] as if we were governing. Instead, we lied in the morning, we lied in the evening. I am through with this. [...] We have obviously lied over the past one and a half, two years. It was absolutely clear that what we were saying was not true. [...] And all this time we have done nothing for four years. Nothing. You cannot mention a single major government measure that we could be proud of. [...] If we have to square up with the country on what we have done for four years, what will we say?* (FT, 2006)

This resulted in riots and nearly brought down the government. Gyurcsany, however, survived the immediate reaction, which some attributed to his transparency.

In addition, the idea of a social function of ignorance is much less applicable to companies. It would be rather hard to claim that companies should be spared the need to be transparent because otherwise society might not function so well. It is true that the collapse of Enron and the loss of the many jobs that entailed might have been avoided if the truth had not come out. But again, it is hard to imagine that it would have stayed forever hidden. One of the reasons why it takes effort to maintain ignorance is that people do in fact value transparency for its own sake and want to tell the truth. In the common phrase, 'the truth will out'.

There are, however, some limits to transparency over corporate affairs. The most fundamental of these is when transparency hurts a stakeholder. This applies even when what is at stake is simply an individual employee's desire for others not to know their personal details. When that stakeholder is an individual, then the need for privacy can be regarded as a human right. Companies, of

162

course, can also be stakeholders of other companies and organizations, and, in practice, they too claim the right to privacy, although in this case it is much less justified.

It is also true that some aspects of transparency, such as divulging trade secrets, can seriously damage the commercial prospects of a company. In these cases it is important to balance the needs of different stakeholders against each other. In relation to transparency, the principle must be that the need for transparency of the most vulnerable stakeholder should determine how much is revealed – not the needs of the most powerful, often the shareholder. This can be seen by considering a hypothetical case in which a trade secret involved the manufacture of a product which was toxic or harmful in some way to the public: clearly the interests of the company need to be overridden in the interests of public health.

As I have argued that one of the practical obstacles to transparency is the potential embarrassment it might cause to company managers, it could be suggested that since individual managers deserve the same privacy granted to others, they should be excused the need to be transparent about such matters. However, managers, in the same way as any other individual stakeholder of a company, act in two capacities: for themselves and in their role as a stakeholder. Transparency is required not over some personal detail about the manager, but over their actions as part of a company. What is demanded is transparency over the manager's actions as a manager, not as an individual. Furthermore, if the argument that managers' actions should be so protected were allowed, it could be used to prevent any transparency from a company whatever, which seems absurd.

While transparency is worthwhile if there is a need, where transparency is not fulfilling a need, it is not required. And indeed certain sorts of apparent transparency are not helpful; these may be called 'idiot transparency'.

One way in which idiot transparency can occur is when a surplus of information is displayed. This may be well-intentioned but naive, or it may be manipulative and deliberately designed to conceal. An example of the former may perhaps be provided by 'databombing', a phenomenon which has arisen with some sustainability reports or very large websites which provide so much information that it is very difficult to find what is required. The need is for effective communication. Transparency is a function of communication, not a function of the quantity of information technically disclosed.

It is also possible for transparency to be counter-productive of its intended purpose. An intensively studied example of this is the principal–agent relationship in economics. It is possible to construct models in which transparency creates perverse incentives with respect to the principal. Where a principal scrutinizes only the decision process, rather than its outcomes, the agent has an incentive to appear to make good decisions rather than to optimize outcomes (Prat, 2005). As a result the actual outcomes may be less than optimal. However, this effect has limited application in reality.

More often, a company will fear that what is to be disclosed will be misunderstood to its detriment. This is of course a possibility, although it must be far more common, due to the efforts of corporate PR, that what is disclosed is misunderstood to the company's advantage. Either way, the potential for misunderstanding is real, and it is the responsibility of the company to work with its stakeholders to minimize such misunderstanding. This will involve care in the formulation of what is disclosed. It may also involve preliminary discussions with stakeholders to discover the least misleading way to present it.

On the whole the question 'What are the limits to transparency?' presupposes that transparency is a necessary evil, rather than a necessary good. Only the existence of a power relationship calls for transparency; the absence of a power relationship does not call for transparency. There is no obligation to divulge information for its own sake, except perhaps as entertainment.

THE PUBLIC AND VOLUNTARY SECTORS

This book has focused on transparency in connection with the private sector. How far are the arguments about transparency relevant to other sectors, such as government and the voluntary sector?

The general arguments concerning the need for transparency where power relations exist are of much wider application than only to the private sector. There has, in fact, been a longer concern for, and a richer literature on, the need for transparency over the activities of the public sector. The main argument here has usually been that the purpose of the public sector is to provide goods or services on behalf of the public, so there is a direct appeal to the legitimacy of public transparency over its activities. There is also a long-standing concern over the propriety of public figures, which parallels the concern over ethical behaviour in companies. There is a consequent need for transparency over issues such as the personal, and especially financial, interests of elected officials and their connection with external organizations. This is the other side of corruption and lobbying.

The moral argument concerning the need for transparency wherever there are power relations therefore extends to both government and the voluntary sector. Beyond this, many of the arguments over the general nature of what should be revealed and what may be kept private will be similar. The reason for this is that the organization–stakeholder analysis on which much of the analysis in this book is based can equally be applied to the government, treated as an organization, and to charitable organizations, although some of the details will undoubtedly be different, especially the particular stakeholders involved on one side or the other of the struggle to establish transparency.

For example, the stakeholders generally concerned with resisting transparency over government business may, on occasions, include both politicians and the civil service management. There are usually no shareholders involved, at least directly. Within the voluntary sector, those organizations that have campaigned for transparency from the private sector are being challenged to demonstrate comparable transparency themselves. While there may be similar feelings of embarrassment at stake for the management of large voluntary organizations as for large companies, there are considerable differences as well. And in fact one of the primary stakeholders to whom NGOs owe transparency will be their members and supporters, rather than the corporate sector.

THE POWER OF COMMUNICATION

How far can you go with transparency? There is a considerable philosophical tradition (including Kant and Habermas) which suggests the answer is 'a long way'. The material of this book, however, suggests that the achievement of transparency is a long and contested social process, always currently unfinished, rather than something which has only to be stated to be accepted.

As the need for transparency has a moral foundation, those with power have a moral obligation to be transparent over how they exercise it. This certainly applies to individuals, but it also applies to companies, which have extremely significant power and influence in the modern world.

The response to the demand for transparency has been inadequate. This is true both historically in relation to shareholder issues, and more recently in relation to the impacts companies have over all other stakeholders. Much corporate communication has been beholden to the brand and a perceived need to maintain some moral perfection. This not only frustrates proper communication and leads to 'spin', it is also simply unrealistic because it is unattainable.

It is difficult to gauge how far power has interfered with communication: to the degree to which transparency is undermined, it will have hidden its tracks quite successfully. But it can be possible, for any given stakeholder, to ascertain whether the conditions for successful communication and transparency have been established. It is possible to set out a number of stages of the achievement of transparency between a company and it stakeholders.

The first stage is the recognition of the individual or group in question as a stakeholder. No communication or transparency is possible until a company recognizes the right of stakeholders to be heard.

The second stage involves acknowledged and deliberate attempts to communicate with the stakeholder. This admits many levels of quality, of which some will be more appropriate than others. However, the second stage cannot be transcended until the company can acknowledge that the stakeholder can quite reasonably ask to be involved in setting the agenda for communications.

At the third stage, then, stakeholders can determine the issues about which they feel communication is necessary. Yet all this is a product of stakeholders raising issues; avenues of communication can be shut down as readily as continued.

The final stage is reached when there is a successful attempt to integrate stakeholder communication into the governance processes of the organization. As a result, stakeholders can make decisions on matters that affect them.

No company has yet achieved stage four for all stakeholder issues. Furthermore, any given company will be at a variety of stages in respect of the multitude of issues which it faces. And different companies will be at different stages with respect to their handling of the same issue.

PRACTICAL TRUST

If transparency is a good thing, then no doubt we should aim for as much as possible. But how much transparency is actually possible? Two attitudes to this question present themselves: uncritical enthusiasm for transparency on the one hand and resentful mistrust on the other.

The enthusiastic approach has been appealingly documented by the science fiction authors Stephen Baxter and Arthur C. Clarke. They have written about a world in which universal transparency is established. For them this enabled a dismal past to be left behind:

> an incomprehensible, taboo-ridden age [...] in which liars and cheats had prospered, and crime was out of control, and people killed each other over lies and myths, and in which the world had been systematically trashed through wilful carelessness, greed, and an utter lack of sympathy for others or foresight regarding the future. [In return for transparency a new world opened up:] one smart-looking townhouse, presumably converted from a shop, which had its walls replaced by clear glass panes. Looking into the brightly lit rooms [...] even the floors and ceilings were transparent, as was much of the furniture – even the bathroom suite. People moved through the rooms, naked, apparently oblivious of the stares of people outside. [...] In the new openness, businesses boomed. Crime seemed to have dropped to an irreducible rump. [...] Politicians had, cautiously, found ways to operate in the new glass-walled world, with every move open to scrutiny by a concerned and online citizenry, now and in the future. [...] From the highest to the lowest. Even manners had changed. People seemed to be becoming a little more tolerant of one another, able to accept each other's differences and faults – because each person knew he or she was under scrutiny too. (Clarke and Baxter, 2002)

Unfortunately there is also a world of resentful mistrust. According to MORI, eight people in ten *disagree* that 'directors of large companies can be trusted to tell the truth' (MORI, 2003). Product labelling and advertising is also regarded with suspicion – both for what it reveals and for what it may still conceal! And this is perhaps just the tip of the iceberg of a more general alienation affecting our attitude to all parts of society which David Edwards has described in *Free to be Human* (Edwards, 1995).

In practice, as individuals we hold contradictory attitudes, simultaneously mistrusting companies while also, because we have to get on with life, appearing to deny that anything is amiss. The result is the discrepancy between what people say (that they don't trust companies) and what they do: buy their products, work for them, sell things to them. For companies, the practice is to build the brand ever higher, better and brighter. This defensive denial convinces few and, if it is not counterproductive in the short run, certainly makes any fall from grace that much harder.

So what attitude *is* appropriate? There is of course a place both for vigorous campaigning and for cooperative support, for boycotting products and for working constructively within companies to improve standards.

I believe that if there is to be sufficient change, there is a need for honesty together with a willingness to explore difficult issues. This is certainly necessary from companies, as much of this book emphasizes. Yet it is also necessary from those who challenge companies, whether from within or without, and whether gently suggesting or aggressively campaigning.

This level of self-transparency from all sides is vital if there is to be much movement on corporate transparency. Credibility is lost if a position of perfection is adopted. When companies are attacked for their environmental performance, for example, one kind of defence is to point out the apparent contradictions in the position of their critics, who may perhaps have flown half way round the world just to make an environmental point. In this situation, it is important to remember that there are two individuals involved, as well as perhaps two organizations. Both are caught in the contradictions just described. If either feel they are confronted with a position of moral perfection, it is very hard for them not to respond from the polar opposite perspective. That way lies a sterile exchange of charge and counter-charge.

It is not possible either to absolve ourselves from the corporate world or to pretend that there just isn't a problem. And since we are all stakeholders of companies in one way or another, it is up to all of us to bring about change. In this, transparency can be our greatest ally.

Bibliography

Aarhus (1998) *Convention on Access to Information, Public Participation and Decision-making in Environmental Matters*, EU, Aarhus, Denmark

ABI (2005) *Financial Risks of Climate Change*, Association of British Insurers, London

AccountAbility (2005a) *Stakeholder Engagement Standard*, exposure draft, AccountAbility, London

AccountAbility (2005b) *Towards Responsible Lobbying: Leadership and Public Policy*, AccountAbility, London

Adams, A. (2006) 'The secret agent', *BBC News*, London, 21 March

Alfred McAlpine (2006) *Corporate Responsibility Report 2005*, Alfred McAlpine, London

AMEC (2005a) *Ethical Conduct/Accountability*, Amec, London

AMEC (2005b) *Shaping the Future: Our Guiding Principles*, Amec, London.

Annan, K. (1998) statement about the Aarhus Convention, widely cited, e.g. see www.unece.org/env/pp

Aranya, N. (1979) 'The influence of pressure groups on financial statements in Britain' in T. A. Lee and R. H. Parker (eds) *Evolution of Corporate Financial Reporting*, Thomas Nelson and Sons Ltd, Sunbury on Thames, UK

ASB (2001) *RS1*, Accounting Standards Board, London

Ashley, J. (2002) 'Instead of a debate over war, there's been a national shrug', *The Guardian*, 23 December, London

Bakan, J. (2004) *The Corporation: The Pathological Pursuit of Profit and Power*, Constable, London

Baker, R. W. (2005) *Capitalism's Achilles Heal*, John Wiley, Hoboken, NJ

Banisar, D. (2004) *Freedom of Information and Access to Government Record Laws Around the World*, Privacy International, London

Barkham, P. (2006) 'Secret deal behind a Norfolk town's mystery U-turn on new supermarket', *The Guardian*, London, 29 April

BBC (2006) 'Murdoch "pays no UK tax"', *BBC News*, London, http://news.bbc.co.uk/1/hi/business/the_company_file/299543.stm, accessed August 2006

Begovic, B. et al (2004) *Corruption in Judiciary*, Centre for Liberal-Democratic Studies, Belgrade, Serbia

Beloe, S., Elkington, J. and Thorpe, J. (2006) 'Lobbying in the spotlight', in D. Greenall (ed) *Corporate Social Responsibility Review*, The Conference Board of Canada, Ontario

Berle, A. A. and Means, G. C. (1933) *The Modern Corporation and Private Property*, Macmillan, New York

Bernays, E. (1947) 'The engineering of consent', *Annals of the American Academy of Political and Social Science*, March

Birdsall, N. (2001) 'Why inequality matters: Some economic issues', *Ethics and International Affairs*, no 15, pp3–28

Birkinshaw, P. (2006) 'Transparency as a human right', in C. Hood and D. Heald (eds) *Transparency: The Key to Better Governance?*, Oxford University Press, Oxford, UK

Blum, L. (1980) *Friendship, Altruism and Morality*, Routledge and Kegan Paul, London

Boseley, S. (2005) 'A question of ethics', *The Guardian*, 30 June London

BP (2006a) *Code of Conduct*, BP, London

BP (2006b) *Making Energy More: Sustainability Report 2005*, BP, London

Brand (2006) *What Is a Brand?*, Brand Solutions Inc, Medina, WA

Browne, J. (2004) 'The ethics of business', The Botwinick Lecture, New York, 19 November

Burchill, S. (2005) *National Interest in International Relations Theory*, Palgrave, Basingstoke, UK

Bush, T. (2005) *Divided by a Common Language – Where Economics Meets the Law: US Versus Non-US Financial Reporting Models*, Institute of Chartered Accountants of England and Wales (ICAEW), London

Cadbury, A. (1992) *The Financial Aspects of Corporate Governance*, London Stock Exchange, London

Carroll, A. B. (1991) 'The pyramid of corporate social responsibility: Toward the moral management of organisational stakeholders', *Business Horizons*, no 48, pp39–48

Carroll, A. B. (1999) 'Corporate social responsibility: Evolution of a definitional construct', *Business and Society*, no 38, pp268–295

Carson, R. (1962) *Silent Spring*, Houghton Mifflin, Boston, MA

Chandler, G. (2003) 'The evolution of the business and human rights debate', in R. Sullivan (ed) *Business and Human Rights*, Greenleaf, Sheffield UK

Chomsky, N. (1994) *Manufacturing Consent: The Political Economy of the Mass Media*, Vintage, London (first published 1988)

Christensen, J. and Murphy, R. (2004) 'The social irresponsibility of corporate tax avoidance – Taking CSR to the bottom line', *Development*, no 47, pp37–44

Claessens, C. A., Djankov, S. and Lang, L. H. P. (1999) *Who Controls East Asian Corporations?*, Policy Research Working Paper Series, World Bank, New York

Clapham, A. (2006) *The Human Rights Obligations of Non-State Actors*, Oxford University Press, Oxford, UK

Clarke, C. and Baxter, S. (2002) *The Light of Other Days*, HarperCollins, London

CoC (2006) 'It pays to engage in corporate social responsibility', British Chambers of Commerce, www.britishchambers.org.uk/business_services/csr/index.html, accessed March 2006

Coca-Cola (2006) *The Coca-Cola Company Form 10-K*, Coca-Cola, Atlanta, GA, available at www.thecoca-colacompany.com/investors/pdfs/form_10K_2005.pdf, accessed March 2007

CoE (1999) *Civil Law Convention on Corruption*, Council of Europe, Strasbourg, France

Cohen, N. (2002) 'One way to get very rich', *The Observer*, London, 24 February

CORE (2006) 'What is CORE?', CORE, www.corporate-responsibility.org, accessed March 2006

CPI (2006) 'Lobbywatch: Interpublic Group of Companies, Inc.', Center for Public Integrity, Washington, DC, www.publicintegrity.org/lobby/profile.aspx?act=firms&year=2003&lo=L001940

CR (2006) 'Non-financial reporting status of the FTSE100: March 2006', Corporate Register, London

CSR (2006) *What is CSR?*, www.csr.gov.uk/whatiscsr.shtml, accessed March 2006

Cumbrians Opposed to a Radioactive Environment (2006) DTI Select Committee Report, Hansard, London

Davies, N. (2002) 'Cosy relationship keeps corporates happy but could cost £20bn in taxes', *The Guardian*, 23 July, London

De Maria, W. (2001) 'Commercial-in-confidence: An obituary to transparency?', *Australian Journal of Public Administration*, no 60, pp92–109

De Maria, W. (2006) 'Brother secret, sister silence: Sibling conspiracies against managerial integrity', *Journal of Business Ethics*, no 65, pp219–234

Desai, P. and Mitra, P. (2004) 'Why do some countries recover so much more easily than others?', *Festschrift in Honor of Guillermo A. Calvo*, IMF, Washington, DC

Dodds, F. and Strauss, M. (2004) *How to Lobby at Intergovernmental Meetings*, Earthscan, London

Donaldson, T. (1982) *Corporations and Morality*, Prentice Hall, Englewood Cliffs, NJ

Donnelly, J. (1989) *Universal Human Rights in Theory and Practice*, Cornell University Press, Ithaca, NY

Dow (undated) 'Bhopal', Dow Chemical, www.dow.com/publicreport/2001/worldclass/bhopal.htm?filepath=&fromPage=BasicSearch, accessed October 2006

Drabek, Z. and Payne, W. (2002) 'The impact of transparency on foreign direct investment', *Journal of Economic Integration*, no 17, pp777–810

Economist (1999) 'Rupert laid bare', *The Economist*, 20 March

Economist (2000) 'Gimme shelter', *The Economist*, 27 January

Edey, H. C. (1979) 'Company accounting in the nineteenth and twentieth centuries', in T. A. Lee and R. H. Parker (eds) *Evolution of Corporate Financial Reporting*, Thomas Nelson and Sons Ltd, Sunbury on Thames, UK

Edwards, D. (1995) *Free to be Human*, Resurgence, Totnes, UK

Edwards, J. R. (1989) *The History of Financial Accounting*, Routledge, London

Egyptian Delta Land and Investment Company Ltd *v.* Todd (1928) A.C. 1 ed. London

Elkington, J. (1997) *Cannibals with Forks: The Triple Bottom Line of 21st Century Business*, Capstone, Oxford, UK

EMAS (2001) Regulation (EC) No 761/2001 of the European Parliament and of the Council

English Bill of Rights (1689) 'Bill of rights: An act declaring the rights and liberties of the subject and settling the succession of the crown', text available at www.constitution.org/eng/eng_bor.htm

Evenett, S. J. and Hoekman, B. M. (2004) *Government Procurement: Market Access, Transparency, and Multilateral Trade Rules*, World Bank, New York

Everett, M. (2003) 'The social life of genes: Privacy, property and the new genetics', *Social Science and Medicine*, no 56, pp53–65

Faccio, M. (2003) *Politically Connected Firms*, University of Nashville, Nashville, TN

FAO (2004) 'Milk and milk products', *Food Outlook*, no 4, December

Fauset, C. (2006) *What's Wrong with Corporate Social Responsibility?*, Corporate Watch, Oxford, UK

FCC (1997) *Complaints about Broadcast Journalism*, Federal Communications Commission, Washington, DC

FLA (2005) *Workplace Code of Conduct*, Fair Labor Association, Washington, DC

Florini, A. M. (1999) 'Does the invisible hand need a transparent glove? The politics of transparency', Annual World Bank Conference on Development Economics, Carnegie Endowment for International Peace, Washington, DC

FoE (2002) *Failing the Challenge – The Other Shell Report*, Friends of the Earth, London

FoE (2005) *Corporate Accountability*, Friends of the Earth, London

Franklin, B. (1789) Letter to Jean Baptiste le Roy, 13 November

FRC (2003) *The Combined Code on Corporate Governance*, Financial Reporting Council, London

Freeman, E. R. (1984) *Strategic Management: A Stakeholder Approach*, Pitman, Boston, MA

French, P. (1979) 'The corporation as a moral person', *American Philosophical Quarterly*, no 16, pp207–215

FSA (2006) *Handbook*, Financial Services Authority, London

FT (2006) 'Excerpts: Hungarian "lies" speech', *Financial Times*, 19 September

GCC (2002) *About Us*, Global Climate Coalition, http://web.archive.org/web/20020610081640/www.globalclimate.org/aboutus.htm, accessed October 2006

Gibson, K. (1995) 'Fictitious persons and real responsibilities', *Journal of Business Ethics*, no 14, pp761–767

Gibson, O. (2003) 'Mobile porn "could generate £2.5bn"', *The Guardian*, 22 January, London

Glennerster, R. and Shin, Y. (2003) *Is Transparency Good for You, and Can the IMF Help?*, International Monetary Fund, New York

Goyder, G. (1961) *The Responsible Company*, Blackwells, Oxford, UK

Gray, J. (1998) *False Dawn: The Delusions of Global Capitalism*, Granta, London

Green Alliance (2001) *Masts, Mobile Phones and Health*, BT, London

GRI (2002) GRI press release, 18 April, Global Reporting Initiative, Amsterdam

GRI (2006) *Setting the Report Boundary*, Global Reporting Initiative, Amsterdam

Guardian (2005) 'Living our values: Social, ethical and environmental audit 2005', The Scott Trust, London

Guardian (2006) 'Living our values: Social, ethical and environmental audit 2006', The Scott Trust, London

Hawken, P., Lovins, A. B. and Lovins, L. H. (1999) *Natural Capitalism: The Next Industrial Revolution*, Earthscan, London

Heald, D. (2006a) 'Transparency as an instrumental value', in C. Hood and D. Heald (eds) *Transparency: The Key to Better Governance?*, Oxford University Press, Oxford, UK

Heald, D. (2006b) 'Varieties of transparency', in C. Hood and D. Heald (eds) *Transparency: The Key to Better Governance?*, Oxford University Press, Oxford, UK

Hemme, T., Weers, A. and Christoffers, K. (2005) *A Global Review – The Supply of Milk and Dairy Products*, International Farm Comparison Network, Braunschweig, Germany

Henderson (2005) *Tax, Risk and Corporate Governance*, Henderson Global Investors, London

Henriques, A. (2004) 'CSR, sustainability and the triple bottom line', in A. Henriques and J. Richardson (eds) *The Triple Bottom Line – Does it All Add up?*, Earthscan, London

Henriques, A. (2005a) 'Corporations – Amoral machines or moral persons?', *Business and Professional Ethics Journal*, no 24

Henriques, A. (2005b) 'Good decision – Bad business', *International Journal of Management and Decision Making*, no 6

Henriques, A. (2005c) 'Three paradoxes and the lesson of materiality', *AccountAbility Forum*, no 5

Henriques, A. (2006a) *Focus on Sustainability and its Implications for CSR*, BSI, London

Henriques, A. (2006b) 'Social footprint – taking time to measure social impact', London, www.henriques.co.uk/downloads/Social%20Footprint.pdf, accessed February 2007

Henriques, A. and Richardson, J. (eds) (2004) *The Triple Bottom Line – Does it All Add up?*, Earthscan, London

Hind, K. (2006) 'Stingy Stones avoid tax on £240m fortune', *Daily Mail*, London, 2 August

Holliday, C. O., Schmidheiny, S., Watts, P. and World Business Council for Sustainable Development (2002) *Walking the Talk: The Business Case for Sustainable Development*, Greenleaf, Sheffield, UK

Holmstrom, B. (1979) 'Moral hazard and observability', *Bell Journal of Economics*, no 10, pp74–91

Holmstrom, B. (1999) 'Managerial incentive problems: A dynamic perspective', *Review of Economic Studies*, no 66, pp169–182

HSE (2006) *Corporate Responsibility*, Health and Safety Executive, London

ICAEW (1925) 'Proof of evidence', *Company Law Committee: Minutes of Evidence*, Institute for Chartered Accountants in England and Wales, pxviii, London

ICEM (1998) 'Rio Tinto – Behind the facade', International Federation of Chemical, Energy, Mine and General Workers' Unions, Brussels

IFAC (2005) *Handbook of International Auditing, Assurance and Ethics Pronouncements*, International Federation of Acountants, New York

Iimi, A. (2006) *Did Botswana Escape from the Resource Curse?*, International Monetary Fund, Washington, DC

ILO (1930) *Convention Concerning Forced or Compulsory Labour*, International Labour Organization, Geneva, Switzerland

ILO (1948) *Freedom of Association and Protection of the Right to Organise Convention*, International Labour Organization, Geneva, Switzerland

ILO (1998) *ILO Declaration on Fundamental Principles and Rights at Work*, International Labour Organization, Geneva, Switzerland

IMCB (2004) *UK Code of Practice for the Self-Regulation of New Forms of Content on Mobiles*, O2 (UK) Ltd, Orange Personal Communications Services Ltd, T-Mobile UK Ltd, Virgin Mobile Telecoms Ltd, Vodafone Ltd and Hutchison 3G UK Ltd, London

ING (2006a) 'Corporate and social responsibility', www.ingdirect.co.uk/html/about/corporate_responsibility.html, accessed April 2006

ING (2006b) 'Community affairs', http://home.ingdirect.com/about/about.asp?s=CommunityAffairs, accessed April 2006

Inland Revenue *v.* Duke of Westminster (1936) A.C. 1, 19, 19 T.C. 490

ISEA (1999) *AA1000 – framework standard*, AccountAbility, London

ISO (2006a) 'Frequently asked questions', ISO, http://isotc.iso.org/livelink/livelink/fetch/2000/2122/830949/3934883/3935096/07_gen_info/faq.html, accessed March 2006

ISO (2006b) 'TG4 convenor report N0035', ISO 26000 3rd Plenary Working Group, Lisbon, Portugal

Jamison, C. and Steare, R. (2003) *Integrity in Practice*, The Soul Gym, Crawley, UK

JCC (2006) *Journal of Corporate Citizenship*, Greenleaf Publishing, www.greenleaf-publishing.com/, accessed March 2006

Kant, I. (1785) *Grundlegung zur Metaphysik der Sitten [Groundwork of the Metaphysics of Morals]*, English translation by Mary J. Gregor, Cambridge University Press, Cambridge, 1998

Kanzer, A. and Williams, C. (2003) 'The future of social reporting is on the line', *Business Ethics*, www.business-ethics.com/nike_vs__kasky.htm, accessed December 2006

Kets De Vries, M. and Cooper, R. (1996) *Family Business – Human Dilemmas in the Family Firm*, International Thomson Business Press (ITBP), London

Kets De Vries, M. F. R. and Miller, D. (1984) *The Neurotic Organization: Diagnosing and Changing Counterproductive Styles of Management*, Jossey-Bass, San Francisco, CA

Klein, N. (2000) *No Logo*, Flamingo, London

Kohan, D. (2003) 'Public policy for achieving transparency and good governance: The experience of Chile', *Global Forum on International Investment – Encouraging Modern Governance and Transparency for Investment: Why and How?*, OECD, Johannesburg, South Africa

Köhler, H. (2003) 'Opportunities and challenges for Central Asia', *Conference for the Tenth Anniversary of the Introduction of the Tenge Almaty*, IMF, Kazakhstan

KPMG (2004) 'KPMG and the media CSR forum', KPMG, London

Krueger, A. O. (1974) 'The political economy of the rent-seeking society', *American Economic Review*, no 64, pp291–303

Ladd, J. (1970) 'Morality and the ideal of rationality in formal organizations', *Monist*, no 54, pp488–516

Lanwehr, R. (2005) 'Tax evasion, fines and corruption in Mozambique', *Global Corruption Report 2006*, Pluto Press, London

Lascelles, D. (2005) *The Ethics of Influence: Political Donations and lobbying*, Institute of Business Ethics, London

Loup, J. (2000) *The UNDP Round Tables and the Private Sector: An Issue Paper*, DIAL, Paris

Lowe, R. (1856) *Parliamentary Debates*, Hansard CXL, 134, London

Lynch, M. (2004) 'Ghost writing and other matters', *Social Studies of Science*, no 34, pp147–148

Margolis, J. D. and Walsh, J. P. (2003) 'Misery loves companies: Rethinking social initiatives by business', *Administrative Science Quarterly*, no 48, pp268–305

Marr, A. (2005) *My Trade: A Short History of British Journalism*, Pan, London

Marsden, C. (2006) *Your Company and Human Rights: What this Means in Practice*, discussion paper, Amnesty International, London

Masia, N. (2006) *The Cost of Developing a New Drug*, US Department of State, Washington, DC

Maucher, H. (1994) *Leadership in Action: Tough-Minded Strategies from the Global Giant*, McGraw-Hill, New York

Mcintosh, N. (2000) 'Is this phone bill too big?', *The Guardian*, London, 20 April

Mehrez, G. and Kaufman, D. (2000) *Transparency, Liberalization, and Banking Crises*, World Bank, New York

Milmo, D. (2001) 'Ten years to recoup phone licences says survey', *The Guardian*, London, 29 January

Mitchell, K. (2005) *Telecom Carrier Capex Growing Worldwide*, Infonetics Research, Campbell, CA, www.infonetics.com/resources/purple.shtml?db05sp.2Q05.nr.shtml, accessed February 2007

Monsanto (2003) 'Monsanto statement regarding Oakhurst Dairy Inc. Filing', Monsanto, St Louis, MO, www.monsanto.com/monsanto/layout/media/03/07-03-03.asp, accessed September 2006

MORI (2003) *British Attitudes To the Euro, Company Directors and Working Life*, Ipsos MORI, London

Moser, P. (2005) 'How do patent laws influence innovation? Evidence from 19th-century world's fairs', *American Economic Review*, no 95, pp1215–1236

Moser, P. (2006) *What Do Inventors Patent?*, working paper, Stanford University, http://web.mit.edu/moser/www/patrat603.pdf, accessed July 2006

Murphy, R. (2004) 'Location, location', *Accountancy Magazine*, March

Nagel, T. (1998) 'Concealment and exposure', *Philosophy and Public Affairs*, no 27, pp3–30

Neighbour, J. (2002) 'Transfer pricing: Keeping it at arm's length', *OECD Observer*, 230

Neus, E. (2005) 'DNA-rights defenders: Get off my genetic property: Money creates conflict of research vs. privacy, *Gene Forum*, www.geneforum.org/node/62, accessed June 2006

Nicholson, D. (2002) 'Could sex save 3G mobiles?', *The Guardian*, London, 1 August

Nike (2003) 'Nike, Inc. and Kasky announce settlement of Kasky v. Nike first amendment case', press release, 12 September, Beaverton, OR, www.nike.com/nikebiz/news/pressrelease.jhtml?year=2003&month=09&letter=f, accessed February 2007

Nike (2004) 'Workers and factories', Nike, www.nike.com/nikebiz/nikebiz.jhtml?page=25&cat=activefactories#, accessed September 2006

North Norfolk Council (2006) 'Report of the chief executive to full council in relation to a land transaction at Cromer Road, Sheringham', North Norfolk Council, Cromer, UK

NOTW (2006) *About Us*, News of the World, London

O2 (2005) 'Understanding your opinions – Adult content', www.o2.com/responsibility/opinions_keyquestions.html, accessed April 2006

O'Hara, K. (2004) *Trust*, Icon Books, Cambridge, UK

O'Neill, O. (2006) 'Transparency and the ethics of communication', in C. Hood and D. Heald (eds) *Transparency: The Key to Better Governance?*, Oxford University Press, Oxford, UK

OAS (1996) *Inter-American Convention against Corruption*, Organisation of American States, adopted at the third plenary session held on March 29, Caracas, Venezuela, www.osec.doc.gov/ogc/occic/corrupt.html, accessed February 2007

OECD (1997) *Convention on Combating Bribery of Foreign Public Officials in International Business Transactions*, Organisation for Economic Co-operation and Development, Paris

OECD (2000) *Guidelines for Multinational Enterprises*, Organisation for Economic Co-operation and Development, Paris

OECD (2003) *OECD Model Tax Convention*, Organisation for Economic Co-operation and Development, Paris

ONS (2005) *Social Trends, 35*, Office of National Statistics, London

Oxfam (2000) *Tax Havens: Releasing the Hidden Billions for Poverty Eradication*, Oxfam, Oxford, UK

PCC (2006) *Code of Practice*, Press Complaints Commission, London

Peslak, A. R. (2005) 'An ethical exploration of privacy and radio frequency identification', *Journal of Business Ethics*, no 59, pp327–345

Pew (2000) *Self Censorship: How Often and Why*, Pew Centre, Washington, DC

Piciotto, S. (1999) 'The state as legal fiction', in M. P. Hampton and J. P. Abbott (eds) *Offshore Finance Centres and Tax Havens: The Rise of Global Capitalism*, Palgrave, Basingstoke, UK

Prat, A. (2005) 'The wrong kind of transparency', *American Economic Review*, no 95, pp862–877

Prat, A. (2006) 'The more closely we are watched, the better we behave?', in C. Hood and D. Heald (eds) *Transparency: The Key to Better Governance?*, Oxford University Press, Oxford, UK

Quintin, O. (2004) Speech to USCIB, European Commission, New York, 23 June

R (on the application of British American Tobacco UK Ltd) and others *v.* The Secretary of State for Health (2004) London

Ramsay *v.* Inland Revenue (1982) W. T. Ramsay Ltd *v.* Inland Revenue Commissioners

Raynard, P. and Murphy, S. (2000) *Charitable Trust? Social Auditing with Voluntary Organisations*, New Economics Foundation, Association of Chief Executives of Voluntary Organisations (ACEVO), London

Riordan, T. (2003) 'A stroll through patent history', *The New York Times*, New York, 29 September

Rio Tinto (2005) 'Legal: Conditions of use of the Rio Tinto web site', Rio Tinto plc, London, www.riotinto.com/utilities/legal.aspx, accessed September 2006

Ross, M. (2003) 'The natural resource curse: How wealth can make you poor', in I. Bannon and P. Collier (eds) *Natural Resources and Violent Conflict*, World Bank, Washington, DC

Ross, M. L. (1999) 'The political economy of the resource curse', *World Politics*, no 51, pp297–322

Ruggie, J. (2006) *Promotion and Protection of Human Rights: Interim Report of the Special Representative of the Secretary-General on the Issue of Human Rights and Transnational Corporations and Other Business Enterprises*, OHCHR, Geneva, Switzerland

Sala-I-Martin, X. and Subramanian, A. (2003) *Addressing the Natural Resource Curse: An Illustration from Nigeria*, National Bureau of Economic Research (NBER), Cambridge, MA

Sampson, A. (2004) *Who Runs This Place?*, John Murray, London

Samuels, A. (1993) *The Political Psyche*, Routledge, London

Samuelson, P. A., Nordhaus, W. D. and Mandel, M. J. (1995) *Economics*, McGraw-Hill, New York and London

Sappington, D. E. (1991) 'Incentives in principal–agent relationships', *Journal of Economic Perspectives*, no 5, pp45–66

Schlosser, E. (2006) *Chew on This: Everything You Don't Want to Know About Fast Food*, Puffin, London

Shell (2005) *General Business Principles*, Shell, London

Shell (2006a) *How We Work*, Shell, London

Shell (2006b) *The Shell Sustainability Report 2005*, Shell, London

SMH (2004) 'Worry grows over Shell's reserves error', *Sydney Morning Herald*, Sydney, Australia

Smith, A. ([1776] 1999) *The Wealth of Nations*, first edition printed by W. Strahan and T. Cadell, London in 1776; edition quoted from published by Penguin (1999)

Southwood, R. (2004) 'Dash me – An anatomy of corruption in the ICT business – an off-the-record briefing', London, www.kubatana.net/html/archive/inftec/040426balact.asp?sector=INFTEC&range_start=31, accessed August 2006

Stevenson, R. B. (1980) *Corporations and Information: Secrecy, Access and Disclosure*, Johns Hopkins University Press, Baltimore, MD

SustainAbility (2001) *Politics and Persuasion: Corporate Influence on Sustainable Development Policy*, SustainAbility, London

SustainAbility (2002) *Trust Us: The Global Reporters 2002 Survey of Corporate Sustainability Reporting*, UNEP, London

SustainAbility and UNEP (2002) *Good News and Bad: The Media, Corporate Responsibility and Sustainable Development*, SustainAbility, London

SustainAbility and WWF (2004) *Through the Looking Glass: Corporate Responsibility in the Media and Entertainment Sector*, SustainAbility, London

SustainAbility and WWF (2005) *Influencing Power: Reviewing the Conduct and Content of Corporate Lobbying*, SustainAbility, London

Swisscom (2006) *2005 Annual Report*, Swisscom, Worblaufen, Switzerland

Thatcher, M. (1987) 'Interview with *Woman's Own*', *Woman's Own*, 31 October

TI (2002) *Transparency International Bribe Payers Index 2002*, Transparency International, Berlin

TI (2005) *Corruption Perceptions Index 2005*, Transparency International, Berlin

TI (2006) *Global Corruption Report 2006*, Transparency International, Berlin

UK Legislature (1906) Prevention of Corruption Act

UK Legislature (1998) Data Protection Act, Chapter 29

UK Legislature (2000) Freedom of Information Act, Chapter 36

UK Legislature (2001) Anti-Terrorism Crime and Security Act

UK Legislature (2004) Environmental Information Regulations, Statutory Instrument 2004, no 3391

UK Legislature (2006) Companies Act

UN (1948) *Universal Declaration of Human Rights*, General Assembly resolution 217 A (III) of 10 December

UN (1966a) *International Covenant on Civil and Political Rights*, United Nations Office of the High Commissioner for Human Rights, Geneva, Switzerland

UN (1966b) *International Covenant on Economic, Social and Cultural Rights*, United Nations Office of the High Commissioner for Human Rights, Geneva, Switzerland

UN (2003a) *Convention Against Corruption*, United Nations, New York

UN (2003b) *Norms on the Responsibilities of Transnational Corporations and Other Business Enterprises with Regard to Human Rights*, United Nations, New York

UN (2006) *World Economic and Social Survey 2006: Diverging Growth and Development*, United Nations, New York

UNCTAD (2001) *World Investment Report 2001, Promoting Linkages*, United Nations Conference on Trade and Development (UNCTAD), Geneva, Switzerland

Unicorn (2005) *Complying with the OECD Anti-Bribery Convention: Corporate Criminal Liability and Corruption – Exploring the Legal Options*, report by K. Drew (ed) of seminar hosted by the Crown Prosecution Service, 12 December, Unicorn (United Against Corruption), London, available at www.againstcorruption.org/reports/2006-03-UK-CorporateLiabilitySeminar.doc

US Bill of Rights (1791) 'The bill of rights: Amendments 1–10 of the constitution', text available at http://usinfo.state.gov/usa/infousa/facts/funddocs/billeng.htm, accessed February 2007

USDA (2004) *Misuse of Position*, United States Department of Agriculture, Washington, DC

USDOS (2000) *Money Laundering and Financial Crimes*, US Department of State, Washington, DC

Velasquez, M. (1983) 'Why corporations are not morally responsible for anything they do', *Business and Professional Ethics Journal*, no 2

Verschoor, C. C. (1999) 'Corporate performance is closely linked to a strong ethical commitment', *Business and Society Review*, no 104, pp407–415

Vodafone UK (2005) *Corporate Responsibility Report 2004/05*, Vodafone, London

Ward, B. (2006) *Royal Society Letter to Exxon*, Royal Society, London

Webb, R. (2006) 'Mobile wireless operators rapidly building next-gen networks', report, Infonetics Research, Campbell, CA, cited at www.3g.co.uk/PR/March 2006/2815.htm, accessed March 2007

Wheeler, D. and Sillanpää, M. (1997) *The Stakeholder Corporation: A Blueprint for Maximising Stakeholder Value*, Pitman, London

Willman, J. (2006) 'Share register fraud cases on the increase', *Financial Times*, London, 6 May

Wipperfürth, A. (2005) *Brand Hijack: Marketing without Marketing*, Portfolio, New York

Wong, H. and Wong, R. (2002) *Effective Teaching*, http://teachers.net/gazette/APR02/wong.html, accessed April 2006

Wood, D. J. (1994) *Business and society*, HarperCollins College Publishers, New York

Woodstock, T. C. (2002) *The Ethics of Lobbying: Organized Interests, Political Power and the Common Good*, Georgetown University Press, Washington, DC

Worcester, R. (2003) *Whom do we Trust?*, Ipsos MORI, London

World Bank (2004) *World Development Report 2005: A Better Investment Climate for Everyone*, World Bank, Washington, DC

World Bank (2005) *Doing Business in 2005*, International Finance Corporation, World Bank, Washington, DC

WoW (2005) *Caterpillar: The Alternative Report*, War on Want, London

Wray, R. (2005) 'Tease not sleaze on mobile phones', *The Guardian*, London, 24 August

Index